1-13-98

The Civil War Letters of Joshua K. Callaway

THE CIVIL WAR LETTERS OF

Joshua K. Callaway

Edited by Judith Lee Hallock

The University of Georgia Press / Athens and London

© 1997 by the University of Georgia Press
Athens, Georgia 30602

Designed by Sandra Strother Hudson
Set in 10 on 14 Caledonia by G & S Typesetters, Inc.
Printed and bound by Maple-Vail
The paper in this book meets the guidelines
for permanence and durability of the Committee on
Production Guidelines for Book Longevity
of the Council on Library Resources.

Printed in the United States of America
01 00 99 98 97 C 5 4 3 2 1

Library of Congress Cataloging in Publication Data

Callaway, Joshua K.
The Civil War letters of Joshua K. Callaway / Judith Lee Hallock,
editor.
p. cm.
Includes bibliographical references (p.   ) and index.
ISBN 0-8203-1886-8 (alk. paper)
1. Callaway, Joshua K.—Correspondence.   2. Confederate States of
America.   Army.   Alabama Infantry Regiment, 28th.   3. Soldiers—
Alabama—Correspondence.   4. Alabama—History—Civil War,
1861–1865—Personal narratives.   5. United States—History—Civil War,
1861–1865—Personal narratives, Confederate.   6. Alabama—
Biography.   I. Hallock, Judith Lee, 1940–   .   II. Title.
E551.5 28th.C35 1997
973.7′461′092—dc21
[B]   97-1764

British Library Cataloging in Publication Data available

Title page: "Looking for a Friend," by Walton Taber, Courtesy of
American Heritage Picture Collection.

To my children,

ERNEST LEE ALBEE

and

DAVID DANIEL HALLOCK,

who fill the family roles that Joshua filled

sons

brothers

husbands

fathers

And in memory of my father,

DANIEL HENRY CORNELIUS HALLOCK

(1910–1996)

CONTENTS

MAPS

ACKNOWLEDGMENTS

I FEEL remarkably fortunate in having discovered the Joshua K. Callaway letters at the Eugene C. Barker Texas History Center, University of Texas, Austin, when I did. They had only recently been deposited there by his descendants, thus making them accessible to scholars for the first time. I made several visits to the center over a period of years, each time wondering if indeed the letters were as fine as I remembered. Each time I found they were even better than I remembered, and finally I sought permission to publish them.

My quest for permission led me to Joshua's descendants, women and men in whom he would have taken great pride and who are equally proud of their ancestor. Although the collection had been divided into four groups in the care of Doris Kellam Langley and her husband, Ralph, Betty Jo Lyon Jackson, Horace King Lyon, and Thomas C. Douglass Jr., it remained in excellent condition. Each caretaker, appreciating the high quality and the importance of the letters, had taken pains to ensure their safety and preservation. The task of editing the collection for publication has been most delightful and rewarding.

My sons, Ernest Albee and David Hallock, are now about the age Joshua was when he marched off to war. I will be forever grateful that they have not been called upon to make the choices and the sacrifices that Joshua had to make. They, along with their wives, Bella Christ and Annmarie DeStefano Hallock, and my beautiful granddaughters, Jenna Marie Hallock and Kayla Lee Albee, are the joys of my life simply by being there.

In addition to being a joy of my life, Ernest also read and critiqued the manuscript. Being a young man himself, he provided insights into Joshua's thoughts that I had missed. Despite a busy life my sister, Sharon Hallock Boutcher, also critiqued my work. And, as always, Grady McWhiney encouraged and advised me throughout the project and shared my enthusiasm for the collection.

Deborah Fuchs, reference librarian at the Middle Country Public Library, Centereach, New York, helped track down obscure references to nineteenth-century literature.

The Eugene C. Barker Texas History Center carefully copied the entire collection for me, and director Don E. Carleton was patient and supportive as I slowly completed the editing process.

Donald S. Frazier prepared the maps with his usual skill and cheerfulness.

Ingeborg Kelly, Ellen Barcel, Carolyn Kaitz, Annmarie Hallock, E. A. (Bud) Livingston, Marie Hulse, and my mother, Lee Esposito, all helped with the final stages of preparing the book for publication.

A special thank you goes to my closest friend, Ingeborg Linsenbarth Kelly.

INTRODUCTION

ON THE MORNING of November 18, 1863, a young man in the Army of Tennessee persuaded some of his fellow soldiers to accompany him to the top of Lookout Mountain overlooking Chattanooga, Tennessee. Finding the view *"sublime beyond conception,"* he imagined the future. "[I began] thinking how travelers from all countries will come to stand on Lookout Mountain to see the valley of Chattanooga, and how that the poets and painters of future generations will . . . immortalize the scene and the mountain in song and on canvas, and while I was musing thus I could not help feeling a spark of ambition, a desire to make my name as immortal in future history and as classic as that of Lookout Mountain." As he reached this point in his reverie, he observed a general emerge from a headquarters at the foot of the mountain, a speck so small only his movements betrayed his presence. "When I compared him to the mountain and then to the universe," the young man wrote, "and thought of his pride and ambition, I could not help smiling at his impetuosity and sighing at his insignificance. He reminded me of an ant trying to shake the earth, and my ambition cooled off and I would be perfectly content to be at home with my wife and never be thought of after I die." [1]

The young man whose ambition so briefly flared was Joshua K. Callaway, a volunteer in Company K, Twenty-eighth Alabama Regiment. He had been soldiering for nineteen months at the time he wrote this letter and would continue to do so for only another six days.

Joshua was born on September 2, 1834, one of thousands of children born that year whose lives would be shaped by the most cataclysmic event in American history, the Civil War. His parents, Reverend Joseph (born in 1800) and Temperance (born in 1805) Callaway, were both natives of Georgia. They produced five children. Elisha W., the firstborn, arrived in 1828. Four years later Sarah A. Damaris (1832) made her appearance, followed at yearly intervals by Camilla (1833) and Joshua (1834). After a six-year respite the Callaway's last child, Samantha M., arrived in 1841. The 1850 federal census found the Callaway family living in Alabama's Coffee County. In 1857 Joseph and Temperance died in Haw Ridge, Dale County, within a few days of each other.[2]

At age fifteen, Joshua worked as a mail carrier, but there is no record of where or when he received his schooling. The letters he wrote, however, reveal him as comparatively well educated. About the time his parents died, Joshua married Dulcinea Baker. The Baker family of eleven had been living in Coffee County since at least 1846, where the father, John Baker, died sometime before 1850. In the late 1850s his widow, Amelia (Millie) Regan Baker, bought land in Summerfield, Dallas County, Alabama, at a sheriff's sale and moved there with her large household—three of her seven sons, both daughters, and son-in-law Joshua.[3]

They found Dallas County very different from Coffee County. The latter boasted extensive and valuable pine forests, and in 1860 slaves accounted for just under 15 percent of the population. Dallas County must have seemed like another world to the Callaways and the Bakers: located in the rich prairie cotton belt, slaves accounted for nearly 77 percent of the population in 1860.[4]

It is unclear why Amelia Baker decided to move to Dallas County. It appears that several family members taught at Centenary Institute in Summerfield—including Joshua, Irene (Dulcinea's sister), John H. Callaway (Joshua's first cousin once removed), and E. W. Callaway—so perhaps the promise of work prompted the move. The institute, a coeducational Methodist Episcopal Church South college, had been established in 1839, the centenary year of Methodism. The school opened in 1843 and through the next two decades served a large number of students, sometimes having as many as five hundred in attendance. "The work done was not of the highest grade according to the modern standards," a former teacher stated years later, "but it was of a kind that made good men and good women." Centenary Institute was one of several colleges in Alabama. One historian noted that "Alabama had more institutions of higher learning, attended by more students, than had any agricultural state of the North of equal population."[5]

Summerfield is located a few miles north of Selma, a bustling river town. In 1860 Summerfield was home to 1,496 people, more than 72 percent of whom were slaves. Although the activities of the area centered on cotton production, the census attests to the importance of Centenary Institute in the life of the community. Only farmers outnumbered teachers—thirty-two farmers as opposed to sixteen teachers. In addition to those listed as teachers, there was one Methodist Episcopal bishop and nine ministers, at least some of whom, no doubt, worked as educators. Of the total number of whites—413—a whopping 144, nearly 35 percent, had attended school within the past year. Many of these were in their late teens and well into their twenties. The majority of the teachers (twelve) were female, and other than two natives of France, all were southern born.[6]

Joshua and Dulcinea became parents for the first time on April 2, 1858, when their daughter Amelia Temperance arrived. In 1860 Dulcinea gave birth to a second daughter, who, sadly, lived only a short time. In January 1862 Joseph J., their last child, made his appearance.[7] Amelia Temperance appears to have been named after both of her grandmothers, and Joseph J. (John?) was probably named after Joshua's father and possibly after Dulcinea's. Joshua seems to have been very close to his wife's family.

When the War between the States erupted in April 1861, Joshua remained at home until after the birth of Joseph in January 1862. In that same month several Alabama men mounted a campaign to recruit a regiment in response to an impassioned plea from the state's governor. The governor had let out all the stops in his message, urging Alabamians to volunteer in order to avoid the humiliation of a draft. "No man of true patriotism, or of a proper degree of personal or State pride, will stand still in such an hour of danger, and suffer himself forced into the defense of his country, his property and his family." In case this failed to be sufficient, the announcement dangled additional incentives before the would-be soldiers: a fifty-dollar bounty offered by the Confederate Congress, and the promise of the state legislature to see that the families of soldiers were "fed and clad during [their] absence." Colonel J. W. Frazer, Lieutenant Colonel J. C. Reid, and Major W. W. Davies all stood ready to welcome and muster in companies raised anywhere in the state. Within a week of this notice's appearance in the local newspaper, several men from Selma and Summerfield advertised for a few additional recruits to complete the raising of a company. "A chance is now offered to get into service at an early day," enticed the advertisement. "Will you join?"[8]

By the end of March, Joshua could no longer resist the call to duty, and on the 29th he enlisted in Perry County, which borders on Dallas County just a few miles from Summerfield. It is unclear why he did not enlist with the Summerfield/Selma men; perhaps he had left it until too late, and the Dallas company was already filled.

And so Joshua K. Callaway became a soldier at the age of twenty-eight. On April 11, 1862, Joshua joined the rest of the state's volunteers for the new regiment at Shelby Springs, Alabama. Commanded by Colonel John W. Frazer, the unit pledged to serve for three years or the duration of the war. Just a day or two after Joshua reached Shelby Springs, he was promoted to first sergeant, and the regiment headed out for Corinth, Mississippi. Arriving on April 22, they were brigaded with the Tenth and Nineteenth South Carolina regiments and the Twenty-fourth and Thirty-fourth Alabama regiments under the command of General James H. Trapier, forming part of General Jones M. Withers's division in General Leonidas Polk's corps.

For the most part the brigade and the division remained throughout the war as first organized, although there were several changes in commanders. General Arthur M. Manigault became the brigade commander in early 1863, remaining at that post until a severe wound received during the Battle of Franklin on November 30, 1864, forced him out of active duty. On the division level, General Thomas C. Hindman replaced Withers after the Tullahoma campaign, and General Patton Anderson took the command after the Battle of Chickamauga. The corps command passed from Polk to General William J. Hardee to General Benjamin F. Cheatham. For a short time General Gustave Toutant Beauregard served as Joshua's army commander, but on June 20, 1862, General Braxton Bragg replaced Beauregard. Joshua received a promotion to second junior lieutenant on October 28, 1862. His service record contains no demerits, and his evaluating officer rated him "efficient, standing good."[9] The Twenty-eighth Alabama earned the reputation of "a fighting regiment that never failed to give a good account of itself," according to brigade commander Manigault, and a soldier in the Thirty-fourth Alabama, a unit that usually fought side by side with the Twenty-eighth, asserted that the Twenty-eighth was "one of the best fighting Reg'ts in the service" and hinted that the soldiers of the regiment displayed more bravery than did its officers.[10]

The Twenty-eighth Alabama saw a good deal of activity. Its soldiers participated in General Bragg's invasion of Kentucky; suffered many casualties at Murfreesboro; fought fiercely at Chickamauga; were nearly surrounded on Orchard Knob at Chattanooga, escaping only after a desperate fight, and then fought at Missionary Ridge two days later; took part in the Atlanta campaign; suffered severe losses at Franklin and Nashville; and surrendered the regiment's last remnants at Greensboro, North Carolina. The Twenty-eighth participated in many of the important battles in the western theater, and Joshua's descriptions of these events open a window for the reader to view them through the eyes of an observant and literate participant.

Early on, Joshua seems to view his role as a soldier as a great lark, a school holiday, and his letters are full of excitement. "I am enjoying myself finely," he enthuses at the end of April 1862. "I had much rather be here than teaching school." Before long, however, harsh reality sets in, and in March 1863 he cries, "O! how I would love to be a citizen—a *school teacher.*"

Illness becomes a constant theme in his letters. A soldier in Joshua's brigade wrote, "You never saw as much sickness in your life. The doctors are doing all that they can to stop it, by having all the filth around the camp removed, and by having the tents kept clean." He also blamed the soldiers themselves, citing their piggery as part of the cause of their distress. "The worst sickness that we have is Diarrhea," he continued. "When the men are taken with it they report to the surgeon, he commences doctoring them to check it, they take his medicine, and eat every thing that they can get hold of and then abuse the doctors because his medicine fails to have the desired effect. I have seen men report them selves sick and at the same time eat more than two men ought." By November the general health of the soldiers was so poor that this soldier asserted, "I think that if we have a winter campaign that pneumonia will kill more men for us than the bullets of the enemy." The soldiers' fears of illness were well grounded, as many more succumbed to disease than to enemy action.[11]

Joshua was most anxious to experience combat, and on May 10, 1862, he excitedly reports to Dulcinea that he *"saw the elephant."* (To nineteenth-century Americans this phrase meant to see the real thing firsthand.) "However," he laments, "our brigade was not actually engaged, but we *saw* it." Soon, though, the novelty wears off, and on July 20, 1862, he complains that soldiers "are hardly allowed to sigh at the fall of [their] friends and relatives and if we do happen to shed a tear secretly, it is soon dried up to make room for one for some one else." Joshua appears desensitized to the miseries of war, and he seems to sense what is happening to him. "We never will have time to contemplate and comprehend the horrors of this war," he believes, "until sweet, delightful peace is restored to us, & we can take a retrospective view."

Joshua's letters include eyewitness accounts of skirmishes and battles, but, as far as one can tell from the letters, he did not participate in plundering and gathering souvenirs as did many of his fellow soldiers. Following his first battle, although "numbers of [the] men got valuable trophies" from the battlefield, all Joshua picked up was "a pair of socks, & they not mates." On other occasions he sends Dulcinea items such as a small piece of telegraph wire, a bit of stalactite from a cave he visited, or a ring he carved from a shell.

Foraging for food proved another matter, and several times Joshua reports such activities. He seems to enjoy these forays for more than just the delectables he obtains. He describes the countryside and the people he encounters along the way. Most, if not all, of these encounters seem to have been friendly, and on occasion he and his fellow foragers are invited to share a family's meal.

Joshua makes frequent references to the Dallas Warriors. This unit was raised in his home county of Dallas and included several young men from Summerfield. Another frequent reference is to the "Coffee boys." These are people Joshua and Dulcinea knew from their Coffee County days, before they moved to Dallas County.

As do most people separated from home and loved ones, Joshua frequently complains of the lack of mail. He seems to understand that Dulcinea has her hands full with caring for two young children, one a nursing infant, and many household and family responsibilities, but that does not lessen his longing for more frequent news from home. When she or the children are ill, and she is even less likely to find the time or the inclination to write letters, Joshua is especially insistent that she write in order to ease his intense anxiety. At one point, he desperately wants Dulcinea to come to visit him, but she appears to have cited child care responsibilities as the reason she cannot accommodate his wishes.

The letters indicate a constant traffic between the army and home. In nineteen of the seventy-four letters, Joshua mentions that he is sending the letter by way of someone returning to Summerfield or Selma, so a minimum of about 26 percent of the letters were hand-carried. In addition, Joshua mentions receiving two hand-carried letters, and on ten occasions he reports having received items that Dulcinea sent by someone traveling to the army. When these are included, the number of letters or items hand-delivered climbs to 37 percent. These represent the minimum percentages; there may have been times Joshua did not mention by whom he was sending the letter, or he may have received additional letters or items by hand that he fails to mention.[12]

The letters also reveal that Joshua enjoys reading novels, and, surprisingly, he had available to him foreign best-sellers, sometimes within months of publication. A case in point is Mary E. Braddon's *Aurora Floyd,* which was published some time in 1863 and is in Joshua's hands before October of the same year. He also documents reading at least part of Victor Hugo's *Les Misérables* ("Cosette"), Edward Bulwer's *A Strange Story,* and Timothy Shay Arthur's *The Withered Heart,* as well as another unidentifiable novel. Most of these were best-sellers of their day, so Joshua manages to keep up with the literary world despite his military service.[13]

Joshua's letters reveal the mundane aspects of military life. He details the contents of his knapsack, notes his eating and sleeping arrangements, describes his daily routine, mentions games and races and contests, reports on the religious life of the army, gives a glimpse into his tent as several soldiers gather to read their just-arrived letters from home, and expresses opinions of his superior officers.

The editing of the letters has been kept to a minimum. Joshua wrote fluently with an engaging style. Few corrections have been made in spelling, largely because few were necessary. Corrections occurred when Joshua clearly made a slip, for example, writing "may" when he obviously meant "many." Often, before arriving at a destination, Joshua misspells place-names, but usually he corrects himself once he has an opportunity to see them written; these have been left as he wrote them. On occasion a word or phrase was illegible, or part of a letter was missing. These instances are indicated with ellipses.

There are a few short letters to his brother-in-law that Joshua includes in

Dulcinea's letters, one letter to a cousin, and one letter (the only one not written by Joshua) from another cousin.

Overall, his letters reveal Joshua to be first a husband and father and then a soldier. They allow us to share the joys and sorrows, the expectations and disappointments, and the day-to-day life of the common soldier.

The appendix provides brief biographical sketches of two-thirds of the people mentioned in the letters, all who could be identified in some way.

The Civil War Letters of Joshua K. Callaway

CHAPTER ONE

Corinth

April 13–May 24, 1862

THE CARNAGE of Shiloh was finished and had passed into history. General Gustave Toutant Beauregard, Confederate commander, appealed for troops to strengthen his army after its losses of more than ten thousand killed, wounded, and missing. Joshua K. Callaway and the Twenty-eighth Alabama formed part of the replacement troops sent to Beauregard's aid. Company K left Selma on April 10, 1862, arriving in Shelby Springs later that day. It remained there only three days before receiving orders to proceed to Corinth, Mississippi. The company arrived in Mobile, Alabama, on April 15, camped there three days, and on the 19th boarded cars on the Mobile and Ohio Railroad for the 340-mile, five-day journey to Corinth.[1]

After the Shiloh defeat, Beauregard had withdrawn the army twenty-three miles south to Corinth, a strategic location of great importance. Besides the Mobile and Ohio on which Callaway reached Corinth, the Memphis and Charleston Railroad, the only real east-west line the Confederacy possessed, also ran through town. In addition, the loss of Corinth would leave Fort Pillow, the last Confederate stronghold on the Mississippi River above Memphis, vulnerable to the Federals. Beauregard established a formidable defensive line at Corinth that stretched for three miles along a ridge behind a protective creek, connecting the Memphis and Charleston on his right to the Mobile and Ohio on his left.[2]

Upon arrival at Corinth on April 23, Callaway's Company K was posted about a mile and a half from town as part of General Braxton Bragg's command. As Federal general Henry Wager Halleck inched his way toward Corinth throughout the month of May, frequent clashes erupted between

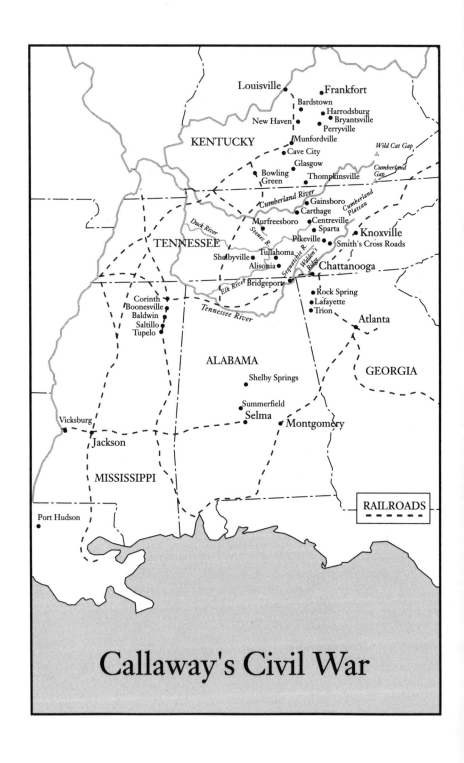

Louisville • • Frankfort
Bardstown •
• Harrodsburg
New Haven • • Bryantsville
• Perryville
Munfordville
KENTUCKY • Cave City   Wild Cat Gap
• Glasgow   △
• Bowling   Thompkinsville   Cumberland
Green   Gap △

Cumberland River • Gainsboro   Cumberland
• Carthage   Plateau
Murfreesboro • • Centreville
TENNESSEE   • • Sparta
Pikeville • • Knoxville
Tullahoma •   • Smith's Cross Roads
Shelbyville • Alisonia •   Chattanooga
Elk River Bridgeport •

Corinth •   • Rock Spring
Boonesville •   • Lafayette
Baldwin •   • Trion
Saltillo •   • Atlanta
Tupelo •

ALABAMA   GEORGIA

• Shelby Springs

• Summerfield
Vicksburg •   Selma • Montgomery
• Jackson

MISSISSIPPI

Port Hudson •   ┌─────────────────┐
│ RAILROADS   │
│ - - - - - - - - │
└─────────────────┘

Callaway's Civil War

Confederate and Federal outposts. On two occasions, May 9 and 19, Union general John Pope moved more rapidly than the rest of Halleck's army and found himself in a risky position near Farmington, four miles east of Corinth. Each time Beauregard attempted to destroy this segment of Halleck's army with coordinated attacks by Bragg and General Earl Van Dorn; twice Bragg attacked with some success, but twice Van Dorn failed to carry out his assigned mission, and Pope escaped unscathed.

Anxious to try his hand at battle, Callaway was delighted to be a participant, or at least an observer, on several occasions, and he detailed his experiences with boyish enthusiasm to Dulcinea. His letters also support one historian's assessment that the attempts to harm the Federals "produced only wasted logistics, due to the constant marching and countermarching."[3]

The Federals, however, were not the most dangerous enemy Callaway faced at Corinth. Like many others who joined Beauregard at this time, Callaway's regiment had received no military training prior to its arrival at the front lines. This meant that, besides being militarily unskilled and undrilled, these new soldiers were "unseasoned," so the diseases that usually ran their course in training camp took their toll at Corinth. "Most of the men were unaccustomed to the exposure attendant upon their new mode of life," explained Colonel Arthur Middleton Manigault, "and [suffered] from diseases generally attendant upon camps and large bodies of men brought together for the first time."[4]

Exacerbating the health situation, the recruits had had no time to learn reasonable sanitary precautions within their camps, and pure water and sufficient food were unavailable. Manigault detailed some of the problems resulting from these circumstances. The area now occupied had been used by the army for months with little or no attention to its policing. As the hot weather arrived, Manigault found the atmosphere "offensive and unwholesome in the extreme." From May 10 on, because of the excessive heat and lack of rain, "the water in the pools or wet weather branches became stagnant or altogether disappeared." What water was available became polluted and contaminated. By mid- to late May at least eighteen thousand soldiers were ill with measles, typhoid fever, and dysentery. Manigault reported that his regiment of South Carolinians, nine hundred strong upon arrival at Corinth, in late May could muster only five hundred, "and many of these were far from robust." They were, he contended, "a fair criterion of the rest of the Army." Manigault also blamed a lack of preparation for part of the misery at Corinth. "I never witnessed a more reckless waste of human life than during this short period," he maintained, "owing to a great degree to the inefficiency or ignorance shown in the management of the Quarter Masters, Subsistence, and Medical Departments." Callaway did not escape illness, but he avoided the medical officers and treated himself; no doubt he came under Manigault's category of "far from robust."[5]

These first letters reveal Joshua K. Callaway as an enthusiastic soldier, eager to "see the elephant," anxious to acquit himself well, and, like so many others, already homesick. He describes what a huge army camp looks like, his first view of Yankees, his first hostile bullets, and, a continuing theme throughout his letters, illness. He introduces his messmates, most of whom came from Perry County, adjacent to Callaway's own Dallas County. These letters also show that it did not take the soldiers long to learn to dig themselves some sort of protection from enemy bullets; Callaway had been soldiering less than two weeks before he was digging. Overall, Callaway seems absolutely delighted to be part of it all.

Camp ———, Shelby Springs, Ala.
Sunday, April 13th 1862

My dear wife, I have been too busy since I came up to write. Today, however, we are resting upon our oars, and after having had a song with my brothers, and noticing that they are all writing to their wives and friends, I have taken it into my head to give you some details in regard to our new and, so far, pleasant sphere and home. We arrived at this place at three o'clock on Friday evening without accident except three men of our company lost their hats on the way and I gave mine to one of them and now have to wear my cap altogether. We are very comfortably quartered in good houses with six good chimneys and one stove. Plenty of good wood and lightwood, and water, any kind you want. We are all well and in fine spirits. However, one man nearly jerked his back out of joint yesterday, trying, like the frog, to beat me jumping. He was very bad yesterday & last night, but I see him up, hobbling about on a stick this morning. It is the first time he has been beaten, and he strained a little too hard.

I am in a mess with five very steady, moral men, one of whom is a great wit and a ventriloquist; hence we have all sorts of fun. He is a printer by trade and of course he is full of yarns and anecdotes. I am glad, ten dollars, that he is in the company.

I can't say when I will be at home. I went out yesterday to see a dress parade, and an order was read out for the reg. to hold themselves in readiness to march, at the shortest notice, for Corrinth [Mississippi], next Tuesday is the day appointed to start; and if we do leave then I shall be at home in a day or two; but since the order originated with Col. Frazer and some other reasons, I think it is all bosh, and think I understand the object of the trick. Col. Frazer is a fine, gallant looking old chap, & a good officer. The Regiment serenaded him last night, and I had the pleasure of hearing several speeches by his staff.

The weather is cold and wet but we ask it no odds now. I have not seen a case of measles or itch yet but both are here plentifully.

> As ever, Your faithful and
> Affectionate
> Josh.

> Mobile, Alabama
> Apr 18th 1862

My Dear D.,

I have been postponing my writing thinking I would get to go to see Weston. ½ an hour ago I asked the col. to give me a pass but before I could get off he got a dispatch to leave for Corrinth at 5 o'clock this evening, and he countermanded it and I am now writing you in a great hurry. There is great rejoicing in camp at the prospect of a fight. We drew our bounty yesterday and I send you $40 by Dr. Vaughan who starts home at 4 o'clock this evening. We are getting knapsacks &c today.

I am well and in fine spirits. Write me at Corrinth soon direct in care of

Capt. Harris, 27th Reg., Ala. Volunteers. I will do my best for a furlough to go home at an early day. I believe I have written all that would interest. When I have more time I will write a *letter*.

May God bless my wife and children, and return me safe to them is the prayer of your faithful & affectionate husband.

J. K. Callaway

(sent to Mrs. J. K. Callaway, Summerfield, Ala., Urbanity of Dr. Vaughan)

Camp Near Corinth, Miss.
Friday April 25th 1862

My dear Dulcinea:

We are at last in camps, regularly, two miles N. E. of Corinth, and I am stealing a moment to fulfill a promise I made in my letter from on board the cars Wednesday.

All is excitement and bustle; and I can now fully realize that we are engaged in a deadly strife. I assure you that an army of 200 000 men is a grand scene to a man who has been so remote from the seat of war.[6] I commenced seeing tents 12 miles beyond Corinth but it being in the night I did not notice how thickly they are camped in that direction, but I have seen it from Corinth to this place (in the woods) and it is one continuous camp—not room to drill a battalion or even a company, and I am told it is so in every direction for ten or 15 miles. Eli can tell you how it looks; and perhaps he can tell why I have not written to any body but you since I left home. I am sorry I ever complained of him for not writing to me oftener. I have no idea how many times I have been called today but I reckon every commissioned officer in the regiment has called me at least once, and it has been raining all day, and our streets are nearly shoe mouth deep in mud. (I hope you will send me my boots by the first one passes), yet I am not wet as I should have been at home. The only difference is, at home I should be out in it voluntarily, and here I am obliged to go, *they draught me.*

You need not be afraid of my suffering from exposure: our tents are very comfortable. There are some asleep in every tent, although it is raining smartly. Two men are snoring in my tent while I write, one of them is a little sick, like about 16 others of our company. In short I am enjoying myself finely. I had much rather be here than teaching school. And then, in addition to my fun, the Yankees are advancing upon us, but what kills my fun from that quarter is, we can't get into the fight. There was a little fight occurred some where about here yesterday, in which we got the worst of it. We are throwing up breast works and felling timber in their way as fast as we can.

I suppose there are several here from Coffee County. Judge Costello is lying at a house a quarter of a mile from our camp, wounded in the thigh, but I have not seen any of them yet. Micajah Harper was killed in the battle of Shiloh. Costello is Captain of a Company here and so is Col. Stark of Elba, in the 18th Ala reg. camped joining our reg. Before I write again I will go and see them.

Tell Eli I will write to him just as soon as I get time. I will not write to Wes till I hear from home. I hear that his company has disbanded.

We have 3 preachers in our Reg. and we have prayer meetings occasionally, and for the first time I can feel that it is *privilege* to worship God, and when Sunday comes I feel sorry that I can't go to church.[7]

Write soon at Corinth. Kiss my children and believe as ever

> Your faithful & affect.
> husband
> J. K. Callaway

P. S. The Adjutant has now called on me for a detail for guard, but I shall close my letter first. Goodbye. Josh.

If there are any letters there for me have them forwarded to me, and oblige your loving J. K.

> Corinth, Miss.
> Monday May 5th 1862

Mrs. D. Callaway:

My dear wife, your welcome letter came to hand 4 days ago, and I should have written you again immediately, but for the fact that we were ordered to prepare 4 days rations and go out on picket guard where we were expected to meet the enemy; and I thought that news that I was going into a fight would render you very uneasy; and I determined to wait till I returned.

We left camp on Friday last under the impression that we were going right into a fight. I was right sick & had been for two days, with fever & diarhoea. They all persuaded me to stay in camp, but I was anxious to see a yankee &

would not be left. The surgeon prepared several litters to carry the wounded on, and we set off & marched about 8 miles, which brought us in 2 miles of the enemy. Our reg. was stationed on the left of the Brigade. We bivouacked one day & night on the ground in a skirt of woods. On the second evening *we* were (that is, Capt. Harris's company & 12 men from another Reg.) sent out still nearer to the enemy as sentinels & skirmishers, in a skirt of woods at the edge of an old field where we could see nearly to the enemies' camp. We could hear them laugh and sing. We had some cavalry between us and them, which we were ordered to support, & if they were driven in were to engage the enemy; and, sure enough, before day the cavalry were driven in & we were drawn up in line of battle, but no enemy came while we were standing, before night. Saturday, we heard the firing of 2 battles, one a pretty severe one, in which we lost 12 killed & several wounded. Sunday morning we got news that we were cut off by them & were ordered to retreat to our camp. I understand that they came in 2 miles of cutting off our whole Brigade. You will find some notes on our scouting expedition enclosed.[8]

My dear, I have no other special news except one or two items. In the first place we have changed Brigades. We are now in Gen. Trappier's Brigade, a S. Carolina affair; and in the second place, our Regiment is known as the 28th Ala. so in writing to me hereafter call it 28th instead of the 27th.

Now my next item is a sad one. My friend, Colwell Johnson got his right leg shot off about 2 or 3 inches above his ankle, a few minutes ago. It was done accidently by a man in another tent. I hear the Drs. have cut it off, indeed it was shot nearly off.

I am not right well yet, but have been doing all the time.

I want you to send me one pair of boots by the first one who passes. Some have passed already. Henry Vaughan got here a day or two ago, but I have not seen him. I understand he is right sick.

I want you to write me how you are getting along, & whether you got that money & my carpet sack, overcoat and gloves. I have repented sending my coat home for the weather is very cool here yet. Corinth is a very disagreeable place, & so is all the country about here. It is shoe mouth deep in the nastiest mud I ever saw, & the water is mean enough to kill an alligator. I gave twenty-five cents the other day for a canteen full of butter milk made of chalk & water made sour with cream of Tartar.

Kiss the children and dream of me tonight. You must write at least as often as I do.

As ever your

Josh

Corinth, Miss.

Saturday, May 10th 1862

Mrs. D. Callaway:

My dear wife, yours of the 4th inst. came to hand the day before yesterday (the 8th) and I should have written you the same day but we were ordered out to meet the enemy that day. The following are the particulars.

We marched out to the breast works, and were then ordered out in advance about 2 miles beyond them. There was some fighting going on, out there, on a small scale, and we expected to engage in it. We passed one dead horse, & met 3 wounded men, which made us think we would get to see the enemy. We went out 2 miles & the yankees retreated & we turned round & started home, & after coming about 1 mile a runner came after us & told us the enemy had turned & were following us. We were then halted and drawn up in line of battle, where we waited about an hour when a courier came & told us they had turned to their own camp. We then marched back to Corinth, where we arrived at midnight. I was completely broke down. I had been unwell for 5 days, and all this tramp was in an awful thick and muddy swamp. Well just as we got in bed we were ordered back, but I couldn't come it; I had taken 2 races, when I was sick, to get a shoot & failed, and as I had been excused from duty by the Surgeon, I thought I'd profit by the advantage. The company, however, went back to the breast works & laid till 7 o'clock yesterday morning & came back, all sleepy & exhausted, and at 8 were ordered out again. Of course I went. We marched 4 miles towards the enemy & got news that they were retreating & turned back, but did not come more than 2 miles before we were halted & turned towards the enemy again, and went nearly at a double quick for 2 miles, when we heard the firing commence to our left & front. We then turned South (towards the firing on our left) & advanced in line of battle, for half a mile through a skirt of woods into an old field, & then turned east and went into the battle. And *then* we *saw the elephant.* However our brigade was not actually engaged, but we *saw* it, and expected constantly to pitch in. We were once ordered to advance and guard one of our batteries against a charge of cavalry, but the charge never came. We whipped them badly, drove them from the field, & numbers of our men got valuable trophies, but, not being allowed to break ranks, I had no chance at anything except what the balance walked over, hence the only thing I got was a pair of socks, & they not mates. We took 1200 prisoners. I saw 7 dead men. One of my messmates, who went across another part of the field says he saw 18. Another saw 25. We saw all those in crossing their line, which being about 2 miles long, there must have been a considerable number of them killed. Our officers & men were all perfectly cool & not at all excited. I could have picked up any number of Blankets and quilts, but my own was all I wanted to carry. A great many of our men threw away their blankets. We got back to camp at Sunset last night. Today I am well except that I am a little sore & stiff from my fatigue yesterday. Capt. Johnson and Dr. Vaughan are both here, but neither of them brought me a letter or my boots as I was in hopes they would. My compliments to Mrs. Capt. Harris. Tell her our gallant little Captain is well, but he was very tired last night, but well pleased with his adventure.

My dear, I hope this letter will be more legible than the one you complain of so much.

Write to your affectionate

J. K. Callaway

Corinth, May 10th

Dear D. I have written you a letter today to send by Capt. Johnson, but I learn Mr. Locket will start to Marion [Perry County, Alabama] in the morning, and thinking he may get through before Mr. Johnson, I will send a few lines by him also.

I am plum strait this evening. I have just got back from the creek where I took a good wash and put on a borrowed shirt; but it is the first clean shirt I have had on since I left home. I also pulled off my green shirt for the first time since I left. It is worn out. Send me any other shirts by the first chance. I believe I wrote you to send the boots I left at Manderson['s] shop. I see some of our boys out who have had the measles. Rube Bennett & Tully Bolling. I don't believe I told you I had the measles this week. But I was up all the time, & took no physics except sage tea, while some who called the doctor have been very sick with them.

I believe I wrote you all the news this morning, however I hear this evening that our forces took 3000 prisoners yesterday, instead of 1200.

I think the prospect for a big fight here is becoming rather less. Some think it will never take place.

I believe I can think of nothing else. Kiss the children for me. Give my respects to Mr. Adams & all who may enquire after me. Tell them I am all right &c.

Your affectionate

J. K. C.

Corinth, Miss.

Tuesday, May 13th 1862

Mrs. Dulcinea Callaway:

My dear wife, Yesterday was my day to write, according to my custom of writing twice a week, but Sunday evening our regiment was ordered out to the breast works, where we staid till late yesterday evening, when we got orders to come back to camp & prepare 5 days rations & be ready to move toward the enemy early this morning, with one hundred rounds of ammunition, to screw up our courage to the fighting point, as we were to attack them & drive them from their position. We were also ordered to pack up all our surplus baggage & ship it to Okalona, a place 10 miles below Corinth on the Rail Road, (where we have a hospital, to which we have sent 20 men from our Company). Last night and this morning I did not have time to write, but since we got ready to march we have been lying about all day waiting for the order. It is now nearly 5 o'clock P. M. & we are still here. There is a rumor in camp that the yankees sent a flag of truce to Gen. Buerrgard [Beauregard] this morning, announcing that the United States had recognized our independence, but this I suppose is a fudge. Everything seems to be quiet this evening, except that we have just now got orders to go to the breast works again to night. The yankees are said to be falling back gradually today. I hope they will continue to draw back.

I am well and in fine spirits. Ready to go out and join in driving them back so as to get some good water out of Tennessee River, or some where up that way.

Well, since we are ordered to go out yonder, I must cut my letter shorter than I intended. I can only tell you how we are located. We are now camped in a nice grove, 2 miles north of Corinth. We have plenty of shade and plenty to eat. The only difficulty is the great scarcity of the water, which is very bad when we do get it. We moved out here last Sunday, we are now in ¼ of a mile of the Breast works.

It seems that you are not getting all my letters. I have written twice a week ever since I came here and have had but two letters from you since I left home. I do not know what is wrong. I wrote you to send me my boots from Manderson['}s shop. I prefer those because they are lighter than those I got at Oakgrove [Chilton County, Alabama]. However, if the weather stays as dry as it is at present my shoes will do me some time yet, but when it is rainy the mud is from shoe mouth to half leg deep.

Well it is now 7 o'clock. We went out to the intrenchments and had dress parade & came back. All is quiet.

I hear this evening, for the first time, that General Price took the yankee telegraph the other day at the battle and telegraphed his compliments to Abe Lincoln.[9]

You have never said whether you got the forty dollars I sent you by Dr. Vaughan. I should like to know in your next.

You ask me if I need my shirts. I do need one very much. I don't care however, about my under shirt now. I have not had on my yellow one since I left Mobile. I wore it all the time I was there, especially when I was strolling about over town. I saw none as pretty as mine. I heard a great many women and children speak of its beauty there.

I want you to let me know how you get along, how much & what you are living on. When your bacon gives out you must get more. Get Mr. Adams or some other friend to attend to it for you. If there are any letters there for me read them, keep the secrets, if there are any and send the letters to me. Let me know if you have heard from Coffee [County], Ark[ansas], or John & Irene. I want to hear from them.

As I have not had room before I will give the name and character of my messmates. Homer M. Ford, William M. Ratliff, William F. Aycock, William C. Osborn, and William R. Cochran; however, Osborn quit our mess last night to go into one with his cousin who has lately come to the company. They are all good sober steady industrious fellows, good soldiers and willing to do their whole duty in camp & in the mess. Cochran is a great humorist and wit, and with all a ventriloquist, hence we have all sorts of fun in our mess. Ford spent 12 months in the Mexican war, & knows all the ropes, so you see we can keep our household in good order. He is head of our mess and we all obey his orders in regard to domestic affairs. Aycock brought a negro with him who does our cooking and washing. We have all our bed ticks filled with leaves and at night we make our beds & spread our blankets and sleep comfortably; though I am sorry to say that our old woman, the housekeeper, (Ford) has been unwell for several days, so that our house, or tent, has not been kept in very good order for some time.

I hope you will accept this for the long letter you asked for. I shall not seal it till morning and if anything happens I will put it in tomorrow.

I will close for tonight by subscribing myself your faithful and affectionate husband

J. K. Callaway

P. S. Wednesday, May 14th. We are all straight this morning. The weather is fine, and we are in fine spirits. The doctors Eilands, from Radfordsville, both got here last night. Dr. Kirksy is here. I suppose you have heard the Oakeses speak of him. No news in Camp this morning. I want you to write me a long letter and answer all the questions I have asked you in former letters. Goodby. Your loving J. K. Callaway

Be sure to kiss the children, and give my love to your mother. My respects to Mr. Adams.

Camp near Corinth
Thursday May 15th 1862

My dear D.

Having written to you two days ago, I decided not to write today, although I had an opportunity to send it by hand, which seems to be the only safe way of getting letters through, for I have written twice a week ever since I left home—but we have received orders to march out 3 or 4 miles to go on picket guard, our company with 4 others leave in the morning to be gone 4 days, which would make my next letter a week from my last, hence I write to night, while my provisions are being cooked.

There is no news in camp except that the yankees are falling back, or are said to be, and the opinion seems to be becoming prevalent that there will be no fight here, and it is thought by some that we will not stay here long. One of our regiment killed a yankee day before yesterday. He was out on picket duty. They took some prisoners.

We are in fine spirits, though several of our company are sick. Indeed, our company only musters 30 men for duty, rank & file. I am quite well and enjoying myself finely, except that it grinds me to think that I am *compelled* to stay here. I've got a dozen masters, who order me about like a negro, but I talk very plain to some of them occasionally. I am all right on the goose.

God Bless you & my babies. Your loving

Josh

Friday Morning, 16th. This is a beautiful morning all is quiet. We start out at 8½ o'clock this morning. I am all right, only I want to see you very much. Kiss my babies.

J. K.

Corinth, Miss.
Monday, May 19th 1862

Mrs. Dulcinea Callaway:

My Dear wife, your favor of the 13th instant came to hand last night, just as we got back from our tramp on picket, and found me well, though very tired. I was truly glad to hear from you, to hear that you were all well, & I was glad to get my boots. Our picketing expedition was a very dangerous adventure, though none of our Reg. was hurt. We were posted at the edge of an old field, 300 yards wide, the yankees on the other side of it. We were ordered to hold our post as long as possible. We lay behind logs & trees & shot yankees & yankees shot us, but we held our post 24 hours. 3 men were stationed together, in order to relieve each other, &, strange to say, we slept some, although the bullets were singing through the trees, sometimes in a few feet of our heads. One Lieutenant in our Reg. got a hole in sleeve, & one point of his star shot off his hat, but he returned the fire and heard the fellow hollow [*sic*] "Oh! Lord," several times. We shot generally at the shaking of a bush or the smoke of a gun, without seeing any body, they being concealed as we were.

We held the field 24 hours, and 2 hours after we were relieved the enemy drove back our pickets & took possession of our line of outposts. We escaped a good drubbing, perhaps, by being relieved as soon as we were for they brought a larger force than ours & a battery of artillery & shelled our men out & took [the] place themselves.

I am well except cold, and in fine spirits. I am glad to know that you feel as well satisfied as you do. May you ever be so. I have no greater desire than to be permitted to return to you, but my first duty is to my country, then to you & if I die in the struggle, be assured I die for you & our little ones. Let me know that you are happy, and I shall be so, for it is you for whom I live. Let it be your constant prayer, faithful & fervent, that I return, and all the yankees in yankeedom can not hurt me, & I shall live to be blessed by you.

Our company are generally moral steady men, but few temptations to vice & I regret that I have no Bible or Hymn Book to read during my leisure moments. We spend our time in cooking, eating, drinking &c, *especially the &c.*

Why don't you let me know if you got the money I sent you by Dr. Vaughan? I sent 40 dollars by him, and your saying nothing about it I fear you never got it.

If you need anything to eat let me know it & I will write to Jack Watters to supply you. If you need clothing buy it with the money I sent you. You must have whatever you want. I have had but 3 letters from you since I left home, though I have written you at least a dozen. I have not had a letter from any one else. I have written to cousin Hosea this morning, and aim to write to Sis & Marie and Nig in a day or two. I want you to send all the letters to me that come to Summerfield for me. I saw some more Coffee boys the other day, from down in my old neighborhood. They say Hope is in the war. He went to Pensacola.

You did not tell me what Hosea's folks nor any one else said. I hope you will excuse this botched up letter. I always have to write on my knee, knapsack, or as I am doing now, on a piece of board across my lap, in a great hurry, & write just as I think. Give my respects to Mr. Adams, Martin's & Montgomery's families. John Montgomery and Capt. Harris are well & I am your loving

Josh

I have not had a letter from Weston yet. I wrote to him some time since. Inclosed you have a bit of my hair which you asked me to send you.

J. K. C.

Camp Near Corinth, Miss.
Saturday, May the 24th 1862

Mrs. D. Callaway:

My dear wife, There has been so much confusion in camp lately that I have forgotten when I wrote you, but, having an opportunity this morning, I will write you a little letter any how. I am well, except a pain in my hip which troubles me when I walk. The boys are all puny, some real sick. Our company can muster only 21 men for duty. Thirty of our men are absent sick. Some at Rienzi, some at Enterprize & some at Macon, Miss.[10] If I get sick I shall go to Macon and stay at Uncle Elisha's. Times are dull, except that our pickets are constantly shooting yankees. Our pickets have fallen back till they are not more than 1½ miles from the breast work. Some think it is done to draw the enemy up within reach of our cannons on the breast work, while others think the yankees are pushing their pickets forward to make us *think* they are advancing while they are really retreating. All this, however, is mere conjecture. This however is true, namely: on last Tuesday (the 20th) we were ordered to prepare 5 days rations, which we did, & left camp next morning early to attack the enemy. Our forces were marching out from 10 in the morning till night. Of course we had an immense army out. The general impression was that the great battle was on hand; but on Wednesday evening we were all marched back to camps. Since we got back I hear that the enemy burnt their tents and retreated before we got near enough to attack them.

I will mention the money again that I sent you by Dr. Vaughan. If you got it you can [buy] anything you want. I know it is entirely unnecessary for me to caution *you* about being extravagant.

You speak of clothing. I should like to have one shirt and one pair of socks.

I have lost one pair, but my yankee socks replaced them, so I still have two pair; but one is worn out at the toe. When you send them be sure to put my initials on each piece.

Yesterday it rained all day. Today every thing is mud. My boots are good to have. Every thing is gloomy. I wrote to sister Camilla yesterday. I have written to cousin Hosea since I heard from you. I want to write Eli as soon as I hear from him. Tell me where he is. I find several men here from my old neighborhood in Coffee. They tell me that Hope is in the war, at Pensacola. I have not heard from Ell Godwin. No idea where he is.

We live sumptuously, on flour bread, Pickled beef and Pickled pork & bacon & meal once in a while. Rice and Rye are our substitutes for coffee. We get plenty of sugar & syrup. Our victuals are generally cooked hastily, our biscuits without soda, our beef hash without seasoning, & of course we can scarcely eat it. I would give a good sum to be at home a few days to eat some of your cooking. The thoughts of your biscuits & old aunt Sally's butter makes my mouth *& eyes* water. May God spare my life & health till I get to see & be with you all again. I *hope* to be there by the 1st of August. Let it be your constant prayer to God to spare me and no man shall hurt me. Yet pray God, that, if it is the fiat of fate that I must die in this war, that I may be ready and resigned. This is *my constant* prayer.

Give my respects to all inquiring friends. Capt. Harris is well. John Montgomery is well. Lieutenant Mims is sick. All the balance of the Summerfield boys are well. When you write give me all the news.

I have not had a letter from Wes yet, though John Montgomery shows me all he gets from him.

My dear D., I am with devoted love your faithful and affectionate husband
J. K. Callaway

P. S. Give my love to your mother & Dan. Tell them to write me a word in your next letter, if they can't write me a letter in full. J. K. C.

[Written across the top of the letter]

I would like for you to write at least once a week to me whether you get letters from me that often or not. Don't wait to get my letters. I have written to you twice a week ever since I came to Corinth, but have not had but 3 letters from you yet. Write once a week any how even if you only say you are well, for to hear that much is well worth five cents every 3 days to me. I hope you will not wait for me to write any more. I[f] you hear from Jim Baker be sure to let me know, for I want to write to him. If [he] is in the war I suppose he will likely come here and if he does I am just as apt not to know it as any way. I expect I have a number of relatives here from various parts, but I can't see them. I have no idea where they are. To hunt a man here is like hunting a needle in a hay stack, unless you know what Reg. he is in. Your loving

J. K.

CHAPTER TWO

Corinth to Tupelo

June 2–July 6, 1862

CALLAWAY'S COMPLAINT about confusion in camp at the end of May is understandable. As the Federals crept ever closer, Beauregard considered his options. On May 25 he met with his senior officers, who advised a withdrawal from Corinth in order to save the army. Beauregard carefully planned the evacuation, which he accomplished with the greatest secrecy. After ordering the soldiers to the front with rations for three days and leading them to believe they would be attacking the enemy, he began sending all of the sick to the rear and moving the military stores and supplies south on the railroad. On the night of May 29 he pulled the entire army out of the front lines and headed south. Beauregard shrewdly left behind a small decoy force that ran railroad cars in and out of town, cheered, and generally created the impression that large numbers of reinforcements were arriving. The ruse worked, and the Federals let them go with only a token cavalry pursuit.[1]

Beauregard first established his army at Baldwin, thirty-five miles south of Corinth, but owing to the barrenness and aridity of the area he moved on to Saltillo, which proved no better. By June 9 the army had moved on to Tupelo, Mississippi, fifty-two miles from Corinth, where the soldiers finally found plenty of good water. Beauregard decided to await developments, but he waited in vain—on June 11 the Federals ended what little pursuit they had mounted.[2]

At Tupelo a major change took place in the army command. Beauregard took himself off to Bladon Springs, Alabama, for a rest without permission from his superiors. President Davis seized this opportunity to remove Beauregard and wired Bragg to take command of the Western Department and the army. Bragg ran a tighter organization than did Beauregard, and the soldiers soon felt the change. Under Bragg's direction, Manigault declared, "many abuses were corrected, discipline and the strictest obedience to orders was rigidly enforced." To the sorrow of many of the troops, Manigault reported, "in the neighborhood of [their] camps were extensive, open fields, well adapted to drill and evolutions of the line."[3] Callaway did not mention the change in army command in any of the extant letters, but he did complain about the stricter discipline and military drill.

This group of letters provides a glimpse of the average Civil War soldier's daily life. Callaway describes stealing cattle from the enemy (not without a fight); he relates his experiences in Beauregard's grand scheme of evacuation; he details a typical day as orderly sergeant of the company; he describes the eating and sleeping arrangements of his mess; he admits the destruction and devastation caused by an army, even a friendly one; he complains of his various illnesses; and religion becomes increasingly important to him. There is a change in the way he refers to his children. In the earlier letters, when he remembered to mention them, they were "the children" or "the babies." Now they become Tillie (or Till, or T.) and Joe.

Included in this section is a letter Callaway received from a cousin. It is the only letter in the collection not written by Callaway.

Camp Near Baldwin Miss.
Monday, June 2nd 1862

Mrs. Dulcinea Callaway:

My dear wife. I have not had time nor chance to write you since last Saturday was a week ago [May 24]. On that day I wrote you and in the evening of the same day we, that is a detachment from our Regiment of 4 companies, the Dallas Warriors & our company among them, & a detachment of about the same No. of men each from the 10th and 19th South Carolina Re[g]iments[4] & Blithes [*sic*] Miss. Regiment,[5] making, in all, a force of about 300 men, were ordered out on picket, under command of Lieutenant Colonel John C. Reid, of the 28th Ala. However we went out to the Breast works on Saturday evening and lay there till Sunday evening, then returned to camp, eat our suppers and went to bed, or to sleep, rather, in our tents, & after having lain on our arms with our accouterments all on for 24 hours. After we had all gone to sleep (about 10 o'clock) we were ordered up to cook 3 days rations, which took till 4 in the morning, and at day light we were ordered out on picket, beyond the intrenchments. The enemies' Pickets seemed to have drawn back, and all day Monday every thing was quiet, and nothing warlike interrupted our retirements & rest (for it was really relief to get off from the noise & excitement of the camp). On Tuesday morning Col. Reid received orders to advance his line of Pickets, which he did by taking some skirmishers to support them. We advanced the line about 400 yds expecting to encounter the enemy at every step, but the movement was executed and we never saw a yank. All was quiet till in the evening, when one of the Pickets came to the Picket camp and reported a bunch of beef cattle, belonging to the enemy, grazing near our picket line. Col. Reid then took about sixty volunteers, myself among them, and went out & drove [them] in to the camp; but when we advanced on them they took fright and fled in the direction of the enemy. But Col. Reid took 10 men and followed them & drove them back, and took one shoot at a yankee who fled from his post. Then all was quiet till Wednesday morning, when the yankee Pickets advanced to within sight of ours, & then the firing commenced, but did not become rapid till about eleven o'clock, about that time it became rapid indeed, and Col. Reid drew up his reserve corps, of about 200 men, in line of battle, the other hundred being on the Posts. The firing continued and the balls whistled over our heads, but we, being under a little hill, were not exposed to danger; after the firing had gone on about an hour two wounded men came in, immediately after which our whole line of Pickets came running in and the yankees following and firing at them at every step, our Pickets ran right through our line & reported a large force of the enemy advancing, which we could easily believe, from the firing. Col. Reid ordered us to scatter and get behind trees, but the Pickets running so & and the Balls whistling so, that some of a South C. Reg. brok[e] & spread confusion through the whole line, but Col. Reid rallied them and formed his line again, & then called for a detail of from 5 to 12 men from a Co. according to the number in a company. There being only 20 in our company he called for 10. Lieut. Edwards who was in command of our company (our Capt. & first Lieut. being sick) ordered me to detail ten men, but being unwilling to take out a certain number and compel them to go, I called for volunteers, & our brave Elias Barron was the first man to step out. Col. Reid then got about 60 men whom he sent out, about 12 o'clock, under Capt. Hopkins as skirmishers. They advanced about 300 yards to the top of a hill, and found themselves in front of three thousand yankees. They exchanged a few rounds with them and were compelled to fall back; and in that retreat John A. Montgomery, my brave and esteemed friend, fell severely wounded in the shoulder and neck, but I hope he will soon be well again.

Col. Reid then ordered us all to advance at once, which order nearly every Alabamian obeyed promptly, but on our left were some South Carolinians who refused to advance at all. Col. Reid then called for some Alabamians to lead them out. Elias Barron volunteered again. I started but Lieut. Edwards having no officers along but himself, called me back to stay with and help him.

We all advanced then about 200 yards and opened fire on them, which they returned immediately, and those South Carolinians retreated again and left our left wing unprotected, which the enemy discovered & filed right round there & opened a cross fire on us, which we stood from 2 till 3 o'clock, about an hour. Then Col. Reid ordered us to fall back, behind trees along, and while we were falling back Elias Barron was walking along very deliberately and one of our boys told him if he did not get behind a tree he would get shot. He smiled & replied "I am not afraid of them" and in a minute a ball struck him in the . . . and wounded him, I fear, mortally. We fell back then across a little creek on a line with the South Carolinians and fought them about one hour, when Col. Reid, who is certainly a gallant officer, got orders from headquarters to bring his forces beyond the breast works. (Col. Reid had sent for reinforcements but could not get them.) In that last retreat, or rather while we were under that cross fire William McMillen, who was another brave soldier, fell mortally wounded, died next morning, Thursday.

In obedience to the order we retreated beyond the breast work. After we all got out, our artillery gave them a shell or two & a few rounds of grape & canister. We were then reinforced with one Regiment and went back to renew the contest, but I suppose the artillery had scattered them. We never saw them any more, although we stayed till eleven Thursday morning, when we were relieved and ordered back to camp. N.B. We went out on Monday morning at day light with barely 3 days rations, which gave out early on Wednesday. When we got to camp we found that all the provisions had been sent off on the wagons on Tuesday. Hence we had nothing to eat except what our sick men had kept in their haversacks, which they divided cheerfully. We were then ordered out to the trenches where we lay till 10 o'clock at night when we joined in the march evacuating Corinth. We marched all night Thursday night and all day Friday & rested Friday night. My load consisted of my knapsack, with 1 Pair pants my fancy shirt, one pair socks 1 pair draw- ers 1 pound tobacco 1 Pair boots some paper an empty haversack, canteen of water, gun, cartridge box, 40 rounds of cartridges &c &c; and all I had to eat from Thursday night to Saturday noon was 4 biscuits one cup of coffee and a piece of beef about half as large as my hand; about noon Saturday I broke ranks and stopped at a house and gave two dollars for twelve biscuits 3 of which I eat and gave the others to the balance of the company. At 3 o'clock Saturday we camped and went out foraging. I got some buttermilk, 2½ pounds of ham 3 pones of bread, which I *bought*. I then found a hen's nest with four eggs which I *pressed* into service. I then called at a house & found a pan of honey & eat as much as I wanted. It was then dark & I was 2 miles from the camp. I started back and on the way I came upon a negro milking some cows. I stopped & tried to buy some milk, but she refused to sell it. I then took the bucket from her with about 3 quarts of milk in it right warm. My three loaves of bread were in my haversack[.][6]

Camp near Baldwin, Miss.
Thursday night, June 5th 1862

Mrs. Dulcinea Callaway:

My dear wife, since I have an opportunity to send it by hand I will write you a short letter, although it is now ten o'clock, & it must needs be short. Lieut. Edwards has resigned and starts home early in the morning, and will carry it for me.

I received your letter of the 25th May yesterday. I was truly happy to hear from you, for it really seemed that you had forgotten me. I hope you will not punish me so again. Write to me twice a week. Surely you can afford to spend two hours twice a week to afford me so much pleasure, and *then* have time to do all that spinning you speak of. I like long letters and a number of them.

I am glad you are so attentive to prayer meeting. I hope you will continue so, and be sure to remember me in [your] prayers, which I know you will, and whe[n I] get home I think I shall take more pleasure [in] church going than I ever did before. I have [not] heard a sermon since I left home.

We have orders tonight to prepare to mo[ve] again to morrow. We have been here now fiv[e days] almost without shelter. We have two tents to the whole company, all the balance being burnt at Corinth. We are camped in an old field where the [sun] shines very warm but we have erected brush arbors and stretched our blankets till we have helped the cause very much.

I saw John Grice today, of the 26th Ala. He says he saw Hope Powell the other day. He is in the 33rd Ala. Regiment. I asked Col. Frazer this evening for permission to go to Baldwin tomorrow to see him. He said I could go if we did not leave, but I suppose we will move. I think though I will get to go any how. If I do I will let you know when I write again, which will be when we get to the next stopping place.

I have news here that France has recognized our independence,[7] and that Johnston and Jackson has [sic] whipped the yankees out of Virginia;[8] and that peace is almost inevitable soon. I hope this [is] all true. I have no idea which way we will go when we leave here. We may go to Tennessee and we may go towards Alabama.

The health of the Company seems to be improving. There are 34 men here. The balance are scattered from here to Mobile. We have lost four men out of the company,[9] namely Henry Farror, Marsh Skinner and William Ratliff. The Company held a meeting the other day and passed some resolutions concerning their deaths. You will see them [in] the Selma Reporter.

My dear, I hope you will write me [so]me more long letters. I love them long and [fu]ll of love and religion. Oh! that I could [be] where I could see you occasionally, but I [hav]e no desire to quit the army till our inde[pe]ndence is established. Which I hope will be soon, after which I will return to my loved ones and enjoy the sweets of liberty, home and family.

I am well and as usual enjoying myself. I pray that this may reach you all well &c. My compliments & respects to all who may think enough of me to inquire after me. My respects to my old friend Mr. Adams.

I am, my love, your faithful and loving husband

J. K. Callaway

P. S. I am glad truly that T. is so fond of her book. I hope you will push her along. Twenty kisses on this for you & her. Kiss Joe for me. I hope he [is] well. J. K.

Camp Near Tupelo, Miss.
Monday, June 16th 1862

Mrs. D. Callaway:

My dear wife, I have been waiting for two days for Hope Powell or Dan Savage to visit me, thinking to write while they were here, but they have not come yet. I believe I told you that they and a number of others from Coffee are in the 33rd. Hope has been discharged, and if not already gone home, he will go in a few days. He and Dan Savage promised to come and see me before he left.

My dear, I am not very well today, though much better than I was yesterday. I have severe cold, and yesterday I had high fever with "awful" pain in my head & bones generally. In the evening I sweated off the fever, and last night I took a regular night sweat & this morning I have severe aching in my back and loins, all of which, together with my constant labor this morning, makes me feel very weak & but little like writing. I have gone through my regular routine of business this morning and marched half a mile to an old field & drilled two hours & come back and made out a regular report of all the Quarter Master Stores lost by our company in the evacuation of Corinth; and it is not yet eleven o'clock. Mine has been no lazy life since I became a soldier, to prove which I propose to give you the order of my business, which I know you will agree is laborious, but for the faithful performance of it, being always at my post and my written reports being always correct and neat & clean, I have the reputation of being the best Orderly Sergeant in the Reg. Some of our co. say the best in the world.

Every morning at day light the drum beats Roll Call. I get up then, form the company, call the Roll & then put the company to cleaning up the camp, sweeping out the street &c, after which I have to make a list of the names of the men who report themselves sick. I then gather them all up, who are able, and march them down to the Surgeon's Office and have them examined and take a list of those who are excused from duty, and then march them back to quarters. I then make out my morning report and carry it to the Adjutant; I then come back & record the names of the men who are detailed for any kind of service—guard or fatigue; by this time it is 8 o'clock, the time for Guard Mounting. I call out those detailed for brigade guard, inspect their arms (guns & ammunition) and march them out and stay till the first guard mounting is over. I then go back and call out those detailed for camp guard, inspect their arms and march them out to the *second* guard mounting and stay till it is over. By this time it is 9 o'clock and the drum beats for company drill. I then parade the company, call the Roll, & form the company properly and we go out and drill till eleven o'clock. Then if there are any returns to make, or reports, in writing, I have it to do; if there are any provisions to draw or Quarter Master Stores to draw I have to make out the requisition. I also have to record all the general orders and some of the Articles of War (all those affecting the private soldier) and read them at Roll Calls. These I have to write whenever I can.

H. M. Ford, of our company, is now Regimental Commissary, and I do nearly all of his writing, making out his returns, making requisitions for the Regiment &c. (By doing this I have an opportunity to know the eating strength of the Regiment, which is 511, about 600 being absent sick.)

By this time, and *generally* before I get through, 3 o'clock comes, & I then parade & form the company, call the Roll and we go out on Battallion Drill till 5 o'clock in the evening; we then come in & I finish, if I can by supper, doing my work. At 8 o'clock the drum beats tattoo. I then form the company and call the Roll again, and if I lack anything of having done all my work, I finish after every body has gone to sleep. I sometimes write till midnight, especially if I write a letter. Now during all this time I am called a hundred times by the officer of the day, Sergeant Major, Adjutant, Quarter Master, Commissary, & others for men to do something about the camp—bury a dead horse, or man, to fill up some hole, or *something*.

Surely it is no wonder that I don't write any more letters than I do.

Now I will give you some idea of our eating and sleeping. Our boy is getting to be a very good cook. He bakes good biscuits, nice light bread and cooks ham & beef steak very nicely; Rice is very easily cooked, molasses is not to be cooked nor sugar. He makes very good coffee. So our victuals, what we get, is nearly as well prepared as if we were at home. Yesterday we had a mess of irish potatoes with butter on them. They were sent to Mr. Graham, of Oakgrove, by his mother, and he divided them with us; he also gave us some fine Pickled beets, the first Pickles I ever saw that I loved, but they were splendid. All this for a Sunday dinner. If I could have been at home & eaten it with you I should have enjoyed it "hugely." But as it was, away from you and sick too, I didn't enjoy it much.

Our Sleeping is not so good. We have only 4 tents in the company. My mess has one of them. Our house hold furniture consists of 1 trunk, 1 gun, 4 knapsacks, 1 Sword & a bedstead. You see a representation of the bedstead at the top of this page, with us asleep on it. It consists of 4 forks driven in the ground, about a foot high, with poles laid in them similar to the head & foot of a bedstead proper. Then we lay 5 poles length ways, leaving a space of about 18 inches between each couple. Then we skin hickory saplings & stretch the bark across these poles, about 6 inches apart, as you see the fine marks in the picture. This bark gives way where it is tied, in drying, and swags, some pieces more than others. We spread half our blankets on this rack for a bed & cover with the balance. It is like lying on a fodder rack between 2 logs 18 inches apart. Knapsacks for pillows. Most of the company sleep on scaffolds made of poles altogether, under a large brush arbor we have in our street. My mess has a brush arbor in front of our tent, which answers the double purpose of a portico and a dining room; our kitchen is out doors; our smoke house, dairy &c is under the bed. We keep house on a grand scale! I tell you we have a gay time! But not withstanding all these hardships, I enjoy myself finely; but when I get sick, which, thank God, has been but very little, so far, I get down in the mouth, take the blues, and want to go home. I have always been thankful for good health, but since I have seen so much suffering and death I am a thousand times more thankful than ever. I hope you will continue to do as you have been doing, pray for the preservation of my health and moral character. I am a believer in the power of prayer.

Perhaps you expect me to give you some items of news, but I cannot tell you anything that is reliable. I hear a great deal of "camp news" but don't know where it starts from. I suppose that some of our generals have gone to Richmond.[10] The Yankees are going back to Tennessee River. France & England are about to interfere in the war. Peace is about to be made and a hundred and one other reports favorable to peace, but no one knows where they start.[11]

I am of the opinion that this army will be divided and sent in various directions, some, perhaps, to Alabama, some to Tennessee and Kentucky and some to Virginia. But I hope none will go near Summerfield, for a country could hardly have a worse curse or plague than to have a large army march through it. We completely eat it out as we go. The locusts of Egypt were not more destructive.

My private and very humble opinion is that the war will end this year. Indeed I shall not be surprised if the fighting is about done now. I think this opinion is founded on good reasoning. Pray that it may be so!

I believe I have said all I can. Hope and Dan Savage and several others requested me to give you & your mother their respects. Frank Green also sends his respects to you. I got a letter from Mr. Oakes 3 days ago. He says he has not heard from you since I left. I promised to notice your mother's letter more at length in this letter but I have so engaged with the other subjects that I had forgotten it, and now I have not got room. Tell her I appreciate it very highly and would like to have another. She speaks of my ability to look at the best side of a bad picture & wishes she had more of the gift, but [I] always thought she had more of it than anybody else. I hope she will continue to remember me in her prayers. Give her my love. Give my respects to Mr. Adams. And I would be glad if you would make some arrangements with some one who writes to the Dallas Warriors to let me hear from you through them. There are letters from Summerfield every day, but I never can hear a word from you only when you write me.

I wish you to send by the first one passing, one shirt and one pair of socks, and believe me Your faithful & loving

Josh Callaway

P. S. I will send you a copy of my report this morning. This itself is not so laborious as keeping my other lists and reports, by which it is made. You have it enclosed.

Lovingly   J. K. C.

I hope Joe is well by this time. Take good care of him. I want to see him again.

N.B. The Columns marked "N.C. Officers" are for Non Commissioned Officers. You see I don't report any body absent without leave or in arrest. There has never been any body absent from our company without leave, and

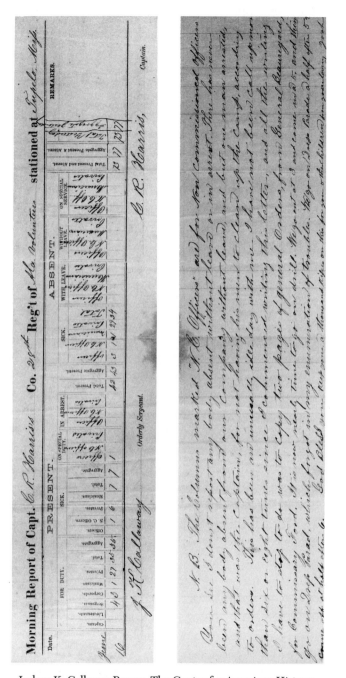

Joshua K. Callaway Papers, The Center for American History,
The University of Texas at Austin

but one man arrested, and that was the Captain, for not having his men to clean up the camp according to orders. This has been an unusually idle day with me. I have not been call[ed] up more than six or eight times since I commenced writing this letter, and all the writing I have to stop to do was to copy two pages of General Orders, from General Beauregard, for Commissary Ford. It is now nearly time to go on drill. We go out at 3 and come in at 5 and *then* go on Dress Parade which [I] forgot in my enumeration of troubles. We go on Dress Parade at half after 5 & come off at half after 6. God Bless you. Keep you a thousand kisses on this for you & the children from your loving Josh.

Camp Near Tupelo, Miss
Thursday, June 19th 1862

Mrs. D. Callaway:

My dear wife, Yours of the 16th inst. came to hand yesterday, and found me well. I have been a little sick. I had fever Sunday, & Monday morning I reported for duty and they put me through pretty tight and Tuesday I had chills & fever, and Wednesday I went to duty & have been all right ever since.

I am glad to hear that the baby [Joe] is well, or better, I was afraid to hear from [of?] him. I am also glad that your letters can get through so very quickly. Your last came in less than two days.

I wrote to Eli yesterday after I got yours. I have written twice to Weston & have not heard a word from him yet, except that John Montgomery let me see all the letters he got from him. Now I hear from him only through you. I want you to tell him when you write to him that if he don't write me I shall give him a good bumping when I see him. He may never have received my letters; possibly I did not direct my letters right, but I directed according to John Montgomery's instructions.

I am glad to hear that he is well, I hope he will enjoy good health hereafter.

I cannot give you any news. It would be folly to write the thousand and one rumors that are afloat in camp, with no certainty about the truth of any of them. I suppose you have heard of the rumored intervention of England, France & Spain; but this, although it may be true, is as yet only rumor. The report says that those powers have offered five proposals for peace—that the Federals have accepted three of them and the Confederates all of them.

I have heard but one sermon since I left home. It was preached by the Rev. S. B. Carson, of Holly Springs, Mississippi, from the 21st verse of the 22nd chapter of Job.[12] It was an able sermon, and doubtless did some good. He preached in another Regiment. One Sermon in three months! Isn't that horrid? Especially when we consider that we have several able ministers in our own Regiment, such as Capt. II. A. M. Henderson. I suppose we have a Chaplain (Hardy Brown) but he has never been in the Reg. more than three or four days & didn't preach then.

We have prayer meeting in our company about twice a week. We had prayer last night, or I should have written to you.

My Dear, I could fill a volume (a little one) with execrations upon the "in[hu]manity of man." I have learned an important lesson by coming to the war. I learned more of human nature and deception than I ever cared to know, though this is one of the *best* Regs. in this respect.

As the mail is about to close, I must wind up my letter. As usual I have not time to think, but have had to hurry and fill up the sheet with whatever has passed through my head while a hundred men have passed by the tent and asked me some foolish question.

I am glad that you feel so cheerful as you seem to do. I have seen & am constantly seeing the most desponding & patriotism killing letters imaginable, written by women to their husbands in this co. or Reg. generally. May the Lord Sustain you and give you that strength of mind & stability of character (which you are almost remarkable for already) sufficiently to keep you above despondence. How can I do otherwise than be contented under such circumstances. Indeed I almost grumble, sometimes, at my own want of courage when I read your letters. I believe I wrote you that all our officers are absent sick or gone home. Lt. Edwards resigned on account of bad health. I hope to hear from you soon. Your loving   J. K. Callaway
[Envelope—return address: J. K. Callaway, Co. K 28 Ala Regt.—sent to: Mrs. J. K. Callaway, Summerfield, Alabama]

[The following letter was written to Callaway by a cousin.]

Tibbee Station
May 10th 1862

Dear Cousin,

Your letter to father was received by him and given to me a few days ago while on a visit home, to answer. He has allways been a slow correspondent, and now is so overcome with the present calamities, particularly the suffering of the poor soldiers, as to almost unfit him for anything. As you know, perhaps, a hospital has been established at Macon, and not only the hospital and wards but many private families are entertaining our sick braves. Oh! how distressing to witness their suffering, and the death of many of them. Poor things, away from home and friends thus to die. But where the soul of the nation is engrossed in our countries [*sic*] cause, her defenders all ways meet with kindness, though it be from stranger friends. When your letter was written you were at Corinth. Do you think of Beauragards [*sic*] movements as the boys in Virginia remarked of Gen Johns[t]on? When asked by a citizen where they were falling back to now? Replied "They did'nt [*sic*] know unless to Mexico." What do you think of our prospects now? Tis useless though, to ask a soldier, for universally they are sanguine of success, and I think this very fact is one of the most cheering features in our case. If our soldiery are certain and determined on victory, we certainly must & will be successfull. As to our *final* success I have never had a doubt, even in the most gloomy hour, but certainly "This is a time that tries mens souls."

I have one brother and an only brother in the army in Virginia. Was not sixteen years of age when he entered the service. I see his regiment was in the battle of Chickahominy [Virginia] [13] but not a word have we heard from him. His time will be out in July and he expects to return home for a short time, as the Conscription law does not take him. But how anxiously I await to hear the casualties of that battle. I have also two brothers-in-law in the army at Corinth. Perhaps you may be able to see them, if posted near them. One of them, Mr. Beauchamp is assistant Quartermaster of that division. The other Mr. Stokes is in Tuckers Miss. Regiment. I don't know the No. of the Regt or the Company. Pa received a letter from Cousin Thomas Callaway, son of Uncle Joshua. He was in the 9th Texas Regt. Perhaps you have found him out before this. Pa has not heard from Cousin Hosea since last fall, before the Yankees had invaded his state at all. The men were in arms *then,* and I reckon the women and children are *now.* I feel all the time that I could fight bravely if I only knew how, and if they do kill my brother, think I will find out how. It seems to me revenge can-not be a sin in this war.

Cousin Joshua, you must write to us. Direct your letter to Pa at Macon. I will be there before many days, and if you get sick or can get a furlough come down to Macon and recruit. Pa inquired of some Texans for Cousin Thomas. They said he was sick at Corinth but they would'nt [*sic*] let him away. I wish so much he could get to our house, where we could nurse him. With many prayers for a preservation of your health, I remain

> Your Affect. Cousin
> Mary J. S. Callaway

> Camp Near Tupelo
> Monday, June 23rd 1862

My dear D:

I thought I would write you last night, but could not for want of a candle. This morning I didn't get time till it is now so late my letter will not get off till tomorrow. I should have written earlier but we had "battallion drill" earlier this morning than common. I have just got in from a three hours heat commencing half past six. I am very warm and tired, and feel a little unwell from cold.

There being no news stirring in camp I cannot make an interesting letter; the only thing of consequence to me is we've got to "*move*" again. I do not know what sort of a place we are going to or where it is, I only know that it is about ¾ of a mile west of our present encampment. There is a detail of about 60 men gone there to dig wells today. This is very disagreeable for we have cleaned off our ground, camp & parade ground nicely, built brush arbors, bedsteads, table &c, and dug thirteen wells, from 9 to 18 feet deep & got plenty of good water. The poor soldier knows nothing of the object of these moves, all he knows is that the order is issued & if he complains he is insulted if not punished. All he dare ask is, "what will you have me to do?" To all this, however, he soon becomes accustomed, and, if, naturally ambitious and resolute, he is jolly at all times and under all circumstances. And when off of duty and in his quarters, if you were to hear him talk on politics, tactics, domestics, "foreign intervention," national policy, republicanism, &c, you would almost think he was a *free man!*

The health of the co. is not as good as it was when I wrote before. The Dallas Warriors, I believe are all well.

Capt. Harris & Lt. George are both at Macon sick & the company is without an officer. Sergt. Aycock was brevetted two weeks ago to the rank of Lieutenant, and his appointment will probably be permanent.

Yesterday I went over to the 33rd Ala hoping to see Hope Powell, but he is gone home. Dan Savage is gone off on a sick leave, I don't know where. I saw a good many of the Coffee boys whom I had not seen before. I saw P. D. Costello, Sidney Warren (of Haw Ridge), Ian Carmichael, Joe Goyers & several others.

Peace is the general theme of conversation, yet nobody desires it except it be on honorable terms.

I am in correspondence with Uncle Elisha's daughter.

My dear, it is a long time between letters. I *certainly* don't get a letter from you every week. I think you might write twice a week. If I had time I'd write to you every day. Try to let me hear from you a little oftener.

Give my love to the family. My respects to Mr. Adams & family also to Mr. Montgomery's family.

And believe me as ever

Your faithful and affectionate
Josh

P. S. You will perhaps wonder where I get such fancy envelopes. This is one that a young man, in another company, gave me for writing a letter for him to his sweetheart.

I saw Warren Wilkerson yesterday. He asked me to give you all his respects when I wrote again.   J. K. Callaway

Camp—Tupelo, Miss.
Saturday, June 28th 1862

Mrs. D. Callaway:

My Dear Wife, Your affectionate letter of the 22nd reached me yesterday; not having had a letter from you since the 18th I was unusually glad to get it and . . .[14] to hear, I was more than glad to hear all was well.

I am not very well myself, though I still keep able to do duty. I have had three severe chills and fevers in the last two days, . . . feel a good deal like having a fever this morning; but have been taking quinine two days and hope I shall avoid a spell of chills & fever.

I hope this will find you all well and . . . There is very little news in camp. I *don't* hear as much talk about "foreign intervention" now as I did a few days ago. We hear that the battle . . . , but know nothing about . . . of course, that we are "giving them gull."

One of our Regiment, who was taken prisoner at Boonesville,[15] got into camp last night and tells a good story of his escape. He is a Lieutenant, but the yankees never found it, or perhaps he would not have escaped at all. He says that himself, and three others were kept in an old house and guarded by six men, between here and Corinth. One of the prisoners, a man from Florida, had occasion to go out in the night and asked the Sentinel to open the door, which he did, and at the same time held a piece of plank in his hand, and as the prisoner stepped out he snatched the plank out of his hand and knocked him down with . . . , and *our* Lieutenant jumped on him & took his gun from him, & the other five guards being . . . in a tent a little way off, they left. After getting off, they changed their clothes and went to a house, and when any yankee would come they would pass as citizens. After boarding a few days they attempted to make . . . , but could not pass the yankee line of Pickets. They then turned and went way round in another county, and passed *round* the picket line. He says . . . well. Buell's Army . . . to Memphis. The men who guarded them told that if all hands felt as they do the war would soon stop. But . . . officers say they will fight us ten years or drive us into the Gulf of Mexico. This looks like we will establish our independence yet, they having determined to fight us *ten* years only, and we having determined to resist a hundred years.

Hardy Brown got home two days ago, and says the people about home are generally well, but that everything looks much more gloomy than when I left.

The Dallas Warriors are generally well, that is those from about Summerfield. Mr. Overton is well and is a jolly old soldier. If you see his family tell them about him, & tell them to let me hear from you when they write to him.

Captain Hopkins and Lieut. Mims are at home & will probably bring my things. Mr. Hargrove will perhaps come before they do & if he does, he will bring them. Don't hesitate to ask anybody to do it, & if you do send them don't send that coarse shirt. I'll never get rid of the one I've got, & if you can send me a pair of summer pants. When I start again I shall throw away my old brown ones.

My respects to all who may inquire after me. I want to hear from John Montgomery. If . . .

I have not heard from W. F. yet.

My love to your Mother and Dan, and a thousand kisses & a world of love on this to you & the children from

Your faithful & Loving

J. K. Callaway

Camp Near Tupelo, Miss

Sunday evening, July 6 1862

My Dear Wife,

I must drop you a short letter. We have just received orders to prepare two days rations and be ready to march at half past 4 o'clock tomorrow morning. It is said we are going to a place called Saltillo 8 miles above this on the Rail Road, though the order does not specify our destination, and from this fact together with several other circumstances, some conjecture that our destination is some point unknown to us, perhaps in Tennessee or Alabama. I think, however, we will go to Saltillo, though we may not stop there long.

I heard a very good sermon today preached by Capt. Nabors of our Regiment.

The victory at Richmond was celebrated here yesterday by the firing of 13 guns by each Division, however, I only heard those of two Divisions.[16]

I wish you and W. F. to write me soon, address as before, Tupelo, Miss. My love to all the family. Mr. Overton is well.

This leaves me tolerably well, and may it find you all well and constant in prayer for your loving

J. K. Callaway

Mrs. J. K. Callaway

Summerfield

Wes,[17] I should like very much to have you visit me in camp, if you don't go to Virginia.[18] It would afford me particular pleasure to see you just now. Write me tomorrow and let me know what you think of it.

The Lord preserve our lives and health, and bless us with a speedy peace is the prayer of Yours in haste

J. K. Callaway

W. F. Baker

CHAPTER THREE

Tupelo to Smith's Cross Roads

July 13–September 1, 1862

JOSHUA CALLAWAY speculated in his July 6 letter that his regiment's move to Saltillo, about nine miles north of Tupelo on the Mobile and Ohio Railroad, portended a further move to an unknown destination, perhaps into Tennessee or Alabama. Little did he know that his commander, General Braxton Bragg, had planned an unprecedented transfer of an army by rail in preparation for a strike northward into Kentucky.

Bragg had hoped to be able to strike a blow against the enemy from his position at Tupelo. The Union army that forced Beauregard to abandon Corinth had been split up. While much of it continued to threaten central Mississippi, General Don Carlos Buell posed a more immediate danger as he crept along the Memphis and Charleston Railroad toward Chattanooga, Tennessee, gateway to the heart of the South. The commander in east Tennessee, General E. Kirby Smith, lacked the forces to deter Buell, so Bragg decided he should join forces with Smith and together they would invade Kentucky in an effort to free the state from the yoke of Union domination. This hoped-for penetration of the enemy's communications would create chaos and confusion by disrupting supply lines and further dividing the Federal forces.[1]

Eliza (Elise) Brooks Ellis Bragg, Braxton's wife, may have prompted his decision to begin his march north from Chattanooga. On June 8, 1862, she reminded him that the modern systems of transportation—railroads and steam navigation on the rivers—could be used for military purposes. "Why not," she queried, "take our army round into Tennessee & thence into Kentucky?" Having earlier sent a division to Chattanooga by rail, Bragg felt confident of his ability to move his entire infantry force by the same means.[2]

Other factors also encouraged Bragg to change his base of operations. It proved difficult to provision the army at Tupelo—the army wagons were badly deteriorated, and Corinth's loss had cut direct rail communication between the East and Mississippi. In her letter of June 8 Elise had also reminded Bragg of his quite desperate straits regarding food for the army: "You leave our enemy in your rear—true, but is not that better than an enemy in your midst, starvation."[3]

Bragg had additional reasons for deciding to invade Kentucky. In early July General John Hunt Morgan had taken off on a highly successful cavalry raid into the area. Morgan reported the Kentuckians eager to take up arms for the Confederacy, a conclusion supported by Kentuckians who had already cast their lot with the South. These Confederate Kentuckians assured Bragg he would be welcomed with open arms in their home state. A final factor may have been the pressure Bragg felt from fellow southerners who expected their generals to undertake offensive moves rather than sit on the defensive.[4]

And so, on July 23, Bragg began the movement of thirty thousand soldiers from Tupelo to Chattanooga, largely by railroad. It took the first troops six days to arrive at their journey's end—a "776-mile trip over six railroads" that was "admirably carried out and in record time." Bragg had moved his troops "farther faster than troops had ever been moved before," uniting "two armies whose direct line of communication had been severed by the enemy." Bragg had successfully exposed Buell's flank and rear and now menaced all of the Union armies in the West by his threat to their communications with the North. "The Confederates," asserted biographer Grady McWhiney, "thanks to Bragg, now had a chance to regain all they had lost."[5]

Joshua Callaway provides an eyewitness account of this grand movement. But before leaving Mississippi, he reports suffering from jaundice and complains about the lack of food, the miserable health of the entire army, and of Bragg's "military despotism." His spirits lift, however, when he takes part in the epic railroad journey, which he describes in detail, including a visit to relatives in Atlanta. The Chattanooga area provides better foraging opportunities for the soldiers, and Joshua tells of one of his excursions. The last letter in this group is written from Ray County, Tennessee, thirty-five miles north of Chattanooga. Joshua is in high spirits and reports the army healthier and anxious to meet the enemy. He also warns Dulcinea that she may not hear from him for some time, perhaps as long as a month—an excellent estimate, as it turned out.

Camp Near Saltillo Miss
Sunday, July 13th 1862

Mrs. Dulcinea Callaway:

My Dear D., I expect you are becoming uneasy on account of my unusually long silence. I wrote you before we left Tupelo and should have written again before this but we have had no mail since we got here. I was becoming very impatient to hear from you, but just as I had decided that I could wait no longer Capt. Hopkins arrived with a letter from you, dated July the 6th.

I am *glad* to hear that you are all well. May the Lord continue to preserve your health.

I hope Till will soon be able for business.

Capt. Hopkins did not bring me any clothes, he says he told one of the boys he would bring them but he don't remember whether they carried them over to him or not. You don't say in your letter whether you sent them by him or not. If, however, you sent that coarse shirt I shall not complain if they are lost. I should like to have a lighter one of some kind, white, linen bosomed shirts are very common, though colored ones are more so. I am not particular about pants. Anything for coolness. And while you are sending be sure to send a handkerchief or two.

I am glad to hear that Eli is wounded in the *leg* instead of the body. I hope it is not very bad; and I also hope he will get home soon.

There is no news stirring in camp, hence I can't tell you anything that you have not heard.

I want you, *without fail* to subscribe for the "Daily Reporter." Take it for six months, commence immediately. You can subscribe in your own name or mine as you please, perhaps better in your own. Commence tomorrow. Wes will attend to it for you.

I hope you will not have to spend many more weeks alone. The impression seems to be very prevalent in camp that peace is at hand. God grant it may be so! *if* it is on *honorable terms.*

I am glad to hear that John Montgomery is getting well. I hope I shall see him in camp before a great while. Give him my respects.

When you write let me know what Wes and Dan are doing. Tell Wes if he has any notion of joining the army to be sure to come here first. I want to see him before he does it.

Mr. Overton is well. Perhaps he heard from home through Capt. Hopkins. I have not seen him since the Capt. arrived.

I am forgetting to tell you about our move. We left Tupelo at 6 o'clock Monday morning last, and got here at 4½ in the evening, after a march of about 18 miles over the dryest and hottest road that I ever saw. The dust rose in such a dense cloud that, at times, we could not see a man twenty paces; and to breathe was almost suffocation. We rested about two hours in the middle of the day. Great numbers of men gave out, and did not get into camp till next day; and, in fact, I heard of two or three who died on the way, but none of them belonged to our Regiment. I stood it very well, from the fact that my knapsack was hauled. I carried nothing but a sword. We are now camped in a nice grove and have excellent water.

I am still unwell. I have been taking the jaundice for three days and it has just now made its appearance in my eyes and skin. If I get sick I shall do my best to get home or at *least* to Uncle Elisha's.

My love to the family. All remember me in your prayers. My respects to all who may enquire after me. Tell Wes to give my respects to Messers Gregory & Hawley. Tell Hawley I have been thinking I'd write to him but have not yet.

My Dear, remember me constantly in your prayers. Kiss the children, don't let T. forget me. And believe me as ever

Your Faithful, Affectionate

J. K. Callaway

P. S. I want you and Wes both to write me immediately, if not sooner. Direct to Saltillo, Miss.

J. K. C.

Camp Near Saltillo, Miss.
Wednesday, July 16th 1862

Mrs. D. Callaway:

My Dear wife, According to my custom, I will write you this morning. As has been the case for three or four weeks I am not exactly well but am up. The jaundice is showing itself very plainly now. It makes me feel mean, weak and puny, but does not, as yet, make me really sick.

The dearth of news still prevails. We hear nothing worth writing or talking about, except that it is generally supposed that we will remain here several weeks. I hope I shall be able to get a short furlough in the time although it is impossible at present. You needn't look for me till you see me.

This morning the weather is dark and cloudy, looks very much like rain. The farming interest in this country has suffered for rain, but it is now raining nearly every day. Vegetables are almost out of the question. Soldiers know nothing about them. I have had one mess of Irish potatoes and one of beans this season. I have eaten two or three green apples and as many peaches. I have had half of one *good* apple. I see but very few orchards in the country, and those I have seen are all very small.

The hardest work we have now is drilling. Our camp is nicely cleaned off. We are camped in a beautiful grove, on the side of a little hill, near Saltillo, on the M[obile and] O[hio] Rail Road, in Itawamba County. We have good spring water in abundance, though it is nearly a quarter of a mile from camp.

I have inquired of several citizens if they know of such a place as Tremont, but have not found a man who had ever heard of such a place.

I hope you will write immediately and let me know if you have heard from Eli. I am very anxious about him.

Capt. Hopkins thinks he left the clothes you sent to him for me at home. Send over there and get them & send them by somebody else. I wish you would find out from John Montgomery if he knows what went with our man, Elias Barron, who was wounded when he was and sent off with him. If he does I want to know all about him. We have not heard a word from him since he was wounded.

We have not been paid off yet, nor do we have any idea when we will be.

I wish you would let me know what disposition you have made with what money I have sent home. How much you have on hand &c.

Tell Wes to be sure to write to me. I would write to him this morning, but I could only repeat what I have written to you, & then I have no paper, ink, Envelopes nor stamps.

Mr. Overton is well but he is very uneasy about his folks, he hears conflicting reports about the state of his wife's health. I hope you will write the exact state of her case.

Give my love to the family. My respects to friends generally. And believe me

Your faithful and Loving

J. K. Callaway

P. S. I got a letter from Cousin Priss Gardenery of Macon County and one from Mary Ann Wilkerson yesterday. They both sent their love to you. Well, I will send the letters to you.

Be sure to write this evening. Lovingly

Josh

Camp Near Saltillo, Miss.

Sunday evening, July 20th 1862

Mrs. D. Callaway:

My Dear wife, I received your letter of the 13th yesterday. It found me still unwell, but today I feel much better, perhaps from this fact, towit: I eat a very hearty dinner. We had a nice fat goose and some roasting ears, the goose baked and the corn boiled, and a nice apple pie for a dessert.

You would scarcely know me, I am very yellow, my eyes look like a dog's. I look like an indian all over.

The news department is blank, except that at inspection this morning there was a dispatch read, stating that the Confederates whipped the yankees at Murphreesborough. Took 1200 prisoners, killed 200 to 300, took a battery of Artillery, 300 wagons and $250,000 worth of stores, and lost 16 killed & 25 wounded.[6]

I am truly sorry to hear that Eli is wounded. I know your mother sees a great deal of trouble, but I know at the same time that she can bear more than almost any other mother. May the Lord sustain her in her affliction!

We are all nothing more than the subjects of a military despotism now, and have no right to think, and are hardly allowed to sigh at the fall of our friends and relatives: and if we do happen to shed a tear secretly, it is soon dried up to make room for one for some one else. We never will have time to contemplate and comprehend the horrors of this war until sweet, delightful peace is restored to us, & we can take a retrospective view.

The health of the company seems to be a little better. Capt. Harris is at home. I must promise to write a long letter *next time.* I must say a word to Wes. Mean time give my love to the family. Kiss the children & believe me your loving husband   J. K. Callaway

W. F. Baker, Esq.[7] Dear Brother, Yours of the 13th came to hand yesterday and I hasten to answer it. I have no news except what I have written to D[ulcinea]. If I could see you I could interest and amuse you for a week, but I can not undertake to do it on paper. Indeed if I were to write all I know, it would forstall me in the pleasure of *telling* you when I get *home,* which I hope to do before many months.

I should have loved to have been under the steps that "Moonlight night" you speak of but if I *had* been there I guess I should have been at home. I hope you will enjoy your self the balance of the war. See the women and Kiss D[ulcinea] & T. & Joe.

Mr. Overton got a letter from his son Tom yesterday stating that he and John were both wounded *slightly* in the leg, & are getting well rapidly. The old man is in fine humor. I regret to hear of the death of Thos. Beaty.

Give my respects to Mr. Montgomery and family, also to Mr. Adams's family. I hope you will give my compliments to all my friends.

Write me all the news. Tell me what Gregory & Hawley are doing, if they are doing much business. Also if neither of them is a conscript, give them my respects. Tell Hawley I am going to write to him in a few days.

Well I believe I have written all I know. I hope you will excuse my short letter. I will write you a better one next time. Overton, Bryan Dallas & Andrew Boggs are all in my tent talking with some other fellows. All well.

Be sure to write soon, this evening, and believe me your

Friend & Brother

J. K. Callaway

Bryan, Andrew & Overton send their respects to you.

Josh

Camp Near Saltillo, Miss.

Saturday morning July 26th 1862

Mrs. J. K. Callaway:

My Dear wife, I have an opportunity to send this to Selma by Mr. Gay. I send with it my morning report, which I want you to take care of for me.

I am *very* well and getting *better.* I hope I shall get to weighing 160 yet.

I am very impatient to get a letter from you. I have not had one since I wrote you before. Surely you don't write twice a week.

We are expecting orders to leave here every day. It is said that we are going to Chatanooga. I suppose we'll go to Mobile and take the Mobile & Pensacola Rail Road to where it intersects the Montgomery & Pensacola Road and then go up by Greenville. We may go by Selma, but if we do I have no idea that anybody will get to go by home. If you find out when we will be there, which I will let you know if possible, I want you to meet me there. It will certainly be very bad to have to pass so near home and not be allowed to stop, but a soldier soon learns to expect nothing but peremptory orders, and to be punished if he looks sour.

We are all well. Mr. Rogers is getting well. I suppose he will be sent to the hospital. I see Hardy Brown pass out yonder. I suppose he is well, he looks so. I believe all the D[allas] W[arrior]s are well who live at Summerfield. Mr. Overton is very well.

There is not a particle of news of any kind stirring. We are listening every day in almost breathless impatience to hear something highly important, but it has not come yet. We are being paid this morning, eight of the companies were paid yesterday. No telling when we will get our wages, perhaps not in another 4 months. There is this advantage in not being paid: we are sure not to spend it.

I hope I shall get a letter or two from you before we leave here.

Give my love to your mother and the family. Let me know if you get any letters. My respects to all enquiring friends, tell them I am in fine humor and expect to be at home in four or five months.

Kiss T. and Joe for me, and believe me as ever your faithful affectionate

J. K. Callaway

Montgomery, Ala
Wednesday morning Aug 6th 1862

Mrs. D. Callaway:

My Dear wife, I snatch a moment this morning to write you. I am in fine health & humor, notwithstanding the fatigue & exposure of six days & nights. We left Saltillo last Thursday at 3 o'clock P. M. on a box car without seats. There was another company in the same car so that we were very much crowded; most of us having to stand up. At night about ten of us took our blankets and climbed on top to sleep but about midnight it set in to raining and ran us back inside and we stood on our feet the balance of the night. We got to Mobile at 8 Friday night, marched from the depot to the wharf where we slept & took another train. Early Saturday morning we embarked on board of a steamer, ("Dick Keys") and went over to the Depot on Ten Saw River where we lay from Saturday morning till Monday evening 8 o'c[lock] waiting for transportation, at which time we embarked on board an open platform car, which would have been very comfortable had the weather been fair, but about 9 o'clock it set in raining; but I wrapped up in my blanket and lay down on a seat (a plank) and slept all night. Awoke the next morning perfectly wet. We got to Montgomery last night at 7 o'clock, although it rained all day. This morning we all have our blankets and clothes spread out in the sun, to be ready for it again at 3 o'clock this evening. The Regt. has lost five men since we left Saltillo. One died very suddenly on the cars last Friday. Two were killed by lightning last Monday, the cars ran over one yesterday, making four killed. One fell off the cars yesterday while running fast. I suppose he will die. When I have time I will write more at length. My love to all. God bless you all.   Your loving

Josh

P. S. I send you ten dollars in this, & I want you to let me know if you get it. Write at Chattanooga Tennessee. Write tomorrow.

J. K. C.

Camp Near Chickamaugee, Tenn [Ga.]

Monday Morning Aug 11th 1862

Mrs. D. Callaway:

My Dear Better Half, I should have written to you before now if I had had time. We got to Chickamaugee last Friday night. Saturday we moved from the Rail Road to our camp and spent the day fixing up, however I found the 33rd Ala. as we went on to the camp, and after we got there I slipped off and went back and saw all the boys from Coffee & Dale, among them Burrel Stakes & his son Henry & Lam Godwin & Counts Baker & some others whom I had not seen before. Counts Baker had just come from home. He says our relatives there are all well, he saw some of them. He says E. D. Godwin is teaching again at the Camp Ground.

Yesterday I went out in the country foraging, but all I got was my dinner & as much fruit as I could eat for which I paid 50 cents. The other boys bought some ducks & geese & chickens & brought them in and cooked them up last night for breakfast & dinner today, but after they went to sleep somebody stole the whole pile. The boys are *"charging"* considerable this morning but can't *collect much.* We went out about five miles, saw a good deal of the country. We ascended a very high hill from which we could see many miles. We saw the "Lookout Mountain" on Tennessee River, and the village on its top. The scene was truly romantic, especially to one who had never before been in a mountainous country. The people are a little wild in their appearance too. My foraging expedition was a pleasant trip, although I did not fare as well as Dan did when Eli sent him to see Miss Jane. I got two glasses of sweet milk but no butter.

You will learn from Eli how I spent my time on the way. The Misses Callaway at Atlanta are interesting ladies, one of them is a widow. Their mother is a very nice old lady & fond of company. Her son Thomas is a handsome young man. I did not see Joshua, although he was in town. The old man is in Florida. Those whom I saw of them are intelligent & educated.

I believe I have written all that would interest you. What I have not written in this I wrote to Eli. I am well and in fine spirits, enjoying myself finely, only I am vexed to think I could not come by home. But I hope I shall see you in three months. The Lord bless & keep you all till I do see you is my prayer. My highest regards to the Misses Montgomery & my friends generally, my love to the family. A thousand and one kisses on this for you & the children. Inclosed is a pretty for T. Tell her to keep it till I come home.

Your faithful & loving J. K. Callaway

P. S. The Dallas Warriors are all well. Tell Wes to write me this evening with you.

Joshua

Camp Gladden Near Tynersville, Tenn
Wednesday Aug 13th 1862

Mrs. Dulcinea Callaway:

My Dear wife, I have managed to procure ink to write to you ever since I wrote that accursed letter from Corinth that made you cry, but now it is time to write you again and I am obliged to write with a pencil. No ink to be had, none in camp.

I believe I neglected to acknowledge the receipt of your letter of the 27th ult. It went to Tupelo & then followed me here. I got it on Sunday morning after we got here Friday night.

I am very well, thank the Lord, & trust this will find you so. I can not but acknowledge the hand of Providence in the preservation of my life & health while I was passing the ordeal in Miss[issippi] where so many thousands who were much stouter than myself were sick & dying. I shudder when I think of the suffering and death that I witnessed while at Corinth. I hope we will never be stationed at such another place. While there everything was gloomy. The men looked sick and sad. I seldom heard an animated conversation or saw a soldier smile, but my ears were constantly saluted by the groans of the sick & dying. The Regiment could muster only about 100 or 200 men, the companies being from 8 to 15 strong; but now all is life & mirth throughout the camp everything is "merry as a marriage bell" the companies can muster from 30 to 50 men ours being about the weakest muster, 32, and we have one sick man, but he keeps up.

Every thing seems to encourage me. The Rebels have cleared the yankees out of Missouri,[8] Stonewall Jackson has whipped Pope again[9] & they have been whipped once or twice in Tennessee.[10] There are now about 5 soldiers playing harts here in the grove (in the camp) and I am hurrying to join them. My Dear, all this improvement in prosperity is owing to the faithful fervent prayers of such innocent, devoted creatures as yourself. The Lord help you to pray! and may he continue to hear you.

The Dallas Warriors, I believe, are all well. We are now camped in a pleasant & apparently healthy country, in a beautiful grove of black jack, post oaks & a few pines, perfectly level & have plenty of good water, though it is a little limy but cold. I am enjoying myself as usual.

My love to the family & respects to friends. Kiss the children & write to me soon at Chattanooga Tennessee camp.

J. K. Callaway

P. S. If you get this before Baley leaves send me a shirt & some socks by him. Tell Wes & E. C. to write to me. Tell me if you know of . . .   Joshua

Camp Near Tyner's Station, Tenn
Sunday morning, Aug 17th 1862

Mrs. D. Callaway:

My Dear wife, it is time for me to write again and I have been so fortunate as to procure some ink. I hope my pencil written letter was legible.

My dear I am in *fine* health, unusually stout; and I can say of a truth that I am in good spirits; probably from this fact: to wit: Capt. Harris arrived last night accompanied by Lieut. George & 4 of our men who had been home two or three months. We have felt the need of officers greatly since our officers have been gone, and their presence of course adds to our already good humor; and another thing which helps us is our foraging expeditions in the country. I must tell you of one trip of this sort I took last Thursday. Two of my comrades & myself left camp at 8½ o'clock and walked four miles into the country before we found any thing but just before we despaired we came to a good looking house with a fine orchard beyond. We called at the house and got permission to go to the orchard and help ourselves. After eating so much fruit as we chose we filled our haversacks. I filled mine with *soft* peaches, thinking we might stagger on some sweet milk. After filling we walked across an old field, to a clump of large trees where we expected to find a cool spring which we did, and a nice spring house too, and in the house we [saw] two large stone pitchers full of the richest looking milk I ever saw, being covered thickly with cream. After taking a draught of the cold water that gushed out of the hill among the rocks, we took a path which led from the spring to the top of the hill that overhung it where we found a good house surrounded by some shrubbery and wild flowers arranged in rural style, all enclosed by a rail fence, altogether indicating plenty, comfort and happiness. Of course we went in, and found a clever old man & lady, and two interesting daughters-in-law whose husbands are in the Confederate Army. We bought one pitcher of the milk (a little over a gallon,) for which we paid a dollar, we then paid a quarter for a large peach pie and enough of sugar to sweeten our peaches. Now you may *imagine* how much milk and peaches I ate and how I enjoyed it but I'm sure I can't *tell* you. After eating our milk & peaches dinner was prepared, which consisted of home made Bacon, Beans, Cabbage, Cucumbers, Sweet milk, Irish Potatoes & Butter and such other vegetables as a soldier craves, but of which he is deprived in camp, and a dessert of fruit pies & cream sauce. Well, after all the eating was over we had a lively, animated conversation for a couple of hours with the ladies, during which the land lady entertained us with musick on the Flax wheel, which was a *show* to me, I having never seen any flax spinning before. When we began to talk of leaving the land lord brought out some watermelons, and you ought to have seen us eat "em." I didn't tell them I had a family & one of my companions *was* and *is* a single man, (Rube Waters). Perhaps we made some impression. I am sure I made an impression on the milk & peaches & the dinner. You may tell Eli that my forage was fully equal to his as long as it lasted. I am enjoying myself hugely.

All that mars my fun is that I can't go to see my *dear* ones at home. But my pleasure is heightened by the fact that we are to begin an onward movement today or tomorrow. The order to strike tents was announced last evening 6½ o'clock. We struck all but two, built bonfires all over the camp, had a grand illumination & speeches from Col. Frazer, Col. Reid & Adjutant Lee. The old camp was made to ring with shouts of applause. Dr. Winn also made a speech. The Sturdy old 28th seemed almost frantic with delight at the announcement of the fact that the march was to be onward to *independence* or *death!* If this *is* the *cool determination* of *every* Confederate *soldier* and our fathers, mothers, wives, brothers, sisters & children will continue to unite their fervent prayers with ours, I have no doubt that by the end of the next three months, victory will have perched upon our banners, our soldiers will drink draughts of cool water from the springs of the Monongaheley and Ohio Rivers, we will quit following our battle flag, stepping to the top of the drum, morning reports will be exchanged for Salutations and Kisses from our wives & children, rubbing guns with greasy rags will be exchanged for clean towels on which to wipe our *now* dirty faces, *dirty* Blankets spread upon the cold damp ground with knapsacks or roots for pillows will be replaced by soft feather beds with *clean* sheets & good pillows and dirty, greasy "haversacks with two days' cooked rations" will be exchanged for good warm breakfasts prepared by the fair hands of our own dear wives & sisters or mothers. What a heart thrilling contemplation! May the Lord help you *all* to *pray!* and the God of peace and Liberty hear and answer your prayers!

My dear, I am not disposed to grumble at you for not writing, but I do think I might get a letter from you once a week, especially if you get four from me before you write.

Remember me affectionately to your mother and the boys. My best wishes & respects to all enquiring friends, especially Messrs Montgomery's, Mc-Gehes's, & Adams's families also to Mrs. Overton, tell her the old man is in fine health, all boys well. Kiss the children, write this evening to Chattanooga & believe me, as ever, your *faithful* and *affectionate* husband.   Joshua K. Callaway

> Camp Gladden, Tennessee,
> Near Tyner's Station,
> 10 miles South East of
> Chattanooga, Hamilton Co.
> Wednesday noon, Aug 20/62

Mrs. D. Callaway,

My Dear D. I received six Letters from you all yesterday, two from yourself, two from Eli, one from Wes & one from El. & "Sis" which last I will enclose to you rather than try to tell you about them. But you never will tell me whether you get the letters I send you from my other correspondents. Let me know if you get them.

I have no news to write except that I am well, and that we are still lying here with our knapsacks packed ready to start at a minute's notice. Our tents are down and gone & have been for several days and we are bivouacking on the ground, expecting orders to march every hour. It is said that we will cross the Tennessee River five miles from here & wait there till our wagons come up which were sent across the country from Miss. but have not come up yet. I suppose they will be in in a few days. Every thing seems lively and all hands seem to be in good humor, pleased at the idea of the move. We are all anxious to see more of Tennessee, to get higher up. There is trouble before us no doubt. Long hard marches, cold weather and perhaps hard fighting. But our watchword is victory, our motto is independence & liberty.

Give my love to the family. Tell Wes I am much obliged to him for going to see Esquire Oakes for me. I hope he enjoyed the trip. I have not received any letter from Mr. Oakes yet. Tell Eli to accept my warmest regard in place of a letter this time. I want to send El. Godwin's letter in this and if I write too much myself there will not be room for it in the envelope. I hope you will all accept it in place of one from me. Tell Dan not to think that I have forgotten him because I don't speak of him by name, for I think of him every time I speak of the "Shebang," "The Concern," the family.

Tell T. I think of her a thousand times tell her to be smart; did she get the pretty I sent her? I'll *bring* her one when I come home. Kiss them both for me, write me at Chattanooga and believe me as ever, Your faithful, loving   J. K. Callaway
P. S. I believe all the Summerfield boys are well. Mr. Overton is in fine health I think. My compliments to Miss Boggs. Her brother is well. When I write again I will write any thing he may want.   J. K. C.

> Camp Near Johnson's Ferry,
> Tennessee River. Sunday morning,
> Aug 24th 1862

Mrs. Dulcinea Callaway:

Dear D., I am at a loss to know how to write you. I know, however, that I am very well, this I suppose interests you more than anything else. The company I believe are all well, i. e. all who are present—40 in number. The Dallas Warriors I think are all well. I promised to write particularly concerning Andrew Boggs in this, for the accommodation of his sister, but I am in a *great* hurry. Suffice it to say he is well & is a clever soldier. Mr. Overton is also very well. We left Camp Gladden last Friday—the 22nd—and marched 8 miles, in slow time, to Johnson's Ferry near Harrison. We got across the River at dark, marched 2 miles by 9 o'clock and camped at the prettiest spring I ever saw in my life, affording plenty of the best water I ever drank, but the next day, Saturday, we had to move back a mile to camp with our Brigade. We are now camped on the side of a mountain, have a beautiful view of the river, which is half a mile off, for several miles up it. We also have a splendid view of the country on the opposite side of the river. It rises gradually, like a picture raised on the opposite side from the beholder for his accommodation, till the hills mingle with the sky and the view is lost. I regret that it is not a mirror that we might see this roofless army in the centre of this beautiful landscape.

The scenery is "grand gloomy and peculiar," but oh how it hurts to have to use river water and bring it half a mile up this mountain, after having left such good water. One Steamer has "passed in review" since we camped here yesterday. I see 3 rafts going down now.

Col. Frazer has had one unionist [11] arrested since we crossed the river. A great many have gone from this country to Lincoln's army, and a good many *more look* like they might be going to Lincoln, or the devil, one before long.

I have no war news to write, peace talk seems to have played out, and being in for the war, we are satisfied any where.

Tell Eli that I have received his note, by Mr. Bell, since beginning this letter, to prove which I will send this to him in the same envelope.

Breakfast is now ready and I must stop. Give my respects to my friends generally. Tell Eli & Wes to write to me. When I get time I will write to them.

My love to the family. Kiss the children for me. Tell T. who wrote this letter.

Write to me at Chattanooga and remember me in your prayers and believe me as ever Your loving husband

J. K. Callaway

> In Camp at Smith's
> Cross roads, Ray Co. Tenn.
> 35 miles North of Chattanooga
> September 1st 1862

Mrs. D. Callaway:

My Dear wife, as I can get a letter off I will write although I have to afflict you with another pencil written letter, for I have no idea when I shall have another opportunity, perhaps a month.

We left Camp near Harrison's Ferry last Saturday, marched 8 miles, and camped at a large spring, which covers about ¼ of an acre & is 110 feet deep, left there at 4 o'clock Sunday morning, marched 17 miles & camped at this place yesterday, (Sunday) at Sunday sunset, were mustered for pay last night,—but have not been paid yet.

I am in fine health &, as usual, in good humor. We are advancing on Buell and he is said to be retreating to Nashville, but I hear this morning that the yankees are evacuating Nashville. We are waiting here for the artillery and wagon trains to get over the mountain. They have stalled ahead of us; we may be here a day or two, but I shall not be surprised if we leave this evening or tonight. The troops all seem to be anxious to overtake the yankees; I think the old 28th would make [their] sign now in battle.

I got two letters this morning—one from Hope Powell & one from Joseph Chancey & Samantha. They are all well but complain of very hard times & great scarcity of salt &c. Samantha says she has a very fine promising boy, nine months old and can walk. Hope has been unwell ever since he got home from the war. He lives where Amos Chancey used to live. He & Joe both live there.

In regard to the clothes you speak of, you must judge what I need. I have two good pair of pants—the pr. that Mrs. Palmore gave me & a pair that I got from Jeff Davis,[12] uniform pants—two good coats. I have the two shirts—two pair of drawers that I brought from home—of course they are worn out, except the old brown coarse one, and I am tired of it. I gave $1.50 for an old one two weeks ago and tore it up last night for gun rags for Company K. The socks that I brought from home are gone long since. I have one pair, however, that was given to me at Tupelo, Miss. but I have worn them constantly for 3 weeks without washing, and they are pretty well worn out. You see that I need a shirt or two and one or two pair of drawers, two pair of socks. And I want you to send my boots. I sold those I had because they were too small. I got ten dollars for them. My shoes are worn out nearly.

The Summerfield soldiers are all well. No news. My love to your mother, the boys. My respects to *every body*, address me at Chattanooga. Kiss my babies, be contented when you know I am so, & remember me in your prayers. May the Lord spare our lives & give us peace in the prayer of you faithful, loving

J. K. Callaway

CHAPTER FOUR

Kentucky Campaign

September 27–November 9, 1862

IN HIS September 1, 1862, letter, Joshua warned Dulcinea of the probability that he would not have an opportunity to write for perhaps a month. As it turned out, his estimate proved quite accurate—the next letter is dated September 27, in which he chronicles his adventures during the first part of the Kentucky campaign. Exactly a month later, on October 27, having returned to Tennessee, Joshua summed up the whole experience from his point of view.

The Army of Tennessee endured hard marching, short rations, lack of clothing, and many disappointments during the campaign, but good health and high morale carried the soldiers through. "The army," General Manigault asserted, "when it started on the expedition, was not as fully equipped and provided as it should have been. Many suits of clothing and pairs of shoes were wanted. . . . Our supply train contained not more than twenty days' provisions. . . . Our commanding general had many difficulties to contend against. He could not supply himself with everything, and the different departments in Richmond gave him no assistance."[1] Despite these problems, General St. John R. Liddell reported in mid-September, "So far, our march had been delightful. The season was propitious, dry weather with pleasant days and cool, bracing nights. The constant movement and change of scene in a high country, sometimes mountainous, had improved the health of the troops. Their spirits were buoyed with the brightest hopes of success. They had the fullest reliance upon the skill of their general. His previous military reputation had justified every fair promise for the future."[2]

The route General Bragg chose for the invasion of Kentucky took the army

across Walden's Ridge, along the Sequatchie River to Pikeville, and over
the Cumberland Plateau to Sparta, Carthage, and Glasgow. From this point
Bragg sent a Mississippi brigade to Cave City to cut the railroad from Bowling Green, a Federal supply line. After completing this mission, the brigade
commander proceeded, without orders, to Munfordville, the site of a Federal
garrison. The first attack on the garrison having failed, Bragg felt compelled
to follow up with his entire army in order to obviate "the impression of a
disaster to rest on the minds" of his troops.[3] A soldier in Company H of the
Twenty-eighth Alabama reported, "On the 16th of September we marched
toward Munfordville to attac[k] the fort, garrisoned by 4500 yanky soldiers.
On the 17th the Fort and Garrison is surrendered, unconditionally." Callaway's regiment saw little of the excitement. Colonel John Frazer, commanding the Twenty-eighth Alabama, reported his troops took position on the side
of a mountain to the right of the Munfordville Road, from which point they
marched to the brow of the mountain to support skirmishers. The regiment
suffered only one slight injury, and Frazer reported the troops and officers
remained "calm, cool, and cheerful during the entire day and obeyed every
command with great alacrity and promptness."[4]

Bragg hoped Buell would choose to attack him here, but Buell showed no
immediate inclination to do so, and short rations soon forced Bragg to withdraw from the Munfordville area. The army moved on to Bardstown, where
it remained for several days under second-in-command General Leonidas
Polk while Bragg proceeded to Frankfurt to confer with General E. Kirby
Smith and to install a pro-Confederate state government. Bragg had two
goals in mind for this installation: to convince the people of Kentucky that
the Confederacy could protect them from Federal invaders, and to allow
Confederate conscription of Kentuckians.

The lack of enthusiasm of Kentuckians to join his forces greatly disappointed General Bragg. Hoping for thousands, he received but a handful. A
Confederate captain responded to a rumor that thirty-two regiments had
been raised in Kentucky by declaring: "We found indeed 32 men who were
willing to be Colonels, 32 willing to serve as Lieut Cols and Majors, any
quantity ready to tack on their collars the bars of a Captain or Lieut, but few,
very few willing to serve in the ranks." Manigault asserted that perhaps two
hundred Kentuckians took up arms with the Confederates, but that "of these

the greater part deserted so soon as it became apparent to them that the army was retreating." [5]

Bragg's hopes for Kentucky soon came to nought, largely through Polk's incompetence and refusal to obey orders. Despite repeated commands from Bragg, Polk failed to move the forces under his command to unite with those accompanying Bragg. The resulting clash at Perryville, Kentucky, on October 8 proved to be a "limited tactical success" for the Confederates. It could not be termed a victory as nothing had been achieved other than 3,396 Confederate casualties and 4,211 Federal. [6] Once again, as at Munfordville, Callaway's regiment did not participate in the battle.

The army withdrew the night of the 8th to Harrodsburg and then moved on to Bryantsville before heading for Cumberland Gap on October 13. During the retreat toward Tennessee, Callaway's regiment finally engaged the enemy. On October 17 General Joseph Wheeler, covering the rear of the army with his cavalry force, called for infantry to assist in checking the Federals. Manigault's brigade answered the call, going into position at Wild Cat Gap. Manigault deployed the Twenty-eighth Alabama, "a fighting regiment that never failed to give a good account of itself," as skirmishers. When the Federals attacked, the "deadly and well-directed fire" from the Twenty-eighth sent them back "in confusion and surprise." Although Manigault had expected the skirmishers to fall back, "the brave 28th would not yield an inch, and successfully held the entire [Federal] force in check throughout the day." [7]

After the Wild Cat Gap affair, Callaway and his regiment followed the rest of the army into Tennessee. On October 24, having completed a two-month march totaling 518 miles, the Army of Tennessee reached Knoxville, where it rested for several days. At the end of October Bragg began moving the army by rail from Knoxville to Chattanooga, and from there to Murfreesboro, where it established winter quarters. On November 22 Callaway's brigade set up a comfortable camp on Stones River, about two miles outside Murfreesboro. [8]

The Regimental Return for October 1862 succinctly summed up the experiences of the Twenty-eighth Alabama during the Kentucky campaign. "The command accompanied Genl Bragg in the campaign through Kentucky during the month," stated the Record of Events. "It was not in any General engagement but participated in several small skirmishes." At Wild Cat Gap, the regiment suffered "the loss of 2 privates killed & one 2d Lieutenant seriously wounded." The latter casualty may have led directly to Callaway being promoted from first sergeant to junior second lieutenant on October 28.[9]

Joshua Callaway's letters concerning this period describe his marches and privations during the Kentucky campaign. He was so ill for some time during the march that it was feared he might die, and for the next few weeks he continues to complain of lingering symptoms. He proudly announces his promotion and asks that Dulcinea send him clothing, along with his old "carpet sack," as his promotion entitles him to carry baggage. As usual, he is hoping to get a furlough so he can spend some time at home.

Camp Near Cox's Creek
Nelson County Kentucky
Saturday Sept. 27/62

Mrs. Dulcinea Callaway: Dear wife, I told you in my last that I might not write you in a great while so I hope you have not suffered any great uneasiness.

We have been marching ever since the 30th of Aug. and to give you all the interesting incidents of the march would require a volume. Suffice it to say, at present, that we have marched about 300 miles in 19 days (having actually marched but 19 days), captured one fortress (Munfordsville) and 4500 prisoners.[10] Are now in 32 miles of Louisville. Our route has been as follows: from Harrison due north to Smiths Cross roads, thence North across the mountains, (Wauldon's ridge [sic]) to Pikeville, thence across the Cumberland mountains to Sparta, thence to Gainsborough, Centreville, Thompkinsville (here we entered Kentucky) Glasgow, Cave City, Munfordsville, where we took so many prisoners, New Haven and Bardstown—having passed through the following counties: viz. Hamilton, Ray, Pike, White, Putnam & Jackson in Tennessee—Monroe, Barron, Hart, Larue & Nelson Kentucky. With these notes you can take a map and point out our line of march. For a detailed account of this *wonderful* march I must refer you to a letter which I expect to write when I get a quire of paper & a week to write. We are all well and strange to say the men all look stout & hearty. I have stood the march like a veteran. We threw away our knapsacks & all our clothes, except one spare shirt, at Sparta on the 4th of September. We have not suffered with hunger but two days. Corn is worth from 25 to 30 cents, Bacon from 4 to 6 cents, wheat from 50 to 75 cents, eggs 3 to 10 cts pr Dozen, chickens from 5 to 10 cts, Butter from 8 to 15[,] milk nothing.

My Dear I am exceedingly anxious to hear from you but there is no chance to get a letter to me now, and it is very uncertain whether you ever get this. There is a squad of Cavalry going from our command back to Tennessee and I understand they will go to where they can mail this.

I have not time to write more. Kiss the children. Give my love to the family.

All of you continue to pray for me as I know you have done. Don't write till you hear from me again, which may be one or two months hence. May the Lord spare & preserve us is the prayer of Your faithful and Affectionate Husband

J. K. Callaway

Camp Near Bardstown
Nelson County, Kentucky
Tuesday Sept. [30] 1862

Mrs. J. K. Callaway:

My dear wife. I thought this morning I would write you a long letter, but so many of the company wanted me to write for them that I shall not have time to write [but] few words[.] Indeed they are calling for them now.

I wrote you a short letter last Saturday but I fear you will never get it. I will write you a full history next chance I have to send one off.

I am well and in fine spirits and am in great haste your loving

J. K. Callaway

[Envelope: From Lieut. J. K. Callaway, Co. K, 28th Ala. Vols, [to] Mrs. Dulcinea B. Callaway, Summerfield, Dallas County, Alabama, Kindness of the Boy Logan, Postmarked Selma, Ala, Oct. 19]

Camp Near Knoxville, Tenn.

Oct. 27th 1862

Mrs. D. Callaway:

My dear wife, As Mr. Brown is going to start home in the morning I will write you a short letter; though it is so cold & so late I can not write much. We have had a big snow. The ground is covered about ten inches. It began Saturday & covered the ground with 3 inches & yesterday it was very cold and a little before night it began again & this morning it was about ten inches deep, but the sun has been shining all day and it thawed rapidly; but it is very cold to a parcel of soldiers who are nearly naked and bare footed.

My dear, I scarcely know what to say about our tramps through Tennessee & Kentucky. I have not room on this small sheet to tell you of half that we have seen and suffered.

I know you must be anxious to know all about it and I am determined to tell you all when I have time and room. Suffice it to say at present that we have marched nearly seven hundred miles, traversed Tennessee & Kentucky in various directions, have met the yankees at several points, been at the taking of about six thousand prisoners & a great amount of army stores, suffered [a great amo]unt of cold, hunger and fa[mine], have been on forced marches nearly all the time, day & night, and finally have had to evacuate Kentucky. We are now resting our weary bodies, for a few days, eight miles north of Knoxville, not knowing how soon or in what direction we will have to move.

The "unkindest cut of all" was that we had to throw away our knapsacks & all our clothes at Sparta, Tennessee, on the 5th of September, and consequently we are now naked, bare footed, dirty, filthy and lousy (with body lice only) beyond description. We have never been paid off yet. My little old blanket has long since failed & but for the kindness of my messmates who let me sleep with them, I should long since have "gone under." [It all feels] really that we are "naked, poor, despised, forsaken." Yet, *thank God* most of us are well, only two of the company have died in all the round whereas when I think of it I wonder that *any* could endure so much but we have endured it cheerfully and are still resolved, by the grace of God, to be free. Several of the company have been sick. I for one was very low for several days. The whole company thought I would die. I thought myself my time had come.

For 5 days I could not sit up. I lay in the wagons & was jolted over about 130 miles of rocky mountainous road, when it seemed every jolt would take my life. I wept, cried, prayed, thought of home, wife & children, blessed & cursed the teamsters, the wagon masters, the Quartermasters, the generals, the yankees and the war generally, but never took any medicine. And my heart is now [11]

Camp Near Knoxville, Tenn.
Wednesday Oct 29th 1862

Mrs. Dulcinea Callaway:

My Dear wife, Capt. H. M. Ford starts home tomorrow after clothes for the Company and this letter must be devoted to that subject. I will tell you in the first place what I want and then how to send it. However I will first tell you that I was elected Lieutenant yesterday, hence I am entitled to a certain amount of baggage to be hauled; then I wish you in the first place to take my old Carpet Sack & if you can't get a key to fit it send it any how.

I want my overcoat, my boots, 2 pair of drawers, 2 shirts (such as you can parade), as many socks as you have on hand, one or two pair of pants & a comforter or night cap; it is very disagreeable to sleep bareheaded. I have ruined two or three hats sleeping in them. I shall want a uniform suit if one of the boys will go up to Mr. Palmore's he can probably get enough of jeans from Mrs. Watters or someone else to make them. I know my dear that it is imposing on you to send to you for so many things, but I can do no better. If you can get the cloth you will not have time to make them to send them by Ford, but you can make them at your leisure and send them by the first one who passes, Indeed you might do better to send all the things by Lieut Mims who will go after clothes for Capt. Hopkins Company. I hope I shall be able to get a furlough after a while, but I can not do without the clothes till then if I can possibly get them before.

I believe I have said all I can about clothes. Indeed all I have said is mere guessing. You can tell much better how to manage the business than I can.

I suppose you are out of provisions and I am sure I can't tell you what to do. I learn that we are to be paid off in a day or two & if we are I can send you some money, but to send the money is all I can do. I hope some friend will invest it for you. I will write to Mr. Palmore to engage all the corn and meat he can from those who owe me tuition in his neighborhood. Spend as much money as you please for whatever you want.

I hope my wages will support you while I am in the war. If so I shall be satisfied. May God bless & protect you.

I will now tell you something about my health. I wrote you about my being sick. I was sick about 7 days. All the boys thought I would die. I looked like a ghost. I was so poor that you might see my back jaw teeth all the time. My eyes were almost out of reach in my head and as big as a cows'. You would not have known me. Now I am as fat as a bear. My face is as full as old Jimmy Savage's, my eyes nearly closed. I would cut an inch right on the shin. Feel like I'd weigh 200 pounds, and by the way I believe it helps my looks; but I fear I am not sound; I am too weak to be in good health.[12]

I will write you again in a few days, for today goodby   J. K. Callaway

Camp Near Knoxville, Tenn.
Thursday Oct. 31st 1862

Mrs. D. Callaway:

My Dear wife, I am crowding you now with letters, though I shall not be surprised if you get this before you do any of those which have preceded it. Lieut. Mims starts home tomorrow. I have just been talking with him. He has just promised me to call on you while he is at Summerfield, and as I wrote you he will take pleasure in telling you anything you wish to know. Then lay off your timidity and ask him as many questions as you please. He will bring all my clothes. Then for fear that you have not got my other letter I will tell you what I want & how to send it.

Being an officer, I am entitled to a certain amount of baggage to be hauled, hence I want my Carpet Sack and if you can't get a key to lock it you must tie it up. I want my overcoat, my boots, two pair of pants, 2 pair Drawers, 2 shirts, such as you have, 2 or 3 pair of socks, my old sheep skin vest, if it is worth sending; some gloves, a comfort to wear around my neck and a woolen net cap to sleep in, if you have such a thing. Now if you can get the jeans to make my uniform and send it I should be very glad. Lieut. Mims will tell you how to make them, i. e. how to cut them, and if you can't get them ready to send by Mims make them & send them by the next one who passes. I suppose I have called for enough to fill the Carpet Sack. If you have anything else that you think I would like to have send it, especially a Bible or hymn book, or both, and if the Carpet Sack will not hold all tie some on outside, and if the Carpet Sack is too bad to bring you can probably buy one at Hawley's for a reasonable price if you can spare the money, but if the old one will hold things till they get to me I can get a knapsack. You must exercise your own discretion & judgement, in which I have the utmost confidence.

There was a small lot of clothing issued to the Regiment this morning. I got 1 pair of drawers & 1 shirt, of good stout domestic, and 1 pr of socks.

As to my health I can not say much. I am too fat. I fear I am a little touched with dropsy.[13] I am weak, stiff, and clumsy, but to a stranger I have the appearance of being in extraordinary health. Lieut. Mims will tell you all about me. The Boys are all in pretty good health, though they have not near got over those awful marches, though they are in good humor.

The snow has all melted and the weather is fine with a heavy frost every morning. Everything looks cheerful. I can not but hope that better days are coming. May the good Lord hasten them and protect and provide for you and our little ones is the daily prayer of your faithful and loving   J. K. Callaway
P. S. I have not had a letter or a word from you since the last of August. I am very impatient and uneasy. When you write tell me all about Eli & Wes & Dan and every body else. Kiss the children and love yourself for me.

Josh

My respects to all who may ask about me.

Monday Evening Nov 9th
My Dear. I must write a little now. I am making an effort to find out where you can get some pork.

Mr. Suther will call on you as he goes home. Ask him about pork. He says Mr. William J. Russell will have pork to spare. Joe Phillips tells me that "Dick Shoat" will have pork to spare. Both of these men are said to be very kind and gentlemanly. You can get Mr. Adams or [John] Beaty to see them for you. Mr. Suther says he will speak to Mr. Russell for you himself as he goes home. Do you ask Mr. Suther if he will or has.

I am very well, thank God. The weather is getting very cold, and threatens to snow. I will not put the money in the letter but will let Mr. Suther carry it in his pocket and instead of fifty I will send 77 dollars. I believe I will send my cotton pants home by him. I don't know yet whether I will or not.

God bless you, my Dear wife. Tell T. and Joe that pa thinks of them many a time. Write just as soon as Mr. Suther gets there. Yours devotedly

J. K. Callaway

Tuesday morning Nov. 10

I am very well. The weather is very cold and clear. Mr. Suther will start at 9 o'clock.

I will send one pair of my cotton pants.

Here is a kiss for you, on my name at the bottom, be sure to kiss there yourself. God bless my Dear

J. K. Callaway

CHAPTER FIVE

Shelbyville

February 1–May 1, 1863

JOSHUA'S LINGERING SYMPTOMS enabled him to obtain a furlough. During his absence, on December 31, 1862, and January 2, 1863, the Army of Tennessee fought a battle at Murfreesboro, Tennessee, and then fell back to Alisonia, where Callaway rejoined his command on January 8, 1863.[1] The next day the brigade moved north again, setting up camp near Shelbyville, Tennessee, on the Duck River. Here they remained until late June, keeping an eye open for a Federal advance.

Following the Battle of Murfreesboro, or Stones River, General William S. Rosecrans kept his Federal troops in position there while he planned and prepared a further invasion southward. Polk's corps, which included Callaway's unit, covered the left center of the Confederate line. The Triune Pike, a likely avenue of advance for Rosecrans, became the responsibility of Polk's corps. Each brigade in the corps took it in turn to serve at the outposts situated several miles from the main line, which meant that Callaway's brigade went out once every four weeks. An occasional enemy reconnaissance broke the line, but rapid reinforcement quickly sealed it again. Brigade commander Manigault believed this duty beneficial to his soldiers, "relieving the monotony of camp life, furnishing useful and valuable instruction to the men, keeping them on the alert and rubbing off the rust which otherwise would have resulted from a life of comparative inactivity." He found that "after a tour of this kind the health of the Brigade benefitted, and the spirits of the men improved."[2]

For a while during this period the Twenty-eighth and Thirty-fourth Alabama regiments were consolidated under the command of the Twenty-eighth's Colonel John C. Reid. Soldiers in the Thirty-fourth found life quite different under the authority of their new commander. "Our regiment is under stricter discipline now than it ever was before," declared the Thirty-fourth's orderly sergeant. "Our boys have been in the habit of doing pretty much as they pleased. Sometimes they will slip off to keep from drilling. Col. Reid puts them under guard and makes them drill about six hours every day for about a week. The boys are all heartily tired of the consolidation & more so of Col. Reid." [3]

By now Joshua is heartily tired of the war. Whereas in the early days he was happy to be away from teaching, now he declares he "would love to be a citizen—a *school teacher*." He describes his winter quarters; relates tales of foraging expeditions and camp amusements; recounts his part in turning back an attack along the Triune Pike; complains of military drilling and the poor health of some of the men; reports a review of the troops by General Bragg, taking the opportunity to describe and to give his opinion of his commanding general; and begs Dulcinea to visit him. In March, Dulcinea fears she is pregnant, and Joshua commiserates with her in typical nineteenth-century euphemisms.

This section includes a letter Joshua wrote to his cousin-in-law, Nathaniel (Nat) Pace.

Camp Near Shelbyville Tennessee
Sunday, Fey. [*sic*] 1st 1863

Mrs. D. Callaway:

My Dear, Dear D., It has now been a week since I wrote you, but it is not the result of negligence, but the want of time; we have been very busy building huts and chimneys. And I am now, like every body else, housed up in my tent by the fire. You have no idea of the amount of comfort it adds to our condition to have chimneys to our tents. It is now raining and cold and I am very comfortable. Our huts are built by setting puncheons on the ground and letting [them] come together at the top on a ridge pole, which is supported by a couple of forks, like the rafters of a house; and then throwing dirt all over it. The ends are stopped up in the same way leaving a space wide enough for a chimney and a door. T[he c]himney, in order to extend above the top of the hut, must be a little higher than my head. The hut, when finished, looks just like old Billy Oakes's potato bank would if it had a chimney only ours are a little taller than his, being high enough for a man to stand nearly strait in them. Some of the men say here after they will build chimneys to their potato cocks to keep them from freezing.

My Dear, I have no news, unless you would like to hear of the Consolidation of the Regiments. The 28th & 34th Ala. Regts. are united which causes the companies to be consolidated. This Company and Captain Butler's from Perry Co. and Captain Hopkins's are all thrown together. Capt. Hopkins is to be the Captain and his 1st Lieutenant, P. G. Wood, is to be the first Lieut., & Lieut. Fowlks of Capt. Butler's Company, is 2nd Lieut. and myself 3rd. All the other officers are to be sent off on detached service of some kind. We have not yet taken the prescribed positions. I am yet in command of my company. I could have been put on detached service if I had wished, but fearing that I might be sent to some command in Virginia or Miss[issippi] or some other disagreeable business, I preferred to stay with my Company.

Well, I promised to tell you what my forage man brought me. He brought me a turkey for which I paid 3 dollars, and a chicken for one dollar. I heard last night where I could get some butter and milk, five miles off, and I aim to go or send after it tomorrow if it is not raining.

I hope you will get the paper I sent you. If you do, I wish you to preserve it till I come. There are some excellent pieces in it. A splendid essay on poetry, which I want you to read carefully; and on the last page is a very thrilling piece of poetry, addressed "to my wife." I intended to mark it but forgot it. I want you to read it and consider it as if written by me, as a testimonial of the undying affection of your faithful husband.

J. K. Callaway

P. S. My love to your mother and the boys. Kiss T. & Joe for me, and all of you pray for me without ceasing. No news here. Everything is quiet. If you hear or see any news of importance let me hear it. I am listening every day for something very important. God give us peace and save us all and our country!

Josh

Camp Near Shelbyville, Tenn.
Wednesday, Feby. 18th 1863

My Dear Wife,

I have only time to write you a short letter this morning. I am very well, thank God, and hope you are so.

I have no special news for you. Everything is quiet, and the indications of a move have partially vanished.

Monday morning our company went out 3 miles into the country to guard some bridges, which being in a very rich and densely populated section of the country we had a very pleasant time, except that it rained all the time; we were however quartered in some stables, cowsheds and haylofts so that we were dry and comfortable most of the time. We were relieved yesterday morning by other companies, and returned to camp, which we found, of course, a perfect slop and to mend the matter, last night, the rain fell in torrents, as if the "windows of heaven were opened and the fountains of the great deep broken up", and this morning our tent was about two inches deep in water and every thing perfectly wet. My Carpet Bag and its contents are soaked. I shall try to dry them by the fire as best I can.

I have not been paid for the month [of] January yet but expect to be in a few days. If you need any money you have only to let me know. Have you ever heard any more of that committee money yet?[4] I expect that has played out. But with the blessing of God I am making enough now to support you. All I ask now is a speedy peace and a safe return home to you, and I expect to be a happy man. The Lord hasten the time when I am to realize these anticipations; and hope from the signs of the times it will not be long, for I have great faith in the strong reaction that is now taking place in the north-western states.[5]

Remember me very kindly to your mother and the family. Kiss the children for me, write to me a little oftener and believe me your affectionate

J. K. Callaway

Mrs. D. Callaway

Camp Near Shelbyville, Tenn.
Sunday Feby. 22nd 1863

Mrs. Dulcinea Callaway:

My Dear Wife, I am desirous to give you a letter long enough to be a little interesting to you. Col. Alaxander has just arrived from Perry County and will return tomorrow; therefore I will write at my leisure.

I am very well, thank God, and hope this will find you and our little ones better than when you wrote before.

We will go out on picket again tomorrow, to be gone a week, but you must not think that picket duty here is as disagreeable as it was at Corinth. On the other hand we like it here, especially in good weather.

I have no news to give you, my dear. Everything is quiet, the enemy shows no disposition to advance, hence we are having a very pleasant time. As I wrote you I am having a very nice time.

This is a very bad day, Cold and Cloudy, however I see the sun is shining now, and I hope we will have a good time out on picket, and I know we will if it don't rain.

I notice that they are expecting an attack on Charleston today, and if it be so and we can whip them there I hope it will [have] a good effect.

Well, Dear, wait till I go to the Commissary and get some rations.———

Well, I went to the Commissary, but I didn't get any Rations. The wind is blowing and chimney smokes so badly that I can hardly see to write. I have just read a news paper in which I see the "War Spring" in Virginia has dried up, as it always does just before peace. You know, my Dear, that I am not a superstitious man, but I can't help trying to believe in the Spring. If it is so I wish it had dried up three months ago. At any rate every thing seems to lean towards peace, although there is nothing particularly indicative of so glorious a thing as that. We all are in favor of peace, provided we can get it on our own terms, but we are not going to *buy* it.

Well, Major Davies has come in for some information about Muster Rolls and you must wait a little.

I got a letter from Gilstrap yesterday. His younger daughter is married to a man of Columbus, Georgia, by the name of O. A. Fields. Mrs. Gilstrap has been sick but is mending.

Well, my letter will be very dull from the fact that I have been interrupted so often.

And since I can't get time to finish it at once I will close.

I hope you are all in better health, but I don't want you to stop writing to me because the children get sick; that only makes me want to hear from you the worse. I write to you twice every week and don't get a letter from [you] once a week.

Write a little oftener and believe me your loving

J. K. Callaway

P. S. I want you to send me two dollars in postage stamps, don't fail. I have been trying to get some stamps ever since I have been in Tennessee.

Camp Near Shelbyville, Tenn.
Monday March 9th 1863

Mrs. J. K. Callaway:

My Dear Wife, I have a chance to send you a letter by hand again tomorrow and I avail myself of it.

I am very well and in fine spirits, and in fact I have some spirits in me. This morning Capt. Hopkins got a present of a bottle of good wine which he divided, and this evening there was whiskey issued to the men and there was some left which falls to the officers. And hence we have all had a draw, and all hands are very lively.

This time I have some news which will perhaps interest you, to wit: last Friday morning we had orders to prepare two days' rations and be ready to move at a moment's notice; we then began to think about drawing the rations and here came the order to "fall in", which we did without even striking tents, thinking that the yankees must be upon us and that we were either going to retreat or fight. There was great wondering as to what was up, nearly every man in the Company asked me what I thought.

Well we went out on the "Triune Pike" where we have [been] going on Picket. A Party of Yankees—ten thousand—had come out from Murfreesboro and attacked our Pickets. General Forrest—Cavalry Commander—who was away down on our left found it out and dispatched to General Bragg to send a force out to meet him and they would capture the whole concern, and accordingly Bragg sent out this Division numbering about seven thousand, and we had a long march of about 18 miles and back, were out three days and two of them almost without anything to eat; it rained nearly all the time and we were without our tents. The Yankees got wind of us and left in the night in time of a storm and we had our tramp for nothing, so far as we were concerned. Forrest, however, got 2500 of them, and we had the pleasure of looking at them today as we came in tired and hungry. If some old traitorous Citizen had not given them the wink we might have bagged the whole party.

This will account for my not writing to you yesterday as is my custom. This is all the news I have worth anything and hope you will excuse a short letter. As I said before I am very well and hope this finds you all so. My love to your mother, remember me kindly to all who inquiry. Remember me in all your prayers. I never lie down or get up without asking God to bless us all, and committing you and the children to his care. May he guard and preserve us is the prayer of your loving

J. K.

Camp Near Shelbyville, Tennessee
Sunday morning March 15th 1863

Mrs. J. K. Callaway:

My Dear wife, The Lord has graciously spared me to see another Sunday morning; and I know you will join me in thanking him for his goodness. The day is not altogether as pretty as some we have lately and hence about all the satisfaction it brings is in the thought that we are one more week nearer that blissful day that is to establish (I hope permanently) our reunion, but another battle is also nearer, I fear. I am very well and hope this will find you all in the same fix.

I have no news for you. All is quiet in front.

I have just eaten a very hearty breakfast of Biscuit, eggs, and meat. I went out foraging yesterday and only got one dozen hen eggs and half a dozen goose eggs and 7 pounds of soap for all of which I paid $3. I also bought me a fine coverlet for $10.00. The filling is blue and the warp white. I bought a blanket the other day for $4.00, a good heavy blanket. So you see I am now fixed up for cold weather. I may send home my new coverlet after a while.

I will now stop for prayer meeting, after which I will finish my letter. May God bless us in the meeting.

Well, we had meeting but not prayer meeting; we had a sermon by Lieut. Coons of the 28th. I don't think we were blessed much in it. He lacks the spirit and power of religion. A very eager and anxious congregation was disappointed.

My dear, I am at a great loss for some thing to write. Everything is dull beyond endurance. Every theme of conversation has been exhausted. The prospects & probabilities of peace have been discussed till peace itself has become an uninteresting topic. I don't know what we are to do for something to keep up our spirits, unless Old Rosey will come to see us, and I'd rather be dull than to see him, unless I could see him in chains. I dreamed last night of being in a little fight and thought I was taken prisoner. I reckon we will go out on picket tomorrow, and if we do I hope we will come back in better spirits.

I had a letter from William Wilkerson the other day. He says all his folks are well, except Aunt Polly who has been in bad health a long time. Times very hard down there, but the people all in good health.

Capt. Hopkins got a letter from home today bringing the sad intelligence of the sickness of his whole family. He is not very well himself.

I have not had a letter yet from Eli or Wes. Give my love to your mother. Love and kiss the dear children for me. Remember me kindly to my friends who make inquiry. *All* of you pray for me day and night and believe me your devoted   J. K. Callaway

P. S. If you meet with an opportunity send me two pair of socks. I have lost my new fine drawers and will want more soon, and a pair of pants.   J. K.

Camp Near Shelbyville, Tenn.
Tuesday March 17th 1863

Mrs. J. K. Callaway:

Dear One, having a chance to send you a line by hand I will write you a day before my time. I am very well and hope this will find you all so, though I am afraid you are not. I have not had a letter from you since last Thursday.

Now if there is nothing the matter I can't stand such delays. I become impatient and uneasy. I don't believe you write enough.

I have no news, everything is quiet so far as I know. A man came in from the front yesterday who says everything is quiet out there. However he says they captured 3 of old Rosey's Couriers who had dispatches or orders for an attack on our right this morning.

My Dear, you have no idea how sick I am of this abominable war. You can't form any idea how much I would give to be at home. I have offered one of my fingers for a furlough, and a whole hand for a transfer to some post, and all but my life for peace. Will peace ever be made! Alas! I fear not, or if at all I fear it will be a long time first. However, I live in hope. "Hope on, hope ever."

We are having fine weather now. The Spring I think is open, but the trees are not putting out yet.

The Regiments are filling up considerably and I think they will be sundered soon.[6] I don't know though that it will do me any good. I don't care anything about promotions. I wouldn't give a fig to be a Lieutenant general, if it were not for the sake of the big pay. But O! how I would love to be a citizen—a *school teacher.*

If I ever do get out of this war, I'll bet I never get into another, for more than a month at a time.

You will perhaps imagine—rightly too—that I have got the blues *somewhat.* I have not thought of anything hardly for a week except you and the children which thought of course always goes with that of peace. Oh! how overwhelmingly delightful it would be to sit down at home, in the shade with those we love so dearly. I long to be there. I'd give a mint of money to lie down on a pallet in the parlor today and have the children play around and on me! God bless them and restore me to them! But as I can not enjoy all that bliss but am compelled to stay out here, far away from everything that is dear to me, in order to keep the vandal enemy from invading our home, may God sustain me, and sanctify the calamity to the good of us all. I hope you will all pray for me constantly. Kiss the children for me. Give my love to your mother and write often to your

Devoted

J. K. Callaway

Camp Near Shelbyville, Tennessee, Mch 19/63

Mrs. J. K. Callaway:

My Dear Wife, Your long looked for letter of the 8th inst. came to hand today, and found me very well, except cold, and drowsyness which comes of my being up last night on guard.

The health of the men is not good as I would like to see it, but no one is very sick.

I am sorry to hear of your mother's ill health and hope she [is] well.

I have not heard a word from Eli since that little note he sent me through you, but am and have been looking for a letter from him and Wes both every day for several weeks. If I knew Wes would not write to me I'd write to him, but I can't write to Eli because I don't know where he is. We hear vague rumors here that Longstreet's Command is in, or going into, Kentucky. Some, however, have heard that he is in North Carolina, and others at Charleston. I am very anxious to have a letter from Eli & Wes both. I wrote to Wes once since he went to Mobile.

The stamps you sent are stuck together. I am afraid I shall lose some of them. I have not tried to get them apart yet. I am very much obliged to you, my dear, for them. It will save me a good deal of embarrassment. I can now write to my friends and prepay the postage. And if you choose, and will furnish me in stamps, I will prepay my letters to you. Anything in the world to please you, *even if it were a kiss.*

I am, as usual, at a great loss for something to write. Everything is very dull. The only amusement in camp seems to be footracing. A young man (Rogers) has been beating everybody who ventured to run against him and has won a good deal of money; but this morning he got beat. There were some eleven hundred dollars bet on the race.

Well, the drum now beats for Battalion Drill, and I must stop till we come in again.

Well, we had a fine drill. I should like for you to see such drill as we had this evening. Four thousand men, a line half a mile long, in an old field containing some three hundred acres, and very level. The men all knowing exactly what to do. I know it would be a show to you; but, being worn out with it, I dread for the hour to come, and find no pleasure in it except in looking at the hosts of pretty women who turn out these beautiful evenings to see us.

To give you some idea of how tired it makes me, I will say we started out at 2 o'clock and marched round, through & across that field I have no idea how often, and back to camp, ½ mile. It is now nearly dark.[7]

> Camp Near Shelbyville, Tennessee
> Sunday evening March 27th 1863

My Dear Wife:

I am writing you today just for a flair. Everything is precisely as it was when I wrote before. It is rumored that Old Rosey is falling back to Nashville. I really hope this is true. I have no doubt he is doing something. I hear that our Cavalry passed through Murfreesboro and went four miles beyond. If this is so he must be gone. But he may be going to Vicksburg and cause us to have more hard marching.[8] Oh that peace would come![9]

> J. K. C.

I am very impatient to hear from you. I have not had a letter from you lately and I am writing three times a week.

I hope your dropsy is not keeping you from writing. I can't stand such treatment as this, my darling. I must have a letter from you or some-one. I am very sorry to hear of your probable condition, and hope you are mistaken, but if you are take care of yourself. I may get home in time to be with you.[10]

Remember me with much love to the children & your mother. Pray for me much and believe . . .[11]

> Camp near Shelbyville, Tenn.
> Tuesday, March 31st 1863

My Dear Wife,

Your very affectionate letter of the 24th came to hand today bringing the sad intelligence of your ill health, and I hasten to reply.[12]

I am very uneasy about you and long to be at home, but can not. I do hope you are well. I shall look for a letter from you every day till I hear from you again.

I am *very* well. I weigh 164 pounds, and if [I] continue to have as good a time as I have been having there is no telling how fat I shall get. But you and I must bear in mind that it is only once in a while we get biscuits or chicken pie. We draw flour once in a great while and some times we get a few pounds at the mill. We have had nothing but corn bread and meat now for several weeks till we got 15 pound, while we were out on picket from a mill out there.

We have just come in from picket. We had rather a bad time owing to the cold and rain. March is going out like a lion indeed. Yesterday, the 30th, it snowed considerable. Today, the last day it is very cold and looks like it will snow before morning. The fruit trees, peaches particularly, are in full bloom. I expect they will all be killed tonight. I am sorry to see it.

My Dear, I have no news to give you. I am not able to say whether the yankees have evacuated Murfreesboro or not. I hear a rumor that we will move soon some think to Mississippi, but I have no idea when nor where we will go.

It seems there is no use for me to write more than once a week, as you get them all on the same day. My object in writing so often is that you may hear from me frequently.

Return my love and compliments to your mother, the children and the negroes.

Your account of T. praying for me is heart stirring. Oh that I may be spared to see my darling child on her knees! The Lord is beginning to answer our prayers in their behalf. Angels rejoice to see the little creature praying and Jesus, who said suffer little children to come unto me &c., will answer her prayers. Let us be watchful of her life, and religion, and God grant that the seed of piety, that has begun to germinate so early in her little heart, may culminate in heaven. Tell her that pa prays for her constantly. May we all meet soon in peace is the prayer of your loving   J. K. Callaway

In Camp Shelbyville
Sunday morning April 5th 1863

Mrs. J. K. Callaway:

My Dear Wife, having got done with Inspection I will devote a few minutes to a conversation with you, but alas! I must do all the talking myself.

Well, I promised to write you a long letter today or some other time, giving you my opinion of the war &c. and to commence. (I will give you the best I've got.) Breckinridge has, I fear, been ordered to Knoxville with his Division.[13] And I also hear that all the wagons belonging to this Division have been ordered to the rear in order to recruit the teams a little, the mules being very poor. These things seem to indicate that active operations will commence very soon. And since they are just such orders as were issued just before we left Saltillo for Tennessee I shall not be surprised if we have another Kentucky tramp this Summer which seems to be the opinion of a good many others.[14] It is now certain to my mind that peace "is gone up" for this summer. And since the yankees have not abated any in their resolution to conquer us I see no end to it yet; still I feel confident that the war is now in its "last stage". That if they fail to whip us with their immense Conscript army this year they will be convinced that they can't do it at all, and will be compelled to give it up. Hence I predict that whenever the shock of war does come this Spring it will be awful. It will be the final, Death Struggle of the expiring Despotism. He will be actuated by the energy of despair. He may make his final stroke at Richmond, or at Vicksburg or in Tennessee. There is no telling, but let every body "stand from under"! And if we can foil him at every point during the next six months the defeated & infuriated monster will turn upon himself, gnaw his own vitals and die. The people of the north will become divided, each party will blame the other for the failure and they will make war upon each other for revenge; and anarchy and despotism will reign without a rival throughout the North. The States will all secede from the old union, and one by one they will ask admittance into the Confederacy or else form a government to itself, and all that will remain of the once proud fabric of the United States will be the blood chilling history of its bloody dissolution. Oh, that I and you & our little children may live to see the end, read the history and witness the results of this bloody revolution, the like of which the world has never seen.

Well, My Dear, I did hope to get a letter from you this morning, but the mail has come in and no letter. Your last letter was dated March 24th. I am uneasy about you. I don't believe I'll write to you any more till next Sunday. Then I reckon you'll write. If I was by you I'd hug you & kiss you & *bite* you till you promised to write oftener and if you didn't promise I'd eat you up and then gnaw Joe & T. mightily.

My Darling, this is a *lovely* morning. It is a rich, balmy, juicy morning. Oh, how I long to be at home! to go to Church and worship God with *you*. The Lord restore us to our homes in peace, and make us happy! My Dear, pray without ceasing, for God alone can settle this great quarrel and save us.

I am very well and hope this will find you all so. Give my love to your mother. Kiss the children for me. Oh, how much would I give to see Joe walking! I think of him every hour in the day. But all I say is God bless them. Tell T. how I love her. And I am my Dear, your

J. K. Callaway

Mrs. J. K. Callaway

P. S. I forgot to tell you how I needed some socks. I went to put on some this morning and could only find one but that was so badly worn out that I could not wear it; & it has a hole in the toe big enough to let out three of the biggest toes I've got. So I had to keep on the best one of my dirty ones. Now I've got both wadded up & stuck between my toes to keep them from pulling back up my leg and leaving my foot sockless. And this worries my toes terribly as well as my patience.

I also need a handkerchief. I've only got my old calico one, and its the dirtiest thing you ever saw. Good by for a day or two.   J. K. C.

P. S. No. 2. A cotton handkerchief here is worth from 3 to 6 dollars and a Silk one is worth from $8 to $12.

I must now go to preaching. good by.   J. K.

[Envelope: From Lieut. J. K. Callaway, Co. K 28th Ala. Vols., to Mrs. J. K. Callaway, Summerfield, Dallas County, Alabama, postmark illegible]

Camp Near Shelbyville, Tennessee
Sunday April 5th 1863

Dear Nat,

I have just returned from a visit over to Dan Monroe's quarters, where I had the pleasure of reading a letter from you to him. I was somewhat surprised at your being at Mobile from the fact that he told me some time ago that you were sutler to the 6th Ala. which was surely as pleasant and more lucrative than your present position. (As you say nothing about having a position in your command I take it that you have none.)

I have no very special news. You will have heard, before this reaches you, that Breckinridge's Command has been ordered to Knoxville.[15] I have no idea what this command will do. Hold still I reckon till old Rosey makes some demonstration. The troops seem to be in fine spirits and in pretty good health. In fact the army has never been in better condition. We are getting plenty to eat now but I fear for the future. Some think we will have another

Kentucky tramp this summer.[16] If we do I am exceedingly anxious to get a position at some post. By the way I must tell you that owing to good looks, good luck, good conduct, or something else, I have been promoted to a Lieutenancy, which promotion I bear with a good deal of *grace*. Therefore if *you* know of any body who has a position for a lieut. who is well posted in *all things* pertaining to *Post*, and well drilled in all the tactics, especially the "route step *March*," recommend me.

I am sorry to hear of the ill health of your mother and Mary, which I heard through Dan.

I was at Elba, in December last, and over on Bolens Creek, but I spent three or four days only and hence did not have time to go to Geneva as I should like to have done. J. Hosea was out and I went down with him. I had a letter from him of the 25 January. All his folks were well. John [Hanford Callaway] was at the fall of Ark. Post[17] and was surrendered a prisoner but escaped before the yankees took possession. He was at home when he and his father wrote. John's wife has two sons.

I have written to Cousin Fair but have not received any answer yet. I am going to write to John Brett; I did not know his address till today.

I remember you told me that John Callow was at Mobile. If he is there yet give him my love, and tell him to write me.

I am *very* well. I weigh 164 lb but am as stiff as any old artillery horse. I can march ten miles a day. It nearly kills me.

My family were well on the 30th March. The latest intelligence from my folks in Coffee was up to the 20th. All were well, except E. D. Godwin who has been sick for several weeks. He belongs to a company of Cavalry lately made up by Jessee Oneal of Indigo Head. Ell. tried for a lieutenancy but I have not learned the result of his effort.

Everything seems to be very quiet here, as if peace was made, but I predict that when the shock of war does come this spring it will be awful. Let every body "stand from under". It will be the final death struggle of the expiring despotism, prompted by the energy of despair. I wish to God it was over and Lincoln was dead and I was at home.

J. Hosea knows nothing of E. W. except that he was at Paris, Texas, last fall a year ago with a train of government wagons. I am afraid he has been killed.

Let me hear from you soon. Address me thus. Lieut. J. K. Callaway. 28th

Regt. Ala Vols. 4th Brigade Withers Division, Polks Corps, A[rmy of] T[ennessee], and then if we are not at Shelbyville, the letter will follow up the command.

I am as ever your friend &c.

J. K. Callaway

Nat Pace Esq.
Mobile, Ala.

In Camp, April 7th 1863, Tuesday

Mrs. J. K. Callaway:

My Dear Love, Lieut. Sellick is going home tomorrow, and I hereby revoke my threat of Sunday, not to write any more till next Sunday. I am, as you see, still at the same place and there are no indications of a move. I am also very well. You ought to see me. I have shaved off some of my whiskers, trimmed my hair, had that old tooth pulled out and washed my face; now if I had a hat I'd be fine looking, but this old cap has got to be the ugliest thing I ever saw.

Mrs. Capt. Hopkins arrived at Shelbyville last night and of course he went and spent the night with her. He is as cheerful as a lark this morning. Why in the world didn't you come with her? I almost cried when I heard she was there & you were not. If I had known she was coming I should have been sure to have written you to come with her. Oh! how I want to see you!

I send home, by Lieut. Sellick, some articles of clothing which I shall not need this summer. Two under shirts and some old socks so badly worn that I can't wear them. I have not determined yet whether I will send my overcoat or not. If I do I will speak of it in a Post Script. I also have a nice blue coverlet that I am at a loss to know what [to] do with. I have a good mind to send it home. I have not yet got those things I sent for. I need them very much, especially the socks "and a hat".

I have no news. The weather is beautiful, everything is lovely and I want to go home bad.

I do think J. D. is having a good time of it. Oh, if I could only have such a time! He don't mind the war.

I am sorry to hear of your losing the smoke house. You speak of "taking meat in the house" like you [have] lots of it. How is [it] going to hold out? I wish you'd tell me everything. I ask about everything I want to know, because I can't think of it. I hope you have heard from Dan by this time? How is he?

My Dear, when you write be a little more careful about the date of your letters. I can't make out the date of your last. I will send it back to see if you can make it out. That is, I will send the part containing the date. And I would be glad if you would give the day of the week always as [I] do.

Write to me soon. Give my kindest regards to your mother and the negros. Kiss the children for me, pray for me and remember your devoted   Josh P. S. I will not send my Coat I believe. I will have the things left in care of Mr. Bill Harrison in Selma. He will send them out to you. N.B. The bundle belonging to me has your name on it, written on a bit of paper. The Carpet bag belongs to Corporal Smith as does the small bundle in it. You will write "Col. C. C. Smith" on a bit of paper and paste on it and have it left at Hawley's Store with the little bundle in it, so he can get it. Yours &c.   J. K. C.

Camp 28th Ala, Friday April 16th '63

My Dear Wife:

Lieut. Wilson leaves for Selma tomorrow and I avail myself, as usual. Your favor of the 8th March came to hand today containing 80 cents worth of Stamps for which I am much obliged. I also got a letter from you *Monday sure enough,* which relieved me very much. I am very well, thank the Lord and trust you all are so. The health of the Regiment is very good at this time. The men are as lively as if they had all been home lately. You ought to [see] them hunt Rabbits. A regiment went out yesterday and caught 60. The men form a circle round the thicket & then send some men to drive & when the Rabbit runs through the line somebody picks him up. It is fine sport.

We have just had a general review. Genl Bragg reviewed the troops himself—Withers's, Cheatham's & McCown's Divisions. I have seen some 2000 men this evening in an old field. Quite a number of ladies turned out to see the show. The review gave me a nearer view of General Bragg than I have ever had before. He is about my heighth, Dark complexion, hair grey, beard which is also grey, is about half an inch long. His face looks sad and careworn. I could not avoid a feeling of reverence when he took off his Cap to acknowledge the salute of the Colors of the regiment, although, as you are aware, I am not an admirer of his, by any means.

I understand that all the baggage has been ordered to the rear, together with the tents. We all are afraid of another Kentucky campaign.[18] Further than this I have no news of any importance. I send you a paper which contains all the news I have.

I am sorry to learn, which [I] have, that Lieut. Sellick lost the Carpet Bag. It was stolen from him. I had two of the best knit shirts in it I ever saw. The two cost me $13. My old sheepskin and several worn out socks were also in it.

Corpl Smith had a pair of pants and a pair of Drawers in it. So that it contained at least $30 worth of clothing. I hope you will send those things [with] Lieut. Mims or some one else though I don't need anything now but some socks and a towel or two and a Handkerchief or two. I bought two pair of socks the other day at a dollar a pair—cotton socks.

We have had a good deal of rain in the last 3 or 4 days but it is fair this evening. I hope we will have a good week for picket.

Well, as I have nothing else with which to fill up the sheet I reckon I must tell you that I have just finished reading a romance, the history of an old miser, who, in early life was a member of the British Parliament, but was disappointed in love and all his hope of fame & distinction as a statesman and consequent earthly happiness were blighted and, being heir to an immense fortune he resigned his seat in Parliament and spent his life in taking revenge upon mankind for his disappointment. He sought and seemed to find bliss in the misery he inflicted on others by means of his wealth. He lived a miserly recluse and doubtless died an infidel. We have all doubtless been disappointed & have fallen far short of our expectations in point of worldly happiness but let us not mistake the road a[s] he did. In stead of brooding over our misfortunes and trying to avenge our wrongs, let us find solace in the thought that our affections should be centered on the Redeemer, whose smile will be an eternal feast and to sing whose praise will be our eternal bliss.

Give my love to your mother. Kiss the children for me. Tell T. that pa thinks of her as often as she can think of me. Pray for me constantly. May the Lord give us peace, restore us all to our homes and loved ones and finally save us all in Heaven is the daily prayer of, My dear love, your faithful loving   J. K.

Camp Near Shelbyville, Tennessee
Friday Night May 1st 1863

Mrs. D. Callaway:

My Dear Wife, I thought I would not write anymore till tomorrow or Sunday but there are orders tonight which look a little ominous. It has been understood for several days that we would move about 4 miles to another camping ground and we were all pleased with the thought, of the change, but it is now 9 o'clock at night and the order has just been issued to cook three days' rations which all hands construe to mean a march and perhaps a fight. I imagine however, that we are only going to hold ourselves in readiness to support a brigade which is going out tomorrow to support Vandorn at Lewisburg. Some think we will go to Lewisburg ourselves. Can't tell anything about it. I will leave my letter open till morning and if I learn any more about it I will tell you. I have told you all I know tonight.

This has been a beautiful day & is a beautiful night. Oh, how I would love to be at home tonight with you away from all this hubbub. Everybody is in a stew. The boys are all hollowing and singing, a perfect buzz. There was a May party today out here somewhere but I don't know where it was. Everybody seems to be lively as May.

Your favor of the 26 came to hand today. I am getting letters about as thick as I want them now. You are doing much better. And your letter is a *treasure* to me. It tells me of the Smartness and goodness of my lovely little T. Tell her that Pa prays for her. May the germ of piety that is budding so early in her infant heart grow all through her life! God bless her!

My dear. Where do you sit of evenings? I fancy I can see you sitting, every evening, about Sunset, in the front passage watching the declining day. And it is a source of great comfort to me to look at the moon at night and think perhaps you are at that moment looking at the same object. Sometimes I become so spell bound that I see your Shadow, with children playing around you on the face of the moon. *Then how I do gaze!*

I forgot to tell you that your letter of 24 came in yesterday. You ask me if I would like to have some washing done. I can't say that I would as my clothes are all clean except one pair of socks.

I think Eli is having a hard time. I am sorry for him. I guess he is tired of marching. Wes will have a good time scratching his itch. Is he at Gainstown yet? I have written to him and Eli both since we have been here. I think they might write to me.

You certainly have worked very hard if you have woven two hundred yards of cloth since February. You surely don't charge anything for weaving or you could make something at that rate. Why don't you charge in proportion to the [cost] of other things. I paid three dollars today for enough of leather to half sole my boots, and put on heels. And then paid two dollars to get the work done. The reason you are crowded so with weaving is because you weave so cheap. A Ginger cake such as we used to buy for five cents is now worth a dollar. A yard of domestic is worth a dollar and a half.

I will write to Eli and Wes again and see if they will get it.

This leaves me in fine health. I weigh 167 pounds. Maybe being fat makes me blind! May the Lord give us *peace* and restore us to each other again very soon is the prayer of, My Darling wife, Your devoted husband

J. K. Callaway

P. S. This is the way to back a letter to me. Lieut. J. K. Callaway, 28th Ala. Regt. Manigault's Brigade, Withers's Division, Polk's Corps, Army of Tennessee. I will back an envelope and send it, or a piece of one. A thousand kisses on this for you and the children from your own J.K.

P. S. No. 2. Saturday morning, May 2nd. This is a beautiful morning. We are ordered to be ready to move at 7. I have all my things packed ready to move now and it [is] about 6½ o'clock. We are said to be going only 4 miles to a new camping ground and I suppose 3 days' rations is only to have us ready for any emergency. Everybody is cheerful. It is a little cool but I expect will be warm enough by noon.

May the Lord bless and save us all from our enemies and give us peace.

J. K.

CHAPTER SIX

Shelbyville

May 9–June 26, 1863

THE FIRST SIX MONTHS of 1863 proved to be the most idyllic of Joshua's military service. Although the brigade took its turns at outpost duty and constructing entrenchments, overall camp life could, at times, be quite enjoyable.[1]

In early May Manigault's brigade was detached from Polk's corps to protect the light artillery batteries that had been sent about five miles from Shelbyville for better pasturage and forage. Manigault declared this "a beautiful country and most delightful camp, where we enjoyed the gradual approach of a most charming spring."[2] What Callaway found most charming was the lack of a field large enough to drill the brigade.

While Callaway's unit gamboled "out in the country," the war continued to claim its victims. General Earl Van Dorn, commanding the cavalry covering the left flank of the Army of Tennessee, had spent much of his time at his headquarters in Spring Hill, Tennessee, entertaining the wife of Dr. George Boddie Peters. On May 7, 1863, Dr. Peters took umbrage, strode into Van Dorn's headquarters, and murdered him. In more heroic circumstances, General Thomas J. "Stonewall" Jackson met his end when he was wounded by his own soldiers while reconnoitering after dark on the Chancellorsville battlefield on May 2, 1863. He died eight days later. Callaway notes both of these tragedies.

Joshua continues to miss Dulcinea and is highly disappointed when she declines to visit him. He reports good health and morale among the soldiers, although he himself suffers another spell of ill health in early June; he laments the death of their neighbor, George Overton, who had been captured

87

during the Battle of Murfreesboro; he reports a religious revival brewing; he
relates a tale of being lost in the woods at night while returning from a foraging expedition; and he tells Dulcinea of his success in playing Cupid for a
fellow soldier. Rumors and speculation continue to be the order of the day.

                                          In Camp May 9th 1863 Saturday
My Dear Wife:

I expect you are beginning to think I ought to write to you. I have no
particular news for you except what I suppose you have heard. I know you
have heard of the great victory in Virginia[3] and the one in Mississippi,[4] but
perhaps you have not heard of the death, the infamous death of General
Vandorn. We are all sorry to lose his valuable services, but we are not sorry
to hear of his death under the circumstances. Infamy & shame have black-
ened his fame; and shame & regret are all he transmits to his posterity.
He sealed with his death the shameful name which he had acquired in life,
namely that of a vile seducer.

                                          Sunday morning May 10/63
My dear, I am at a great loss for something to write to you. I have not a
particle of news. All I can say is Oh, how I want to see you. I am very well,
thank God, and hope this will find you all so. We are having beautiful weather
and are enjoying ourselves as well as we possibly could and be so far from
the object of our affection. There are some fool soldiers who have their wives
with them here and although I would not have you here for any amount, (that
is here in camp) yet I can't help envying those poor fellows their happiness.

I have been out in the country several times since we moved out here and
find the people very kind. But I am at [a] loss to interpret the conduct of
some of them. No doubt some of them are strongly union but afraid to own
their partiality.

There is not indication of a fight yet. But the army is in fine condition. The
health is better than ever, I believe, before. The men are all lively. We play
marbles, baste, ball &c. every day. And we drill some too.

Most everybody seems contented. The prospect for a good crop is better
than usual. Victory is perching upon our banner on every field and the army

of Tennessee is becoming impatient for an opportunity to win more glory. (Our brother soldiers in Virginia and Miss[issippi] are outstripping us in the way to fame.) Indeed God and all nature seem to be smiling propitiously on our cause and we all look for a better day soon. May God grant us peace and restoration to our dear ones very soon. A world of love to you and our dear children and your mother from your devoted

J. K. Callaway

D. Callaway

Camp 4 miles from Shelbyville,
on Lewisburg Pike
Thursday night May 14th 1863

My Darling D:

Your favor of the 8th (for which I am much obliged to you) came to hand today and found me very well. In fact it came in yesterday but I was off on guard and did not get it till I came in this morning.

We are, as you see, still at this camp, and the longer we stay here the better we like it. We are separated from the body of the army, there being none but this Brigade out here, and the water is excellent; but the most charming feature about this camp is that there is no old field large enough to drill us in.

Nothing of interest has happened since we came out here, except that there has been one or two picnics and I hear the officers of this brigade are going to give one next Saturday (day after tomorrow). This evening General Bragg, Withers, and Col. Manigault rode through our camps to inspect them, the Brigade was turned out and presented arms (saluted) to the venerable looking old veteran. The health of the Brigade is unusually good. Our camp hospital looks like an old deserted camp. There is not a man in it.

There is no prospect of our moving that I know of. McCown's Division, I suppose, is gone, perhaps to Miss[issippi]. One Brigade of our Division (Withers's) is gone to Columbia.

I should be very sorry to hear that the yankees had got down there but I don't think you need to be very uneasy. I guess General Forrest will gobble up that squad before they get much farther.

I have no news. Of course you have heard of the death [of] Stonewall Jackson.

I am in fine health and, like everybody else, in fine spirits. I do hope this accursed war will close during this year. Oh, that I could see you. While I write a number of soldiers are gathered round a little fire about twenty yards in front of my tent and singing—"There is glory in my soul" &c.—which makes me feel *so sad and lonely*. My all of earthly glory is the hope of our reunion and future happiness together and our indissoluble union in Heaven. The Lord give us peace and return us to our homes speedily! Write often My *Darling*. Give my love to your mother. I hope her health is improved. Kiss the children for me and believe me, as ever, My Dearest love,

Your faithful, devoted

J. K. Callaway

P. S. You are not praying for me now as fervently as you have been. My Dearest don't neglect that duty.

Camp Near Shelbyville,

Tuesday May 19/63

My Dear Love,

Your kind letter of the 13th came to hand today and found me well. I am always glad to hear from you but I am sorry to hear that you should be sick even a moment.

My darling, I think from every indication that we will spend the summer here, and I know that I can't get a furlough and if I could it would only be to see you; therefore I want you, if you possibly can, to come to see me. Leave the children, T. at least, at home and one month's wages will pay your expenses here and back. Old Mr. Callen is coming up here and if he will not bring you in his care then go to Selma and put yourself in care of the captain of a Steamboat to Montgomery and he will see you on board of the cars in care of the conductor who will see you through to this place. And then I shall be a happy Soldier. Perhaps Wes can go with you as far as Montgomery. He can at least help you off. My friend Mr. Adams or Mr. Gregory will take pleasure in assisting you.

I will tell you the following as an inducement to come: Capt. Hopkins has rented a good house with two large rooms and furniture, gets provisions, of course, from the Commissary. Mrs. Hopkins makes from 2 to 12 dollars a day sewing. So you see you can make your expenses here and more clear money than you can make weaving unless you would charge more than two or three bits a yard. If we stay here all summer it will be delightful to me to have you here. Mrs. Hopkins will spend the Summer here; and if we leave here you and her can go back home together at your leisure. Capt. Hopkins is anxious for you to come and says I may go halves with him in the house and that Mrs. Hopkins's servant may do your cooking and washing. He pays fifteen dollars a month for the house. I am anxious for you to come. I would give one month's wages to spend one day and night with you. It would be best to leave *both* the children at home, but I will not insist, especially as I am anxious to [see] them. I will send a dispatch to you this evening. Capt. Hopkins will dispatch for me when he goes down tonight. Come quickly. Perhaps Lieut Mims will come on with you. Bring your trunk and clothes to stay all Summer. My love to your mother and Wes & Dan. Start to me about Monday. I am your loving   J. K. Callaway

P. S. Capt. Hopkins has written for a servant who will perhaps come on as a servant to you. I am happy at the thought of your coming   J. K.

P. S. I send you 20 dollars perhaps you will need it as you come.

Sunday Evening 4 o'clock[5]

My dear, Somehow or other I feel impelled to write more to you but I am sure I don't know what to say. I wrote all I could think of this morning, nevertheless, I feel that constant anxiety to talk to you and writing comes nearer satisfying that craving than anything I can do.

I suppose you are aware of the state of things about Vicksburg[6] & I can tell you nothing. I am sorry to hear that it is likely to fall and sent help thinking that the prospect is not so gloomy as it is represented. In fact, I heard this morning that the yankees at Murfreesboro think Banks and his whole army have been captured by our forces.[7] If Vicksburg falls the yankees will rejoice and our cause will be badly crippled if not lost. God forbid that it should ever fall! We have whipped them in Virginia and South Carolina, and now if we can whip them here and at Vicksburg I think peace must come.

I have been down to the river and into it since dinner. It is a good place to bathe if there were not so many dead horses, hogs, cows &c. and all the offal from two large army slaughterhouses in it above. The water really stinks. I don't think I shall go into it any more. But I suppose I might as well bathe in it as to drink it. However, there is a small spring on the other side, which the men get to by means of rafts, and one on this side, but it is a good way off and very weak. I have not drunk any River water yet, and if we do go on picket tomorrow, I hope I shall not have to drink any at all.

My dear, I hope I shall see you very soon. I believe I have given you all the instructions necessary to enable you to get here. Put yourself in care of the captain of a boat, or get Wes to do it and he will see that you are taken care of.

You need not feel lost or embarrassed at all. I hope to get a letter from you tomorrow, until then I bid you & T. and Joe Good by, Your loving

J. K.

P. S. I must add one more line to tell that a lady has just sent me a bouquet. These ladies all seem to think I am a very clever fellow. You must hurry up here before I become enamored with one of Tennessee's beauties. But in all this wide world over there is none like my own, Dear, Dulcinea.

Picket Camp 8 miles above Shelbyville
Monday June 1st 1863

Mrs. Dulcinea Callaway:

My Dear Wife, Your very affectionate letter of the 23rd May came to hand yesterday and I hasten to reply.

I am *not* very much surprised at your not coming, for I had thought of all the excuses you mention before I wrote, but I thought you had some "calico" that would do to wear up here. I do not think at all hard of you, my dear, but am very sorry that you can not come. Although I thought it uncertain about your coming, yet I could not avoid pleasing anticipation of seeing you soon, and hence your letter has completely nonplused me. I am sad; almost got the blues. You certainly have no idea how badly I want to see you.

I still think we will stay here all summer though we may leave in a week, and if your clothes are not good buy more. That is what, and *all*, I live for, i. e. to feed & clothe you and the children, and make *you* happy. But if I can make myself happy at the same time by bringing you nearer to me I know your loving heart will approve it. But I would not, by any means, have you to leave Joe sick or undertake the trip with him when in your opinion he could not bear it.

You did not say whether you got the money I sent or not. I would have sent more but thought it unsafe. If you need more borrow and I will replace it immediately. I shall send some money home anyhow by the first opportunity.

I am very sorry to hear that Joe is sick. I hope he is well now. And I trust your own health is better than when you wrote.

I have no news. Everything is quiet here. We can't hear anything from Vicksburg. We are very uneasy about it. I can't help hoping that we have or will whip them there; and if we do I think it will go a great way towards making peace.

My Dear, enclosed is a little ring, the workmanship of my own hands; manufactured from a muscle [*sic*] shell, which I hope you will accept and wear for my sake. And if you never see me again, if I should die or be killed, preserve it as a relict not only of me but of the war, of Duck River in Tennessee. I hope to have one ready to send to T. in my next letter.[8]

All the Summerfield boys are well. Lieut Mims arrived last Thursday. He is very well.

Continue to pray for peace & me. I have kissed this ring for you, and want you to kiss the children for me, and write oftener than once a week. My love to your mother and the boys when you see them.

My Darling, I am your loving, devoted

J. K.

P. S. I forgot to tell you that I am very well.

[Envelope: From J. K. Callaway, C. "K" 28th Ala, to Mrs. J. K. Callaway, Summerfield, Dallas County, Alabama, postmark Selma, Ala, May 30, written in hand—Due 5]

> Picket Camp 8 miles from
> Shelbyville Wednesday
> June 3rd 1863

My Darling Wife:

I must write you a short letter this evening although I have not a great deal of news. But I may not have the chance to write any more for some time. I can now appreciate your discretion in not coming to see me. We have orders now to keep 3 day's rations cooked all the time and hold our selves in readiness to move at a moment's notice. Some think we will go to Vicksburg, but I think differently. I think Bragg is meditating an attack on old Rosey. Two

Brigades passed here this morning going to the front. It is thought that the yankees are very weak now at Murfreesboro and hence it is probable that Bragg will advance.

Of course you have all the news from Vicksburg. I have none of importance from there, but hope it is all well there.

It may be that we will not move from here for some time yet but [I] think the chances are that we will leave tomorrow. If we do advance I expect to be in a fight in a few days, perhaps before you get this. May the God of battles be with us & crown us with victory. Pray for me constantly.

I have not got that ring ready to send to T. yet but will send her one before long. Tell her that Pa has not forgotten her.

I forgot to tell you that I got a letter from Eli the other day. He was well when he wrote. I am glad to get a letter from him. I was uneasy about him, had not heard from him since the battle of Chancellorsville.[9] I will write to him [in] a day or two. I wrote Wes twice at Selma, but I understand that they have gone back to Mobile, and if so he will not get my letter.

Wes has been very lucky as a soldier. He has had a real *"hog killing time"* ever since he became one. I wish it may continue favorable for him.

My Dear, I hope I shall hear from you tomorrow and semi-occasionally. May God bless you all and give us peace. Your own

J. K.

Mrs. D. C.

P. S. My Darling, I must apologize a little for not writing more, but, as I said before, I have no news, more than I have written, and then there is a big game of "Town Ball" going on out here and they are all very jolly and I am about to lose it all, hence I know you will excuse me.

A kiss apiece for you all

J. K.

Camp 28th Ala Near Shelbyville
Monday morning June 8th 1863

My Dear Wife, I looked in vain for a letter from you yesterday. I have not one from you since yesterday was a week ago. I am a little uneasy about you. I fear you or some of the family are very sick. Please don't keep me in suspense so long at a time.

I am not so well just now myself. I have been troubled for several days with diarrhoea but have not quit doing duty, and am better now.

I have not got a word of news. Of course you are in possession of all the news from Vicksburg. I heard from some citizens yesterday that Vicksburg had fallen but no one believes it.

Everything is very quiet here. Old Rosey and Bragg both seem to be waiting to see the result of the Vicksburg affair before moving. And if we beat them there as badly as I think [we] will they will certainly be willing to make peace. Though it may bring on a fight here.

I believe I wrote you that I had got a letter from Eli & one from Wes. I wrote to Eli yesterday and shall write to Wes tomorrow. I have not had a letter from anybody from Coffee in some time.

We are still on Picket. We have been out here two weeks already and will remain this week which will make a three week tour of picketing, but some want to stay here all the time from the fact that we have a nice place to camp, but I don't because the guard duty is much heavier.

Tell T. that I have not made that ring yet but still intend to make it. But when I make it if it is a better one than I sent before I want you to keep it and give her the one I sent you.

Yesterday was a very pleasant day but cloudy and the mornings are all very cool here. The fire feels very well until after sun up. This morning is very clear and cool. We have a good deal of rain here lately, and I hope you are not needing rain in Alabama.

The crops all look very well but seem to be late. I have not seen any corn higher than my knees. The wheat will do to cut in a week or so and is very fine. I see some rust but don't think it is doing any harm yet, nor don't think it can. I suppose you are getting some flour. If you have not bought any yet you must buy.

When will your subscription for the paper be out? You renew it.

When you buy flour buy enough to do you the balance of the year.

Well, breakfast will soon be ready and [I] must stop. Give my love to your mother. Kiss the children and remember me kindly to the negroes and enquiring friends. Pray for me constantly, write to me frequently and believe me as ever your devoted

J. K. Callaway

Mrs. Dulcinea Callaway

Picket Camp, as usual

Friday June 17th 1863

Mrs. J. K. Callaway:

My Dear Love, I must drop you a few lines although I am not in much fix for it. I am very well, thank the Lord, but have been on guard for 24 hours and have just come off. I am sleepy & nervous, although I had an easy time on guard. I got a good dinner and supper at a good secesh house. I got a fine mess of Irish potatoes & beans in. I am not sure but what it's my beans & potatoes that makes me feel so bad. I also read a good book entitled "The Withered Heart." [10] It is a good account of a very unhappy marriage, resulting from a misunderstanding of each other's hearts and dispositions. I gathered some very valuable hints and lesson from it Alas! also! how much domestic misery have we all witnessed from the same cause. It caused me to institute a diligent review of my past life in regard to my own dear wife. Have I ever sent a pang to her bosom, by misunderstanding her true woman's heart? I hope not but still I fear. If I have I heartily repent.

I have plenty of cheering news from Vicksburg and Virginia but I suppose you are posted up and I need not go into details.

There is no news here. Everything is quiet. I do hope that the defeats at Vicksburg and Va. will cause them to see their error and make peace.

I have not received any letters from any body since you except old Bill Oakes. His folks are all well and in fine health & spirits. He made 200 or 300 bushels of wheat. You ought to go up & see him now. Miss Jane invited me to dinner with her and as I can't go I will transfer my invitation to you. Mr. Callen brought my bundle of clothes all that you said you sent. I am very much obliged to you. I have got on my shirt and lighter pants now. I like them very much. The darker pants are not as pretty but I think I can do very well till winter. I will send home my over coat and one pair pants by Mr. Callen.

How much money have you on hand? Do you desire more? I have some on hand but expect to draw in a few days and when the men are paid off I can collect a good deal that I have lent out.

I have not heard a word from Coffee in so long that I don't know what to think of them all. Do you get any letters from any of them?

I believe I wrote you that I had received and answered letters from Eli and Wes. I have not heard from them since. I should like to hear from Eli now, and shall [be] uneasy about him till I do hear from—and when you hear from him let me know whether he was in the last fight and how he came out. I suppose you have heard of the death of Mr. [George W.] Overton. He died at Petersburg, I believe, in Virginia.

The wheat Crops up here are very fine indeed. The people are just now in a good way harvesting.

Rain plenty and a fine prospect for a good corn crop although most of the corn is late. I have not seen any higher than my waist.

I am glad, my dear, that you sent the paper &c. I can get them here but not as cheap perhaps as there. Why didn't you send me your ambrotype?

I believe I have written all I know and hence must close. Give my love to your mother and the children. A thousand kisses on this for you and them. Write a little oftener and believe me, my darling wife, your

Very affectionate
J. K. Callaway

P. S. Mr. Callen will start home in a few days and then I will write again. God bless *you* my dear and spare our lives & preserve our health.

Picket Camp, Sunday June 21st 1863

Mrs. J. K. Callaway:

My Dear Love, Mr. Callen starts home this evening and I write by him, not that I have any news but that you may hear from me and hear what I will send by him. I send my old over coat, my jeans pants, two or three old socks and piece of stalactite that I got out of a cave. I believe I told you about going into the cave.

I have no news, as I said. I am very well thank God and hope this will find you so. Everything is very quiet up here. No prospect of a fight or a foot race that [I] know of. I still think we will stay here all the summer. If you could have come up when I first wrote you on the subject I might have spent several happy hours before this time. All the news from Virginia and Mississippi is cheering but I confess that I am still very uneasy for Vicksburg.

Well, Well, My Dear, I beg pardon for saying so often that I have no news, for I have an item that I have no doubt will be of interest to you. It is this. We have had sermons preached by two very able divines lately. One by the

Right Rev. Bishop Elliott of Georgia, an Episcopalian, and one by the Rev. Dr. Palmer of New Orleans, a Refugee, who is an intellectual giant of Presbyterian church, and we will have two today by the Rev. Mr. Watson of Valley Creek Presbyterian Church. But the news is that I think there is a revival of religion brewing. This Regiment is following the example of the others and getting up the "Christian Association", a kind of church. It is a good thing and I hope will prosper.

The weather is very cool this morning. We are, as you see, still on picket. We have had a four weeks heat of it this time, but we are, I learn, to be relieved in the morning. Then we will go back to camp on the River 2 miles from town on the West side. Our camp will not be so pleasant there. We will be right in the swamp and will, I am afraid, have to use river water altogether.

The Crops up here look well plenty of rain and the prospect of more very good. I never saw so much wheat in my life as is made up here. I hope you will get plenty cake. I wish you had some of the sugar that we waste. We get plenty from the Commissary & eat as much as we want and barter it for milk.

O how I do want a furlough. I didn't know how I did love my D. till I was separated from her. Indeed I thought that long separation would cause carelessness. That the longer I staid away the less I would want a furlough, but

> "They sin, who tell us love can die;
> With *life*, all other passions fly; . . .
> But love is indestructible;
> Its holy flame forever burneth;
> From Heaven it came; to Heaven returneth." [11]

I find that the longer I stay away the worse I want to see you, worse if possible, as you say, than ever.

> "Nay, thou art now so dear methinks
> The further we are forced apart,
> Affections firm, elastic links
> But bind the closer round the heart."

My Dear. I hope you will excuse my "love letter" as such a thing seems to be uncalled for & unnecessary, but I must indulge my imagination a little. I hope however that we will soon be united again and until then there will be no objective to an exchange of sentimental love letters.

I shall write to Wes and to Sis today. You see what Eli wrote to Irene about Ell Godwin. I'd rather he had not done it. I think Charles Mizell was doing injustice to us all in telling it unless he believed it which I have no idea he did.

Well. It is now time for inspection and I must close. If you have an opportunity I want you to have your ambrotype taken and send it to me. I would give anything in the world for it. I will not write to you again, Darling, till I get a letter from you. I have to go from one [to] two weeks without a syllable from you and if you go a week without hearing from me you want to complain, and if I was by you I'd bite you good and squeeze you half in two. May the Lord bless us all and soon restore us to each other in peace and happiness. My love to your mother & friends, a great many kisses for you [and] the dear children. Your affectionate Husband   J. K. Callaway

P. S. 1 o'clock P. M. I have just eaten a very hearty dinner of lettuce, fried onions, rice pudding, dew berry pies and apple pies. Now I want to be at home to lie down & play with the children & talk with you. I wish you could have taken dinner with me.

D., I never can think to ask whether Eli took up that note for me that Harrison & Tate had in favor of Mims & Sorsby. Did he? How much was it, interest and all?

Good by My dear

J. K.

Camp on Duck River near Shelbyville
Friday June 26th 1863

Mrs. D. Callaway:

My Dear Love, Your very esteemed favor of the 18th reached me today and found me quite well, and hope this will find you so. I am very uneasy about Joe. But hope he is well. I know he will not want for good nursing. I am sure you and your inestimable mother can raise him if any body can.

My dear, I am at a great loss for something to write. It really seems to me that my letters are all alike, and that their monotony must make them dull, stale and uninteresting. But it is the best I can do. We have some good news from Vicksburg but of course you have all that. Everything is very quiet here except that we had orders yesterday morning to cook one day's rations and be ready to move. It was said that the yankees were advancing but we all suppose that it was nothing more than a foraging party and have heard no more from them. The weather has been very bad for three days, raining almost incessantly. Day before yesterday I got a pass and went out into the country, with a young Captain, to be gone till 4 o'clock P. M. But it rained so that I could not get back by the specified time and we decided to wait till after supper, especially as we had got a very fine dinner, consisting of salad, meat, and bread and some of the best coffee I ever saw. Then dessert was Batter cakes, honey, butter and sweet milk, and then our supper was after the same style. I never saw a meal better prepared or more palatable. But it kept raining till about ten o'clock at night and then the captain determined to stay all night and risk being Courtmarshalled but I determined to go to camp live or die, and set out by myself in the darkest darkness I ever saw. I had at least 6 miles to walk and the road was about from shoe mouth to half leg deep in mud & water. The road was new and blind and in many places nothing more than a foot path and I hardly knew the way even in the day time and where it amounted to any thing at all it was a lane with a big ditch on either side. I fell down and into the ditches frequently. I never fell flat down in the mud, however, but I have a pretty severe cut on my right hand that I got by catching on it to keep from falling flat. And when I was tired to death with slipping & stumbling & blundering over rocks and into mud holes & ditches, and nearly dead for some water I got lost. At last my road seemed to give out and I couldn't follow it any farther, and start in any direction and I would run against a tree or over a log or stump. I then set out to find a spring which I recollected seeing among some big rocks on the side of a hill close by. I got above the spring on the side of the hill and started blundering along back down the hill and when I thought I had passed all obstacles & had a clear route the balance of the way down and had despaired of finding the spring, I stumbled over a large rock and fell into it. But I wanted water too badly to try to get out without drinking; and I stood right in the middle of it and with my hands I dipped up and drank about a quart and rested a little. Well, my thirst slaked I set out to find my road but it was no go. I then thought of a single match which [I] happened to have in my pocket book, but there was not a splinter of any kind in a mile of me that would kindle (there is no pine or light wood in Tennessee) and what good would my match do, which in all probability would not kindle now as it set in raining again pretty hard. It was now about 3 o'clock in the morning, I suppose, and just as I was casting about in my mind, where I could get to sit down and rest till day, I ran my hand into my pocket to get my hankerchief to clear my face of the mingled rain and sweat which was dripping very profusely from it, and felt a bundle of old letters (about a dozen) most of them written by your own sweet hand and which I was trying to preserve. The thought was an action and I drew out one and unfolded it and rolled it up into the shape of a candle and then struck my match and lighted it, and while it was burning I found my path and lighted another, and then another, and another and so on till they were all gone, but as the last one gave out I came into a road plain enough to follow without a light. I soon came to the river at the camp, or near it, and there is no way to cross it except on the tumbling dam (I believe I have told you before that there is an old mill here). Well, I started, but the mud had settled on it till it is so slick that the sun shine slips off. The dam is about 150 yards long. I went but a short distance on it till I came upon a fishing Pole that some body had left on the dam, and which served me as a sort of walking stick and balance pole. Well, after half an hour feeling and creeping & trembling over the tremendous roar of water among the rocks below me, I reached the old mill frame which is but the ruins of an extensive old arrangement. The planks all gone and nothing but the old timbers left, except the great mill part of the concern. It was raining steadily and was so dark that I could not tell positively, without feeling with my fingers, whether my eyes were open or not. I had to go about 30 yards through this old frame. I could not reach the water with my long fishing pole. The frame is very high and the water was roaring terribly below. I leave you imagine how I came through this terribly gloomy ordeal. Suffice it to say I came out unhurt, but not un-muddied and, I must confess, not altogether unfrightened. And am now all right side up and forked end down. When [I] got in I found all my mess uneasy about me, afraid I would undertake to come across there in the night. They say it was almost a superhuman feat. I hope, my darling, that this account of my adventure will be some relief from the dull monotony of my letters if not a little interesting. And I have another Item which will not be out of place, as I have been relieved from the obligation of secrecy.

A very clever young man of Capt. Hopkins's Co., some time ago, fell in love with a young lady of Tennessee and was anxious to court her, but was afraid to undertake it for fear of failing; and having a good deal of confidence in me as a friend and thinking somehow that I would be *the man* he divulged his secret to me and asked me to write to her for him. I did so and he was so well pleased with the letter and the impression it produced he wanted me to continue to do his courting. He says I am the best hand he ever saw on love letters. They are to be married at 4 o'clock tomorrow evening. And, as Phillips owes his success to me, I am invited to be present. But I don't know yet whether I can or not.

In regard to the ring I was afraid the one I sent would not fit your finger and the one I sent to T. will be entirely too small for you.

I had a letter from Wes today but he gives me no news. He and Dan have been lucky indeed. I have never received but two letters from Eli and have written to him at least as often. I heard somebody say today that all the Cadets had been furloughed home. Of course this is not so. If it is I hope to hear of Eli at Home in a few days.

I do hope that this year will close the war. The Lord hasten the day of peace.

My love to your mother and the children. Write to me soon. May God spare our lives, preserve our health and restore us to each other soon in health, peace and happiness is the prayer of your Devoted   J. K.

CHAPTER SEVEN

Tullahoma to Chattanooga

June 29–August 2, 1863

JOSHUA'S IDYLLIC DAYS came to an abrupt end on the morning of June 27, 1863. Several days earlier General William S. Rosecrans had begun his advance against the Army of Tennessee. While feinting at the center of General Braxton Bragg's lines, the Federal general flanked the Confederate right with the bulk of his army. Heavy rains, however, slowed their progress, giving Bragg time to organize a response.

After some confusion, Bragg pulled the army from its nearly seventy-mile-long line of defense to concentrate at Tullahoma, an important road junction that he had decided to protect despite its obvious vulnerabilities. By late afternoon on June 28 Bragg was preparing for battle. But at the same time he discussed with his corps commanders, Generals Leonidas Polk and William J. Hardee, the relative merits of standing or retreating. Polk spoke strongly for withdrawal, whereas Hardee advised a wait-and-see strategy.

Two days later Bragg realized he had no choice but to abandon Tullahoma as the Federals threatened to cut his line of retreat. By 7:00 P.M. Bragg had his entire army headed south. He briefly considered giving battle at the Elk River or at Cowan, at the foot of the mountain, before deciding to abandon Middle Tennessee altogether. The night of July 2–3 the army crossed the mountain, and by evening of July 4 the Army of Tennessee had crossed the Tennessee River and moved into Chattanooga.[1]

General Arthur M. Manigault, Callaway's brigade commander, recounted his troops' confused and fatiguing withdrawal from Shelbyville to Chattanooga:

103

On the morning of the 27th of June, at daylight, the troops evacuated Shelbyville and moved towards Tullahoma, reaching it about dark on the same evening. . . . On the 28th, the Division remained in bivouac, the purposes of the enemy apparently undeveloped. On the 29th, about sunrise, I received an order to form the Brigade and to move rapidly to the front, as the enemy was reported moving on us and within two miles. Marching quickly, in a short time we reached some hastily constructed breastworks about a mile to the north of the village. Here . . . we fell to work strengthening and improving our defenses. Sharp firing was going . . . about two miles in our front, and to our right, our Cavalry and that of the enemy being engaged, our own skirmish line about a half-mile in front of us unemployed, although the Infantry of the enemy was said to be steadily advancing. This state of things lasted all day, and during the earlier part of the afternoon of the 30th, after which time the firing slackened, and finally ceased entirely. We soon learned that the enemy . . . had then reached or were passing our right flank and moving to our rear, evidently with a view of cutting us off from our line of retreat and base of supplies at Chattanooga. . . . At sunset the route was taken up towards Allisonia, on the Elk River, . . . which it was very desirable that we should secure. . . . Marching the entire night, over the most execrable roads, a distance of 18 miles, we reached Allisonia about 7 o'clock the following morning. . . . Here we remained on the 1st of July, the enemy feeling his way towards us. . . . On the morning of the second, General Bragg began falling back towards the mountains, reaching the foot of them that evening, and our trains immediately commenced the ascent. During the night, after much labor and anxiety, they all passed over, and before day, most of the troops had also begun to ascend. Marching all day, we reached within six miles of the Tennessee River, after a march of some 30 miles, and there went into camp. . . . The army crossed the Tennessee River on the 4th of July, a pontoon bridge having been laid down for that purpose . . . about six miles above Bridgeport. . . . On the same evening we . . . encamped . . . near to Shellmound Station. . . . The following day we reached Whitesides Station, and the day after, July 6, Chattanooga. From the moment of our leaving Shelbyville, we had nothing but hard marching, and a most fa-

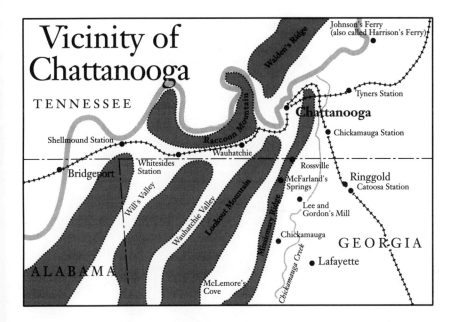

Vicinity of Chattanooga

TENNESSEE

Johnson's Ferry (also called Harrison's Ferry)

Walden's Ridge

Tyners Station

Chattanooga

Shellmound Station

Raccoon Mountain

Wauhatchie

Chickamauga Station

Bridgeport

Whitesides Station

Will's Valley

Wauhatchie Valley

Lookout Mountain

Missionary Ridge

Rossville

McFarland's Springs

Ringgold
Catoosa Station

Lee and Gordon's Mill

Chickamauga

GEORGIA

Lafayette

ALABAMA

McLemore's Cove

Chickamauga Creek

tiguing time of it, in the construction of breastworks, etc. The weather was very warm, and much rain fell. The consequence was that the roads were in a wretched condition, and after the passage over them of some 2,000 wagons and over 100 guns, with the caissons, forges, etc., they became almost impossible.[2]

Having found comparative safety in Chattanooga, the Army of Tennessee went into camps, "and the usual duties of camp life recommenced." Manigault found the climate pleasant, although it was "very hot during the day. The nights were cool and refreshing." As the brigade had few tents, the soldiers built brush arbors for protection from the weather.[3] They also kept busy strengthening the forts around Chattanooga.[4]

Joshua recounts the excitement, drudgery, and fatigue of the Tullahoma campaign. Unlike many others, he praises Bragg for his skill in extricating the army intact, but he laments the loss of the rich middle Tennessee farmlands, as did the rest of the Confederacy, and complains of the lack and quality of the rations now available to the soldiers. He suffers a dramatic weight loss— nineteen pounds in less than four weeks—but he does not specify whether this is caused by the lack of rations, the stress of the retreat from Shelbyville, or further illness. He describes camp amusements, especially an important shooting match, and rather lightheartedly reports the hanging of two young men believed to be spies. On July 24 Joshua receives word that Dulcinea and the children are ill, and he immediately applies for a furlough. When his first application is denied by Bragg, Joshua tries to see him personally but fails in this, too. He resubmits his application and promises to "devil" Bragg until the furlough is approved.

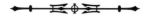

Fort Rains, Tullahoma, Tenn.

4 o'clock P. M. Monday June 29th 1863

Mrs. D. Callaway:

My Darling Wife.

My conjecture on the envelope of my letter of Saturday proved true. We got to this place (Tullahoma) at day light Sunday morning after an awful march through the rain and mud & rested till 6 this morning when unexpectedly to me we were ordered out. The 28th & 2 companies of the . . . are garrisoning this fort which covers about ½ an acre of mud and has 13 guns. A battle is certainly on hand and we have been listening all day for the ball to open and will not be surprised if it begins in 5 minutes but a storm has prevailed all day which has probably kept it off.

I am in a tent and steal a moment to write a line. It may, for ought I know, be the last I may write you. I can only say God bless you all. I will write again and more fully after the fuss is over, if I live. It is raining very hard and may defer a fight for a day or two. I wish it may.

The men are all in fine spirits and seem resolved to sell their lives as dearly as possible. We may all be killed or captured, but our trust is in God and we mean to give them the best there is in us. I know you are all praying for our success, then how can we be other than conquerors.

May Heaven smile propitiously on you and us and bring us all out safely; and conquerors through him who loved us. Your Devoted   J. K. Callaway

Bivouac Near Chattanooga
Tuesday July the 7th 1863

Mrs. Dulcinea Callaway:

My Dear Love, You are perhaps becoming very impatient to hear from me again, and after having just passed through the *fiery* ordeal of another *awful* march I will give you the best I have. In the first place I am very well.

I suppose you got my letters of the 26th and 29th June and shall write accordingly.

We remained in the fort (Rains) till 2 o'clock Wednesday morning July the 1st when we evacuated it. And then commenced a march the most killing to man and beast that I have ever gone through yet. We suffered awfully with rain, mud, heat, hunger and fatigue; but not near so much with hunger in our Regt. as in every other part of the army. Getting into that fort was a "God send" to us. As on Tuesday evening we sent out a detail to cook rations and just as they got ready to begin they were ordered to throw out the rations and pour water on the pots that were hot and have the wagons loaded ready to move instantly and when they got back to the fort and reported we laid violent hands on a few barrels of crackers and a quantity of dried beef, which had been stored away in there, and filled our *haversacks* and *pockets*. After a hard day's march on Wednesday we got to & bivouacked for the night at Alisonia, (the place where I joined the command on the 8th of January last). Left there at day light Thursday morning and reached the foot of the mountain at 4 P. M. where we overtook the rear of the wagon train. We rested till night for them to get up out of the way but they failed, and our Brigade was sent to help them up while the balance of the Division formed line of battle to keep back the yankees & protect the train. We marched in two ranks (one each side of the road) and every man in the Brigade pushing a wagon. I never have seen a set of men and mules so completely exhausted in my life. I actually went to sleep while walking (or rather climbing) along. I sat down by a rock at another time to rest, while the command was halted for some purpose, and went to sleep and they went off and left me although there was a tremendous whipping hollowing and swearing. I saw a driver get off of his mule while waiting for the wagons to move in front & he lay down by his mule & fell asleep and his mule went to sleep and fell down on him and nearly broke his leg.

But we got up the mountain about day light and stopped at sun up to rest and feed the teams but moved on at 6 o'clock, marched across the top & down this side of the mountain and camped in the mud at night. Moved on at daylight Saturday morning. Crossed the Tenn. River on a Pontoon Bridge, at 1 o'clock, where it is nearly a quarter of a mile wide and camped at "Shell Mound." Sunday morning we moved on at daylight and camped at 8 yesterday morning and after a hard march over the slickest mud, & through the hardest rain that I ever was in, and over a spur of the Look Out [sic] Mountain we reached this place tired, sick, worn out, wet, hungry, mad and with our feet blistered & sore; but the men are all cheerful still. We are camped at the foot of this grand old Lookout Mountain 1½ miles from town. The mountain looks grand, majestic, sublime, towering among the clouds. Its summit has been twice hid today by heavy clouds which seemed to rise out of its side and poured torrents of rain on us in the valley while I expect the sun was shining up there. I have not been up there yet but intend to go up if we stay here long. I went to town today but could not find Mace [Mason C.] Kimmey who is there. He was wounded at the battle of Perryville last year.

My Dear, you would doubtless feel disappointed if I were not to give you my opinion of Bragg's retreat. A great many are down on him for it, but I confess that, if I understand it & know anything of the comparative strength of the two opposing armies, he has displayed more of the *general* than in all his former career. Old Rosey laid a very pretty bait for him twice and would have caught many a General but Bragg did not bite. All the troops that he had sent to Miss[issippi] was from his right wing which covered McMinville and held the roads leading to our rear. And when Old Rosey found that they were gone he sent a large force round there to capture Tullahoma and cut off our supplies, while, with another strong force, he made a feint upon Shelbyville as if he would attack us in front, to keep [us] there till he could accomplish his object but Bragg understood him and drew his whole force back to Tullahoma. That trumped ole Rosey and he didn't know how to play his hand, and hence we were lying there in line of battle from Sunday till Tuesday night, waiting to see what he *would* do. He seemed to make up his mind about Tuesday morning and Bragg discovered it in the evening. It was to cut us off at Alisonia 6 miles below just as he had tried to do at Tullahoma, and tried it the same way; (by pressing hard in front); but Bragg wouldn't bite but drew off again and beat him to the mountain and got away, no doubt very unexpectedly to the whole yankee nation and brought out his army safe except perhaps a few stragglers, and to make up for them General Wheeler ambushed the yankees on top of the mountain the day after we had passed and killed and captured 2000 or 3000 of them & drove them back to the foot on the other side.

If they had attacked us in front at either Shelbyville or Tullahoma we would have whipped them terribly but old Rosey knew that and wouldn't come up. Bragg did not have force enough to fight him on equal grounds and if he had divided his army to force Rosencrans back from his flank movement & compel him to fight us in our breast works we would have been badly whipped. It would have taken at least half of the army to even check that flanking force and that would have weakened us so in front that we would have fallen an easy prey to the vandals. Bragg did the right thing and is entitled to great credit for the masterly skill with which he handled his army in getting it out of the very jaws of destruction.

These are the conclusions I come to looking at the thing from my point of view. You know that I am not a Bragg man and may have reason hereafter to change my opinion of the retreat. I am aware that a great many differ with me.

Well, it is now getting late and raining. I will quit till morning. Good Night.

Wednesday morning July 8th

Well my Dear I am on hand and very well, thank God. I had another good night's sleep last night. The weather looks dark and lowering this morning. The top of the Lookout is gone up out of sight among the clouds, "and we shall have rain."

The men are all lively this morning but that is only common. I saw the other day when we were marching our slick roads in time of the rain, and all very tired, a hundred men fall down in the mud; and every time one fell, and grunted under the weight of his knapsack & gun every body else laughed and made some remark. But he would soon laugh at some one else's fall.

Well, I believe I have written all I know. I can't tell you anything about where we will go next, for no one, not even Bragg, I reckon, knows. Some think we are as apt to go to Miss[issippi] as to Kentucky. I shall hold on and see.

I am very sorry that we had to give up so much good country. Corn, hogs & wheat in this state. The Valleys of Duck & Elk Rivers are proverbial for the richness of the soil; and we have lost it all. But I know some men up there who I think will destroy their crops rather than let the enemy have them.

My Dear, I can't tell you what to do about writing to me. I think myself that we will stay here some time, though we may leave in a very few days. You may direct your letters to Chattanooga and they will follow me if we are not here. If we stay here long I should be happy to have you come to see me.

Give my love to your mother and kiss the children for me. I think you have been neglecting your duty. I expected to get a letter whenever we got the mail but have not got it yet.

You will notice that I commenced this letter on another sheet and before I knew it I was writing on this. I am afraid you will not be able to find the beginning. I will number the pages. We had a rumor here last night that Vicksburg had fallen.[5] I hope this is not so. If it is we are badly crippled.

Write to me immediately. And may God bless us all & give us peace is the prayer of your Devoted husband

J. K. Callaway

Mrs. Dulcinea Callaway

Camp Near Chattanooga
Saturday July the 11th 1863

My Dear Wife:

Col. Reid starts home tomorrow morning and I send this by him. I have no very special news.

Of course you have heard all about the fall of Vicksburg and I need not say a word about it. I am afraid to say anything. I fear the War will last for the next 50 years. We were all cheerful and in good spirits till its fall. Now we are sad and depressed. That is the most paralyzing stroke that we have ever sustained. I am now afraid that Lee's invasion of Maryland and Pennsylvania will do us no good.[6] The future does indeed look dark and gloomy. Oh, when will the end be! We are not whipped by any means. But when we reflect that the yankees have taken every place that they have tried on the Mississippi from Fort Donnelson[7] [*sic*] to New Orleans; and every place except Richmond, and now have full possession of the whole of the Mississippi Valley and a good foot hold in *every* state; I say when we or when *I* reflect upon these facts the picture looks gloomy indeed, and I confess that I tremble with apprehension. But Our trust is in God and Our cause is just.

Your letters of recent dates 21st June 1st July were received a day or two ago. I am always glad to get your letters no matter how old they are. But if you will send them to some particular post office they will come quicker, two or three of your last were only directed to the army of Tennessee. You forgot to add Shelbyville. (Chattanooga now) We are camped in a very pretty place and are now having a very nice time but I can't say how long it will last. We may move in a day and we may not move in 3 months.

The weather is a little better than when I wrote you last. Not quite as much rain. We have moved away from the foot of the mountain and are now in a nice Black Jack thicket, in another direction from Trion. Can't see a mountain in any direction. Looks a little like the old camp ground in old Coffee.

I had a letter from Wes two days ago. No news. Dan had gone home as you told me. I am glad he got a furlough. I wish he had a discharge and was up here. He and I could make money like a machine. I got a letter from Nat Pace two days ago. He was well. His mother was very sick. Expected to die.

My Dear I would send you some money but I have not got it. Not expecting to have an opportunity to send it home I have lent it out and now can't get it.

I think you are losing by not buying flour now. I think it will rise rather than fall. Buy whatever you want. Let me hear from you twice a week at least.

Give my love to your mother. Kiss the children for me. Let me know if you got T.'s "little white ring." I sent it some time ago. I forgot to tell you that I am very well.

The Lord bless us & save us and give Peace and independence is the prayer of your

Devoted
J. K. Callaway

Camp near Chattanooga, Wednesday
July 16th 1863

My Dear Love:

I have received two letters from you since I wrote you but they are old, one of them, however, is dated July 5th. It does very well, but not as late as I want. I want one today dated yesterday. I have no news to give you. Everything is as it was. We are building a fort here but have no idea how long we will stay here to fight in it. It has always happened that Bragg leaves all his fortifications.

My dear, I am at a loss to know how or what to write. I have been in good heart all along but now I am depressed. I can't see the end. I begin to feel like I was separated from you forever. Oh! when will I see you?

We may stay here some time and if we do surely you can come to see me. If you don't, I shall try to go to see you. Col. Reid got a furlough for 30 days. Why may not I? But a hundred have tried since he left.

My dear, I am not very well. I had to sit down yesterday evening on Dress Parade to keep from fainting. I have lost about 15 pounds in weight since we left Shelbyville. I have some fever every day or two. My health is declining some way. May be I'll get a sick furlough.

The weather has been a little better for some days. It rains only about every 3rd day now. I got Eli's letter the other day for which I am much obliged to you & him. Tell T. that Pa would make her another ring if he could get a shell, but there are none here. She must trim her little fat fingers. But when I come home I'll kiss them down a little so she can wear it.

Kiss my little Joe for me *hard.* Can he talk?

Oh, how I do want to see him! Surely the war will not last always! Give my love to your mother, & Dan, if he is at home yet. Write me twice a week. Tell me all the news. I hear that Mrs. Childers is dead? I am sorry. Pray for me. And May the Lord give us peace & independence with the remission of our sins, & our home & families is the prayer of your Devoted husband.

J. K. Callaway

Wednesday evening. My dear, I did not get to send off my letter today as I expected and will add a little to it. As I said before I am not very well. I have not eaten anything since breakfast. I am suffering now with headache. There is nothing new today, except the surrender of Port Hudson[8] and of course you have that. There is no telling where our reverses are going to end. It looks to me, as I said before, like we are nearly gone up. But our trust is in God and our cause is just. Let us not be discouraged. I fear we will be on very short rations before the year is out. We are only getting one third of a pound of meat a day now. And sometimes it happens that that is over half bone or so badly spoiled that we can't eat it.

I got a letter from Sis today. All well. Jim Baker was at Home on furlough. Ell is in the 64 Ala regiment, a corporal. Sis says she got a letter from you a day or two ago and had answered it. Hope's family was very sick when she heard from them last. It has not rained today.

Well, that's all. Kiss the children for me & write to me.   Josh

Camp Near Chattanooga, Tenn.
Sunday morning July 19/63

Mrs. Dulcinea Callaway:

My Dear Wife, Time has moved on and brought another sabbath which is my day to write to you.

I have nothing special to tell you. And if I make out a long letter it must be made of nonsense.

I am not very well yet but am so much better that I have almost despaired of getting a furlough. A large number of men and officers from this Regiment have made application for furlough and some of them have been granted. Capt. Hopkins got one for six days to go and see his parents. Lieut Wood asked for one to go and see his family, whom he has not seen in nearly two years, and failed. Capt. Hewett sent up an application which, being founded on the fact that his wife was lying at the point of death, was approved by all the intermediate commanders and disapproved by General Bragg. The Captain then went to see General Bragg in person and got it. Privates can get furloughs when officers can't near reach them.

My Dear, you did not say in your last letter, dated July 12th, whether you got my letter, which I wrote while in the Fort at Tullahoma or not: I would like to know whether you got it or not.

There has been some little excitement in camp for a few days in regard to a big shooting match. The prize being a fine gun valued at $500, some say 1500. There was 5 men from each Regiment allowed to shoot for it. Of course these five were the best marksmen in the Regiment. And the shooting was done by Regt, one Regiment against another, and the old 28th Bore off the prize triumphantly, and then the different marksmen of the Regiment had to shoot for it to determine what particular soldier should have the prize, and one Mr. May of Co. "D" is the lucky & honored one. Oh how his posterity will harp on it. His grand children's children will be proud of their ancestry. None but privates and non commissioned officers had a trial at it.

The weather is fine now and has been for several days. This is a lovely morning, but the weather is not in keeping with our feelings. Our success seems to have come to a stand. General Lee has fallen back on this side of the Potomac. Johnston is falling back on the Tombigbee[9] we are idle.

I feel very much depressed. The yankees have largely the advantage of us. We have received a series of staggering blows. Nevertheless I am not out of heart. As I said before, our trust is in God and our cause is just.

> "Judge not the Lord by feeble sense,
> But trust him for his grace.
> Behind a frowning Providence
> He hides a smiling face."

We are still on short rations, but the meat that we have drawn lately has been so poor (beef) that I might say we are out of rations. But still we are doing finely. I can endure a great deal while I know you and the children are doing well. I sent out yesterday and bought half a gallon of milk for which I paid a dollar. It made me two meals. I could have bought butter milk for half that price. Today we will have some blackberry pies for dinner.

I Promised to make another ring for T. if I had another shell. But I can't get a shell and have made [one] out of a guttapercha button. It is not a very nice one but is the best I can do.

I am not exactly satisfied, my dear, with your writing. I want a letter from you at least twice a week, and if you can't get paper write on anything and if you use anything that I want preserved, as you did before, I will send it back as I do this time.

I hope this will find you all well. I am very sorry to hear of Dan's sickness. Give him and your mother my love. Write to me *today* and occasionally.

May the Lord bless, Preserve and restore us to each other soon in peace and happiness is the prayer of, My Darling Wife, Your affectionate Husband

J. K. Callaway

P. S. Kiss the children for me.

2 P. M. I have just seen a dispatch from Virginia stating that Eli was wounded in the Battle of Gettysburg.[10] But the dispatch does not say positively whether he was wounded on the leg or shoulder, and hence I am in hopes he is not wounded at all. I am writing to him and will send it to you and if you know where he is send it to him. If you do not know keep it till you learn his whereabouts and then forward it. Truly your   J. K.

Camp Near Chattanooga
Thursday July 23rd 1863

My Dear D.:

I am becoming uneasy again. I have been looking for a letter from you every day for a week, and can't get it. Why in the world don't you write, my dear? Are you sick?

I am not very well yet. When I left Shelbyville I weighed 167 pounds and this morning I weigh 148. You see a decline of 19 pounds.

Capt. Reese leaves for Marion this evening and I avail myself of the opportunity to send you a little missive. I hope it will find you all well and you *writing* to me. I hope you have heard from Eli by this time and forwarded my letter.

I have no news at all to write unless it is that we are on very short rations. We had a very little blue beef for breakfast yesterday morning and no meat since. We had bread and cucumbers for dinner, with a little sugar; bread and rice for supper, and bread & water for breakfast this morning. We are cooking collards for dinner without any meat or bread. I went to the commissary a while ago they told me they would issue some beef and meat this evening.

It is very hard to be on such short rations, but we hope for better times. Starvation is much better than subjugation and hence we don't grumble.

Everything here is as it was when I wrote you last. I got a letter from Nig day before yesterday. All well. I am not in very high spirits, yet, about *"the situation,"* but am better reconciled than when Vicksburg first fell. I have never thought for a moment that we would finally fail, but I am almost sick at the thought of the blood, treasure and long war it is going to take before we establish our independence.

My Dear, I want a knife & fork and if I buy it here it will cost me five dollars. Therefore if you have a chance send me one and a spoon. You have not said anything yet about coming to see me. Use your own pleasure, my Dear. Although I am anxious to see you.

Give me all the news and my love to your mother and the children. I hope Dan is well.

Kiss the children and *write, WRITE* to me.

Your loving Josh

D. C.

Camp Near Chattanooga Tenn.
Friday night, July 24th 1863

My Dear, Darling Wife:

Your favor of the 19th Inst. reached me today, bringing the sad intelligence of your illness and that of our dear children. Just as soon as I read your letter I sat down and wrote an application for a 20 days furlough and started it up and if I get it shall be home in a few days, perhaps in a week. But I have not much hope of getting it. I will not hear from it before Monday or Tuesday, if I do before Wednesday or Thursday night. You need not look for me too sanguinely, for I am very doubtful.[11]

I am in tolerably good health, though not very well. I believe I wrote you my weight, (148 pounds).

I am on duty tomorrow working, or rather overseeing, on the fortifications.

I shall look for another letter from you tomorrow and every day till I get one.

I will write to you again as soon as I hear from my furlough, if I do not get it, but if I get it I shall start immediately for home.

There is no news stirring here. Everything remains "status quo" since I wrote.

I hope you will excuse so short a letter when I tell you that Bill Leach has just come from home, and there are six men in my tent some reading letters that he brought them; all reading as loud as they can, and the balance of them talking and laughing as hard as they can. I hope you have heard from Eli before this time. And I do hope you and the children are better.

God bless you, My Dear, and restore us all to health and each other in peace and happiness.

Your loving & devoted

J. K. Callaway

Mrs. D. Callaway

Camp Near Chattanooga

Sunday July 26th 1863

Mrs. Dulcinea Callaway:

My Dear wife, Mr Russell leaves for home at 2 o'clock this evening and I can not fail to send you another letter, when I can send right home, although I started one to you by mail yesterday.

I have no special news, my darling, except two Items, one of which I forgot in my letter of the 24th.

First I am tolerably well, at least getting stout again. This I suppose will interest you from the fact that I have been puny so long.

In the next place, and as I forgot before, there were two yankee spies went up a spout here last Friday, day be[fo]re yesterday, by hanging. They were both very young. I suppose no more than 18 or 20 years old.[12]

I have, however, one other item of news, and a very sad item it is too. Fred Vaughan got a letter today from his brother Henry stating that Eli and Thomas Beaty were wounded at the Battle [of] Gettysburg and left in the hands of the enemy. Joe Overton wrote to John [Overton] today also, that his brother Tom had written home that they were "*mortally*" wounded and left in the hands of the enemy. I am anxious to know how, where and how badly they were wounded &c.

I have not heard from my furlough and am afraid to hear for fear it will not be granted. I am almost hopeless on the subject. I am also afraid to hear from home. Still I am almost crazy to hear. Why in the world do not you write, or, if you are not able why does not your mother write, if it's only a line.

Well, My Darling, Preaching is now about to commence just out side my tent and I must close and join in the service, and ask God to restore us all to wanted health, to pardon all our miss doings, to restore peace and happiness to our country and us to each other.

Your very affectionate husband
J. K. Callaway

Mrs. Dulcinea Callaway,
Summerfield,
Alabama

Camp Near Chattanooga
Wednesday July 29th 1863

My Dear Wife:

I have suffered the most *intense* anxiety ever since the receipt, last Friday, of your letter of the 19th which brought the intelligence of your sickness. I have suffered thus not only because I could not hear any more from you, which itself is enough to kill me, and for which I can see no excuse at all, unless you are all dead, but anxiety to hear from my furlough. I made my application as strong as I could, and yesterday it came back "*Disapproved by Command of Gen Bragg*" and this morning I went to see Gen. Bragg myself but he was not there and I only saw his A[djutant] G[eneral] who told me that personal applications are not allowed. My great uneasiness about you all and my disappointment about my furlough has almost made me sick. I don't know what to be at. I am vexed and grieved. I shall now send my application right back to Bragg and if it is rejected again I'll start a new one and continue to devil him thus till I get a furlough or a letter from you, one.

I am very well besides my uneasiness about home. I must complain of maltreatment by you, for if you are not able to write you can get somebody to write for you. But to write that you are all sick and then not write a word for a week is a grievious sin, and if I were to get news every day of the increasing severity of your illness it would not be any worse.

Mr. Nathan Edwards will start home in a few minutes and I send this [by] him.

I engineered a furlough through for him but I can't work one out for myself.

I have no news. Everything still.

God knows I hope this will find you greatly improved if not well.

Do pray let me hear from you

Your loving

J. K. Callaway

Camp Near Chattanooga

Sunday night Aug 2nd 1863

My Dear D.:

The calm, still, Sabbath evening has again come, and darkness is closing in and beginning to envelop the earth, and fell a strange kind of repose. And while the eternal hum of the army and the incessant creaking of the July flies, together with the lowing of some cows and the barking of a dog, which I hear on the side of a neighboring mountain, are sounding like a mournful dirge, making me feel lonely even in the midst of the army. My thoughts run to my far off home, to dear and perhaps sick & suffering children. Oh! how I long to see them! But, alas! All I can do is to kiss this sheet and drop a tear on it and ask God to protect and preserve them till I can see them.

> "The curfew tolls the knell of departing day,
> The lowing herd winds slowly over the [lea]
> The plowman homeward plods his weary way,
> And leaves the world to darkness and to me."[13]

I believe I told you how hard I was trying to get a furlough. It has not come back yet. I am in the most awful suspense. I am considerably relieved, however, since I wrote last. Friday I got your letter of the 27th informing me that you were all better. (Oh! how grateful I was for that little missive!) and today John Overton got a letter from his mother stating that my folks were "all well except that one of the children was complaining a little."

My application will surely come back in a day or two and if it is granted I shall be at home by the last of this week, but as I said before I have no hope.

My Dear, I have no particular news. You have it all. If I get my furlough I will *tell* you a good many things. If I fail to get it I will then *write* some things that I prefer to tell you verbally.

D. You never have told me whether you got my little pencil written letter which I wrote from Fort Rains. Let me know in your next whether you got it or not. And let me know whether you will try to come to see me or not, provided I will make some arrangement for you an escort and some accommodation for you here.

Mr. Russell, by whom I sent my bible home, will be coming back in a few days and I am satisfied will take pleasure in bringing you up. I will write to him and get him to call on you and see if you want to come.

I will write again when I hear from my furlough, and if I get it I will telegraph.

Do pray, my Dear, don't keep me in such awful suspense anymore about writing. It nearly kills me.

I believe I have written all I know that will interest you.

I am very well. God bless you, My Darling

J. K. Callaway

CHAPTER EIGHT

Chickamauga

August 27–September 24, 1863

JOSHUA'S STRATEGY of deviling General Bragg with applications for a furlough proved successful, and he spent most of August with his family. When he returned to the Army of Tennessee late in the month, Bragg had already begun shifting the troops about in a bewildered response to threats from the advancing Federals under General Rosecrans. Indeed, Joshua's brigade was not where he had left it a few weeks earlier, and such was the confusion in Chattanooga that no one could immediately tell him where to find it. He finally reached his comrades the following day, seven miles from the city, just in time to turn around and march back through town to a new position. This proved an apt beginning to Callaway's participation in the Chickamauga campaign—a series of marches, countermarches, and recountermarches.

During Callaway's absence General Thomas C. Hindman replaced General Jones M. Withers as division commander—"and the change was truly an unfortunate one for us," declared brigade commander General Manigault. "[He was] a scheming, maneuvering, political general. . . . Morally, he stood deservedly low in the opinions of most of the officers . . . the cunningest, most slippery intriguer that I ever met with." The five-foot one-inch Hindman, much given to snug clothing, ruffled shirts, and patent leather boots, did not impress his soldiers, either. "All I have to fear now is our new general," asserted soldier Thomas Hall, who related an incident that proved Hindman a "regular low life rowdy." During a night march, upon finding General Polk's staff camped on the site Hindman had selected for himself, he roused the interlopers by referring to them as "unprincipled curs." "To say the least," Hall concluded, "he was challenged to a duel, which he did not

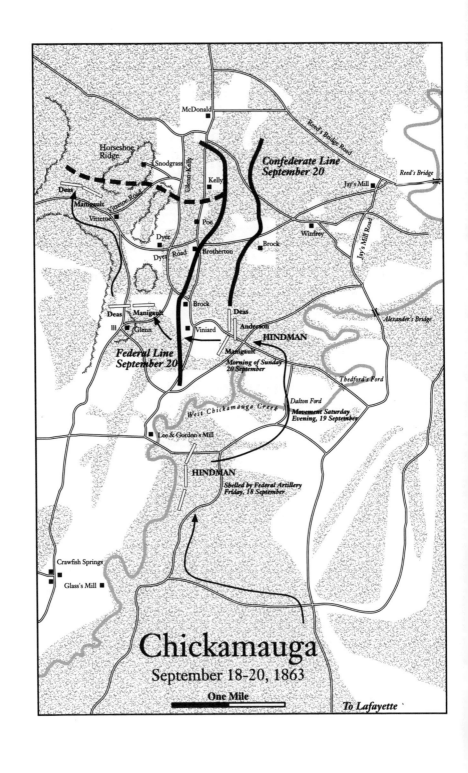

Chickamauga

September 18-20, 1863

One Mile

accept"—thereby proving, in some minds, his cowardice. Hindman's performance during the coming weeks bears out these assessments by his subordinate and by his common soldier.[1]

Bragg ordered the Army of Tennessee out of Chattanooga on September 9, 1863. The troops headed generally south in order to forestall a flanking
movement by the Federals that would sever the Confederate line of communications. Rosecrans had split his army into three widely separated units,
affording Bragg several splendid opportunities to destroy the Northern army
in detail—opportunities that Bragg's subordinates failed to use to advantage.
The first lost opportunity occurred at McLemore's Cove on September 11,
where Hindman's reluctance and refusal to attack the enemy allowed them
to escape; the second came two days later, when General Polk failed to carry
out orders to attack the Federals near Rock Spring. Bragg retreated as far as
Lafayette, where he headquartered for several days before turning north
again with the intention of interposing his army between Rosecrans and
Chattanooga. On September 18 the armies met, skirmished, and jockeyed
for position. Over the next two days nearly thirty thousand American soldiers
became casualties as they fought the bloody Battle of Chickamauga. Hindman's division, under Polk's command during the first day's fighting, fought
on the left of the Confederate line. When General James Longstreet arrived
with reinforcements from Virginia during the night of the 19th–20th, Bragg
assigned him to command the left, and Polk moved to the right of the line
with most of his corps. Hindman's division, however, held its position at the
extreme left of the Confederate line, where they had a hot time of it on the
final day of the battle.[2]

Joshua's report of his adventures during the campaign and battle closely
matches his brigade commander's narrative of events. Manigault wrote that
the division received its first marching orders on August 20, when it crossed
Lookout Mountain and moved several miles up the Wauhatchie Valley. They
camped here until the evening of the 23d. This was about the time Callaway
rejoined the unit, just in time to recross the mountain to bivouac on the far
side of Chattanooga. During this movement Callaway's regiment formed a
rear guard, holding the pass over the mountain. Hindman's division spent the
next week at McFarland's Springs, about five miles from Chattanooga, "a
delightful location at the foot of . . . Missionary Ridge, with a fine spring of

excellent water." On the 30th they moved again to reinforce General D. H. Hill, who guarded the Tennessee River seven miles east of Chattanooga, near the mouth of Chickamauga Creek. The division remained with Hill for three days, during which time considerable fraternizing took place between the soldiers of the opposing armies posted on either side of the river. On September 2 the division returned to McFarland's Springs and on the 8th left the Springs for the last time, marching fifteen miles to Lee and Gordon's Mill on Chickamauga Creek. Here the soldiers bivouacked until early morning on the 10th, when they moved toward McLemore's Cove.[3]

September 11 saw the first failure of Bragg's subordinates to carry out orders as Hindman frittered away the hours planning his own retreat route rather than attacking the Federals, who had made themselves vulnerable by marching into a natural trap. "The opportunity offered General Hindman for distinguishing himself and striking a terrible blow was favorable in the extreme," Manigault asserted, "but he was not up to the work, it being far beyond his capacity as a general." The enemy discovered their peril and quickly withdrew. By the time Hindman ordered an advance, "only a skirmish line and brigade or two of infantry were in [the soldier's] front to resist [them]." Manigault expressed extreme disappointment. "The whole affair proved a miserable failure, altho had there been a proper man to manage for us, I have little doubt but that a most brilliant success would have been achieved. . . . Seven hours elapsed between the time that our line was within two and a half miles of the enemy, and the time that I saw the enemy retreating towards the gap. Our division was stationary for hours, and when moved forward, they were too late to accomplish their purpose."[4]

That night the division made a "tedious and rough" night march to Lafayette, where the soldiers rested until sunset, when once again they received orders for a night march—eleven miles to join Polk at Rock Springs. When they reached the position at daylight on the 12th, Polk ordered the brigade forward to feel for the enemy, but by then the Northerners had disappeared from Polk's front. Once again, while the Confederates procrastinated and argued, the Federals withdrew to safety. The following morning the weary soldiers retraced their steps to Lafayette and remained there until the night of the 17th, when again they received orders for a night march.[5]

At 8:00 A.M. on September 18, Callaway's brigade reached the vicinity of Lee and Gordon's Mill once again. On the extreme left of the Confederate army, the soldiers formed a line of battle near the mills and then moved forward to within a half mile of Chickamauga Creek. An artillery duel began, and as skirmishers pushed forward, sharp firing broke out. "Here we had a disagreeable day of it, the bullets and cannon shot flying unpleasantly thick about us," Manigault reported. The next afternoon he received orders to move rapidly to the right: "The battle of Chickamauga had commenced, and we were wanted."[6]

After marching about three and a half miles and crossing the Chickamauga at Hunt's Ford, the unit went forward to relieve Cheatham's division. By this time the enemy had retreated, leaving only skirmishers, who exchanged shots with the Confederates until dark. The Thirty-fourth Alabama, forming the left of the brigade, found its left wing in an open field. A scouting party of Federals fired a volley into the regiment, which the Southerners immediately returned. The next day a captured Federal captain reported that he had been sent out with a group of about sixty men. Losing his way in the dark, he suddenly found himself in front of the Confederates, who answered the fire of his own men. The captain claimed the volley left only himself and two men unscathed. Shortly after this incident, Manigault's brigade pulled back about four hundred yards to take its position in line of battle "as well as circumstances and the darkness would permit."[7]

Bragg's plan for September 20 called for Polk's wing on the right to begin the festivities early in the morning. The action would then proceed to the left, each section of the Army of Tennessee attacking as those on its right became engaged. Manigault's brigade, on the extreme left of the line, had a long wait. Ready to move at 7:00 A.M., the soldiers awaited the order to advance. "Hour after hour passed, still there was no indication of the fight having commenced," Manigault reported. "Everything was quiet as though no human being was within miles, not even a scattering picket shot. Various were the surmises as to the cause of the delay." The cause, as usual, was Polk's dilatoriness. Hours after the battle should have begun he was enjoying a leisurely breakfast at his headquarters. Finally, about 11:20 A.M., Manigault's brigade began its advance.[8]

Moving through woods and open ground, the brigade advanced upon a Federal position on a hill. The soldiers faltered briefly under enemy artillery fire but then managed to rush the breastworks and wrest them from the defenders. They held for a short time until Federal reinforcements compelled Manigault to withdraw after the Twenty-fourth and Twenty-eighth Alabama regiments "suffered severely" under enemy crossfire. At some point during this conflict a piece of artillery fell into Union hands. Determined to retrieve it, Colonel Reid, commanding the Twenty-eighth Alabama, called for volunteers. Callaway's Company K and Company I, first to answer the call, drove the enemy off and returned the piece to its rightful owners.[9]

Meanwhile, the remainder of Hindman's division, posted to the right of Manigault, along with other units, had broken through the Federal line and was in pursuit. This was the famous breakthrough long credited to Longstreet, but a closer look at the official reports of the battle make it clear that Bragg personally ordered the advance that serendipitously hit the Federal line at the precise point that had just been abandoned by the Northerners through a failure of communications. When the Federals recognized their precarious position, they "retreated precipitately," and Manigault's soldiers advanced "almost unopposed," rejoining the remainder of their division about two miles in advance of their jumping-off point.[10]

As if the soldiers had not had enough fighting for one day, Manigault's brigade now joined the assault on Snodgrass Hill, where Federal general George H. Thomas had established a strong position, and a lasting reputation, with the thirty-thousand Federals who had not fled the field. From 3:00 P.M. until sunset the Twenty-eighth Alabama fiercely attacked and counterattacked. By the close of the day's fighting Manigault reported that "scarcely any order preserved, and no defined line. Regiments and companies inextricably mixed up, and it resembled more a skirmish on a grand scale than the conflict of a line of battle." As soldiers ran out of ammunition, they resupplied themselves from the killed and wounded around them. Callaway's regiment helped drive a large segment of the Federal force into a ravine, where they were captured by another Confederate unit arriving as reinforcements. During the night the remaining Federals withdrew to rejoin Rosecrans, who had his army busily securing its position in Chattanooga.[11]

Manigault declared Chickamauga the hardest fight that he had ever been engaged in: "It lasted longer, and was more obstinately contested than any other. . . . The fire we got under when first we became engaged in the morning exceeded anything I ever before or after experienced. The air seemed alive with bullets." He reported his brigade 2,025 strong as it went into battle. They suffered 540 killed or severely or mortally wounded, 69 slightly wounded, and 47 captured, a loss of 656. One of those killed was brigade inspector Captain Daniel E. Huger, Manigault's brother-in-law.[12]

Callaway's regiment, the Twenty-eighth Alabama, received well-deserved praise. Colonel John C. Reid insisted, "Men never fought more gallantly than did my command." Hindman included the recovery of the briefly captured artillery piece in his report, stating that the "Twenty-eighth Alabama gallantly faced about and brought it off in safety." Sergeant James R. Smith received Company K's acclamation for "gallantry and good conduct in the battle," placing his name on the Battle of Chickamauga's Roll of Honor. Although the official records do not record Smith's deeds on the field, Joshua relates one brief moment of the battle that reveals Smith's heroism.[13]

The Army of Tennessee remained on the field at Chickamauga for two days following the battle, recuperating from the exhaustion and the chaos created by three weeks of marching and two days of fierce fighting. There was much to be done—burying the dead, collecting usable arms and ammunition, gathering together the scattered units. On September 23 Bragg once again put his army on the road, "toward Chattanooga," declared one of Callaway's regiment, "ready to execute any order from [the] General."[14]

Joshua's letters during the four weeks of campaign and battle confirm much of what appears in the official records. He also writes of events that do not appear in official sources, such as nightly prayer meetings and suffering some illness. He complains that Dulcinea does not write to him often enough, fears that she is ill, and becomes concerned when he hears that his children are sick. He writes an amusing account of a deserting officer who, when caught and punished, receives his just deserts. On September 2 Joshua celebrates his twenty-ninth birthday with an introspective review of his life; unfortunately pieces of this letter are missing, so some of his musings are lost to us. From his account of the battle, one suspects Joshua enjoyed it immensely. Two days after the fight he writes a short note to let Dulcinea know he is "alive and well," but in a long letter written four days after the event, his excitement is still evident as he describes his adventures. Even in the midst of battle, he tells his wife, he felt "perfectly calm and serene." Sadly, he reports the loss of a diary he had been keeping. One can only wonder what it would have added to the story told through his letters.

Bivouac on Lookout Mountain

Thursday morning Aug 27/63

Mrs. D. Callaway:

My Dear wife, I promised to write last Sunday, but I never got to my command till Sunday evening. I got to Chattanooga Saturday night but the command had moved and owing to the great confusion no one could tell me where it was. I went to and staid all night at our old camping place by myself, and Sunday morning I went back into town & learned where my Regt. was. Seven miles from town on the Will's Valley Rail Road. I got to it about 3 o'clock in the evening and in an hour had to start back. We are now (our Regt.) on the west side of the Look Out Mountain about half way from the foot to the top, guarding the road which leads across the corner of it to Chattanooga. We have the best position I ever saw in my life. This Regt. can keep ten thousand men from crossing the mountain, can whip them, though I have no idea that they will give us a chance at them here. They will either cross above or below. In either case they will find thousands of veteran rebels to greet them. Everything is very quiet now—this morning—but no one knows how soon—what moment—the conflict will begin. We are waiting on them. And I feel pretty sure of a great victory.

Our wagons are five or six miles from us in rear, and all our baggage is in them. I have neither pen, ink, nor paper here. Hence I have not written before. I know you will be very uneasy before you get this. But I hope you are praying for me. If I had another sheet of paper I would write to Wes, but my friend didn't like to spare this sheet. Tell him to write to me any how and I will when I get back to the wagons, which will not be till this frolic is over.

I got a letter from Hope Powell yesterday. His folks are not well. He has no news.

Remember me constantly in your prayers. I am very anxious to hear from home. How is T? I am very well and hope this will find you all so.

My Love to all. Your Loving

J. K. Callaway

Camp as before
Saturday, August 29/63

My Dear. D.:

As I am writing to Wes I must write you a little.

I have no news except what I have written to him. You will read his and send it to him.

We are having a good time up here. I do hope this will find you all well. I do not remember, Dear, what I paid for the Soda, I sent half a pound and I think I paid $2.50. I am glad you had good biscuits. May you *always* have *plenty* that is *good.* I sent twenty grains of quinine for which I paid two dollars.[15] I hope it will cure you all. The surgeon of the Post was not in when I was in Selma or I might have got it for nothing. But getting [it] at the drug store I had to pay for it.

Let me hear from you soon and often. Kiss the children for me & Pray for me.

God bless you my darling
Josh

P. S. Send me that note against Squire James W. Oakes. Sergt. Rogers will take it up.

Yours &c.
Josh

In Camp, Wednesday Evening
September 2nd 1863

Mrs. D. Callaway:

My Dearest D. this is my birthday. And while I return unto God my sincere thanks for having preserved my life, and for having brought me safely through all the trials and dangers of twenty-nine years I must not forget to thank him also for the inestimable blessing of such an invaluable jewel as yourself. And allow me, my darling, to express my gratitude to you for your disinterested love, the very thought of which, while I . . .[16]

. . . have been lounging about all day, have had nothing to do but review my past life. And the retrospect is in some degree pleasing, but at the same time it is painful. There are many very bright spots in my childhood, youth, and even early manhood to which memory reverts with my pleasing recollections; but there are scenes in my past life which I look back upon with many bitter regrets. The Lord forgive me for the "follies of youth and the sins of riper years!" The neglect of mental improvement in youth is certainly a great sin. And in my case casts its dark shadow beyond the . . . even to the grave. Oh, how . . .[17]

You will observe that you can not tell from the dating of this letter where we are, and I am sure I am not able to tell you where we are. We left our position on the mountain Monday evening at 2 o'clock and marched very hard to Chickamauga, ten or twelve miles, where we arrived about 8 P. M. Left there at 3 or 4 yesterday evening and marched to this place (McFarlands Spring) 12 miles, got here at 9 last night. I was completely broke down and hence I had a fever last night. We are about five miles from Chattanooga. The yankees seem to have drawn off for a while and we have gone into camp again as if we did not expect any more fuss. I have not seen any yankees except at a great distance, across the river in an orchard. George Mims hollowed at them and ordered them out of the orchard. I suppose they thought the next thing would be a ball, and they got out in double quick time.

I have no idea how soon we will be in motion again.

I believe I wrote you that we have prayer meeting nearly every night, but it is now night, after supper, and the horn has not blowed (we have a horn which is sounded for service, reminding one of a camp meeting. Indeed it is a camp meeting.)

May God bless us all. And give us peace and independence.

Let me hear from you constantly. There is nothing affords me half as much pleasure as to read a letter from you.

My love to your mother. Kiss T. and Joe for me. Remember me kindly to any and all who may feel an interest in my wellfare. Tell T. how Pa loves her and wants her [to] pray for him as well as herself.

Your Devoted

J. K. Callaway

Camp Near McFarland's Spring Near (5 miles)

Chattanooga, Sunday morning Sept 6th 1863

My dear Love:

My patience is becoming thread bare. I have not had a letter from you since the one you wrote on Sunday after I left. Of course I conclude that you are too sick to write. I am very uneasy about you my dear.

I have no particular news. We have been lying here for a few days resting, but I suppose our resting is now over. We have just received orders to cook three days' rations and be ready to move at a moment's warning. I do not know in what direction we will move, but I suppose we will go towards the enemy. We have, I learn, got a pontoon bridge across the river just above town. We heard heavy cannonading yesterday up there but have not heard what harm was done. Not much I reckon.

I have not one word of news, my dear. I only write that you may know that I think of you. I am quite well, and hope this will find you all so yet I am very fearful. I am almost afraid to hear from you.

We had prayer meeting last night and have had every night since we have been here. Meeting commenced last Wednesday night just after I sealed my letter to you. I have not had a letter from anybody but you and Wes since I got back. I am beginning to feel lost. Yes, I got one from Hope.

The weather is very dry and the road exceedingly dusty. I got dust enough in my nose and lungs the other day to make a brick. After a little march we all look like a parcel of . . . cats. You can hardly tell one man from another. Everybody's hair, whiskers, skin and clothes are the same color.

My Darling, I bought two papers of mixed needles the other day. After taking out two or three from each packet I send you the balance. I paid fifty cents a paper for them. Much cheaper I suppose than they can be bought in Selma.

I am very anxious to hear something more from Eli. Has Wes and Dan gone back? Give my love to your mother. Kiss T. and Joe for me and remember me kindly to all the old friends & Pray for me constantly. Don't neglect this my love for I feel sure that I can not live unless I am supported by the prayers of my Darling wife. A great many kisses on this for you and the children. May the Lord bless us and preserve us and restore us to each [oth]er soon in peace and prosperity is the prayer of your Very Affectionate

J. K. Callaway

We leave immediately. I don't know where.

P. S. 11 A. M. I have just received yours of the first inst in which you say, "why don't you write?" My darling, I have written twice every week. I am very much obliged to you for your letter. I love you better than ever. All I lack of being happy is your society. God bless you forever.   J.K.

Bivouac Near Lafayette, Ga.
Thursday Sept. 17th 1863

Mrs. J. K. Callaway:

My Dear Wife, By the Grace of God I am yet alive and well for which I am very thankful; and trust this will find you all well, and full of the spirit of religion. Mr. Dacus of our company came in yesterday from home. He saw Wes in Selma the day he left you. Wes told him that you were well yourself but that both the children were sick. I am very sorry to hear that but hope you are all well now. I hope your mother will get to take her trip to Talladega but I should be very sorry to hear her leave you while the children are sick.

My Dear, I thought I would be able to give you some of the particulars of our recent operations but I can't do it now. General Bragg has issued a proclamation or circular in which he says: "Soldiers, you have offered to meet the enemy twice in battle and he has fled from you. It now remains for you to chase him down and force him to fight." Hence we all imagine there is some terrible marching and fighting ahead. The allowance of officers' baggage is reduced to almost nothing. (two blankets and a small valise or carpetsack) No one knows which way we will move. Some think we will go back towards Chattanooga. I hope I shall be able to give you all the particulars after it is all over. I must tell you of a little incident that occurred a day or two before this row commenced: One Lieutenant Tucker of this regiment deserted some time ago, after he had just drawn nine months wages, and carried off a private with him. Owing to President Davis's amnesty he could not be hurt for desertion and was courtmartialed for getting the private off with him. He was dismissed from the service in disgrace. His sentence was read on dress parade. The ranks were opened and faced inward, this being done the major [sent] him to the head of the line and announced that "A man was going to pass down the lines and any man was at liberty to kick his stern who felt like it." He then started him by giving him a tremendous kick behind. Every man, nearly, in the regiment lifted. At first he walked very slowly giving them a fine chance at him. But they hurt him so badly that he began to beg them not to "kick hard," but this only raised the yell of indignation tenfold louder. He then struck a trot and went through in double quick time, to the tune of *"Here's your deserting lieutenant; lift him boys."* The privates seemed to enjoy it hugely. After the show was over he moped off to his quarters and began to prepare to go home in shame and infamy, but just before he was ready to leave the colonel went down and conscripted him. He only lacked two days of being forty-five years old. He is now over the age but he's *"in for the war"*. He is now carrying a musket, a private.

The troops are still in fine spirits. I don't think anybody is afraid of the result.

May God give us the victory. There are some signs of a move soon. We will probably move tonight. In fact I think we will. There is no telling when the fight will come off. Pray for me constantly. I Bless God that I am beginning to feel as of old when the Lord blessed me. I can now go into the fight without that great dread which has hitherto haunted me. I have a good mind to say that I believe that God is reconciled to me through the blood of Christ which interceedeth for me. But I am afraid to say it! Oh, for a little more faith! Pray for me my darling. I love to read the bible. I have just read Paul's letter to the Hebrews. It is a delightful book. Read it, my dear, and may God bless you in it.

I can't tell you when nor where to write to me yet. My love to all.

Grace and peace be with you all, and glory and honor to God.

Yours truly forever
J. K. Callaway

Bivouac near Chickamauga Creek
Tuesday night Sept. 22/63

My Dear Love,

Through the amazing mercy of God I am alive and well for which I hope
you will all join me in thanking & praising & serving the Lord. I have just
passed through the terrible ordeal of a hard battle, and strange to say I am
untouched, although we were in a few yards of their line for several minutes,
at one time, fighting like tigers; and fought them about forty steps for an
hour and a half at another time. We have routed them and run them off.
They are said to be crossing the river and leaving as hard as they can. "Thanks
be unto God who giveth us the victory through our Lord Jesus Christ."

You will see a list of the casualties in the "Reporter." I have not time to
give you the particulars now. I will write at length when I have an opportunity. I write now merely to let you know that your prayers for the preservation of my life have been answered, and to relieve your suspense.

Your kind letter of the 6th, enclosing the note, reached me early yesterday morning, for which I am obliged to you. I saw the old 4th Ala[bama]
yesterday.

It is now 9 o'clock and we leave in the morning at 3. Continue your prayers
for me, the struggle may not be over yet.

I must bid you good night. May the Lord bless & keep us all and finally
save us in Heaven.

Your Affectionate husband
J. K. Callaway

Mrs. J. K. Callaway

Camp of wagon train 28th Ala Vols.
Sunday September 24th 1863

Mrs. Dulcinea B. Callaway:

My Dear Love, Again, through the Exceeding mercy of God, I am permitted to write you. May my poor, ungrateful heart always be as thankful for
God's blessings as now. My gratitude is my happiness.

My dear, I promised you to give you all the particulars of our late movements when an opportunity offered, but I cannot do it now, although I have

ample time, because I have lost the little diary which I kept. I will however do the best I can from memory.

We left McFarland's Spring about the 5th September and moved down to cross Chickamaugee Creek at Lee's & Gordon's Mills, the next day we lay over there and cooked rations & on the next day we moved down the Valley a few miles and went into line of battle lay there till the next day, then moved over to the right and attacked a considerable force of the enemy in what is called MacKlemore's Cove, which is the valley between Lookout Mountain and Missionary Ridge. We drove them out.

We then moved down to La Fayette which is a little town. (the County Site of Walker County, Georgia) After one day's rest we moved out in the direction of Chattanooga and offered the enemy battle which he declined after some skirmishing. We lay there one day and night. Then moved back to La Fayette and rested about three days and nights, and then having, I suppose, driven in all the flanking parties and got the Yankees all together in one body, General Bragg moved forward and attacked them on Chickamaugee Creek on the 18th instant. Manigault's Brigade left Lafayette at five o'clock in the evening of Thursday the 17th. Moved up nearly to the position assigned us by 2 o'clock that night. We then turned into a field and stacked arms & rested till day light Friday morning the 18th when we moved up and formed line of battle parallel to the course of the Creek and in easy range of a battery of artillery which the yankees had planted on the opposite of the creek.

They commenced Shelling us as soon as we began to form, and continued it at intervals all day. One man was killed and about six or eight wounded in the Brigade. One man in the 28th was wounded by a cannon ball rolling on the ground. They saw it coming rolling along and began to get out of its way and some one ran over him and knocked him down and he did not get up till it struck him on the shin and nearly broke his leg. It to[ok] it badly, wounding him severely.

We lay there till Saturday evening. The fighting commenced away down on our right on Friday evening, and was severe Saturday morning it reopened with tenfold fury and increased all day. Late in the evening we moved down to the right and took our place in the line just at dark. It being dark we did not get our line exactly parallel to that of the yankees, and consequently the left of our Brigade (34th Ala. Regt.) swung round *into* the yankee line of skirmishers who fired into the 34th killing one or two and wounding several others. But the 34th returned the fire promptly and killed the whole company of yankees except three men, and the Lieutenant commanding them whom they captured the next day.

We lay there all night, and the yankees drew off about half a mile and formed a new line of battle on a ridge, leaving a line of skirmishers in the place of their line of battle. At 8 o'clock Sunday morning, the 20th, the battle commenced, away down on the right several miles, with increased fury, and kept coming up along the line till at 10 the whole line—which I suppose was some 6 or 8 miles long—became engaged we, being on the extreme left, were ordered forward.

We threw out a line of skirmishers a hundred and fifty yards in front and moved steadily forward not knowing how far off the enemy was. When we had gone about three hundred yards our skirmishers encountered those of the enemy, and as soon as the firing commenced all order and control was lost, the men raised the "War whoop," "the yell," "The battle cry" and away they went like a gang of mad tigers or demons, "Every man a host," in double quick time. We soon ran over our skirmishers and those of the enemy fled as if old Scratch had been after them. Thus we charged fully half a mile across an old field then across a skirt of woods then another old field and into another skirt of woods, with three [of] our Regiments on the right of the Brigade in a corn field perfectly exposed to the enemies' small arms and artillery which they could not stand long but gave way, and then all the enemies' fire was turned upon the 28th and 34th which we didn't stand long. But away we all went as fiercely as we had gone up there.

One piece of our artillery was left on the field and when Col. Reid asked for two companies to volunteer to go back and bring it out, Captain Hopkins's Company and ours volunteered and we went back right in the face of the enemy and brought it off and as the yankees saw fit to let us alone we did them and so it was done without the fire of a gun. Our Brigade was then ordered farther to the right and formed at the foot of a long hill on the top of which was the enemy's line. It was now 2 o'clock in the evening and the battle was raging all along the line on our left and right as if heaven and earth were coming together. A thousand thunderstorms all turned loose together could not equal the noise.

We were now ordered forward and when we got half way up the hill they opened on us with great fury with grape and canister and with small arms. But we moved steadily on till we got in about twenty yards of their line where we halted and went regularly to work. Here commenced a scene that beggars description, and God forbid that I should ever have to witness such another. The carnage was awful. Men were shot down all around me. I was indeed in the very midst of death. We fought them thus close I suppose about ten minutes when, as if by command, our whole line gave way and away we went down the hill like a gang of sheep. There was no line in our rear to support us. We fell back about two hundred yards and rallied and then advanced again to within about fifty yards of our former position when the Regt. on our left gave way again and the yankees swung round into their place giving them a complete cross fire on the 28th. But we held that ground fifteen or twenty minutes and gave way again, but rallied as before and moved a third time to the charge. This time we reached the crest or top of the hill and found ourselves on equal footing with the enemy. Here we stood at least an hour before they gave way. (To give you some idea of how long we fought there I will relate a little incident: One man of our company, J. R. Smith, who stood in the very front of the fight, shot away all his 40 rounds and came back to me for more ammunition and I cut the cartridge box off of a wounded man and gave to him and he went back & shot nearly or quite all that away; And that you may know he was not excited but brave & gallant I must tell you what he said while I was getting his ammunition: There were a good many lying back and skulking behind trees under the hill, and bawled out to them "It's a free fight, boys, come up and pitch in." And just as I handed him the cartridge box a man came up the hill hollowing at the top of his voice, to those who were lying back, to "Rally boys and fight for your country" and spoke to Smith as if he thought Smith was one of them, and Smith took him by the arm and led him off saying, "Come fight side of me, I'll see you out." And led him off. But I soon lost sight of him and don't know how long he stood up.)

The Yankees gave way about dark and fled in every direction. We followed them over half a mile, picking up a great many prisoners, when another Brigade came up and followed on after them.

We now moved back to the top of the hill and "Slept on the battle field" Napoleon's sign of victory. But the Sleep of a victorious army on a field won is not very sweet when we are haunted all night long with the groans and cries of the wounded dying.

I have now seen and experienced "The horrors of war" as well as the spoils and glories. And may God deliver us from so awful a scourge and calamity!

To undertake to describe the appearance of the field after the battle would be time lost. I saw it the next day for four or five miles along the line. The timber was not blown up by the roots, as is in a hurricane, but small trees were shot down and large ones shot through and limbs of all sizes shot off, and trees peeled and scarred all over and everything *full* of minnie balls, grape & cannister, and the ground literally ploughed up by cannon balls. Well, the woods looked like a corn field after a tremendous wind and hail storm.

Now, my Dear, it will perhaps surprise you when I tell you that in the very midst of all this terrible thunder, blood, carnage, slaughter, with my heart lifted to God in prayer and my trust in him and knowing that my wife and a host of others were praying for me, I felt perfectly calm and secure, knew all that was passing around me. Never lost my wits a single moment. And I am proud to say that I don't think I did anything of which you or I or any of my friends need be ashamed.

The Yankees are now in Chattanooga, and we are holding them there. They can't get out on this side of the river without a fight, and if they commence that we will, with the help of God, whip them again. Our line extends from the river above town [to] the river below. We hold the point of Lookout Mountain which overlooks the town and from which we can Shell them to death. But I do not [know] what Bragg is going to do. I don't think though that he will make us storm their works. Bragg knows them and he knows that his men know them. And I fear it would be hard to get men to storm such places.

Our line is on the top of what is called Missionary Ridge, from which we can see all their works and at night all their fires. I am now back with the wagon train in charge of the cooking detail for the Brigade and for the present out of danger. Pray for me.

I am very well, thank God. The mail is going out and I must close. I believe I have written all I know. My love to all. A thousand kisses for you and the children. The Lord bless us all and save us with an everlasting salvation.

Your Loving

J. K. Callaway

Behind the Lines, Chattanooga

September 30–October 21, 1863

IN HIS September 24 letter, Joshua had speculated on General Bragg's next move. Although one member of the Twenty-eighth Alabama declared the soldiers were "ready to execute any order from [their] General," brigade commander General Manigault reported that from the heights above Chattanooga they could see the enemy "at work like beavers upon their defences." Manigault also pointed out, "Unfortunately, we had done most of it for them," a reference to the fact that the works being strengthened had been constructed by the Confederates during their tenure in Chattanooga. Callaway enunciated Bragg's dilemma when he wrote, "I do not know what Bragg is going to do." Assaulting the Federal positions may have seemed a likely follow-up to the rout at Chickamauga, but since his own army had constructed the works, Bragg knew how strong they were. "And I fear," Joshua confided, "it would be hard to get men to storm such places." [1] Besides, Bragg had other things on his mind.

The Army of Tennessee had barely established itself on the heights of Missionary Ridge before Bragg began a wholesale purging of his army. With good cause, he relieved Generals Polk and Hindman almost immediately, and Hill shortly thereafter, for their disobedience of orders during the campaign and Battle of Chickamauga. Shortly after the dismissal of these incompetents, some of Bragg's remaining subordinates, probably led by General Longstreet, who hoped to get command of the Army of Tennessee himself, got up a petition to President Davis complaining of Bragg's decisions following the Battle of Chickamauga and asked that he be removed from command of the army. Davis visited the army in mid-October to sort things out. Despite the complaints he heard from unhappy subordinates, Davis upheld Bragg because, he told the general, "the conference satisfied [him] that no change for the better could be made in the commander of the army."[2]

While Bragg quarrels with his subordinates, Joshua enjoys a pleasant interlude. On assignment behind the lines at Chickamauga Station, he supervises the brigade cooks, telling Dulcinea that he is "chief cook and bottle washer," and he enjoys being the highest authority in the area. His circumstances are comfortable, with plenty to eat and a warm bed, unlike his comrades, who are camped on a rocky hillside with no tents and scant rations. As usual he suffers some ailment for several days. He is increasingly religious, at one point admitting to Dulcinea, "It's the all absorbing subject with me," and he asks her to see about both of them rejoining a church. He discusses Edward Bulwer's new novel with her, complains of the frequent rain, worries over his family's circumstances, and gives Dulcinea directions for cooking beef tripe.

Camp of Wagon Train 28th Ala. Regt.
Chickamaugee Creek Sept. 30th/63

Mrs. Dulcinea B. Callaway:

My Very Dear Wife, I now have an opportunity to send a letter by hand, to Selma, by a negro. And I write, not because I have any news, but that you may know that the good Lord still continues to bless me with life and health for which I hope you will join me in thanking him. Everything is precisely as it was when I wrote last. So if you will read that letter today you will know how we are all getting along. Except, however, that there is some prospect of rain today. It is now 2 P. M. and sprinkling a little.

I have not been so much gratified lately as I was a while ago when I got a letter from Eli and one from Wes both dated the 9th. I am truly glad that Eli got home. I hope he will get to stay at home till he is exchanged.[3]

His letter brought the good news that you are all better. I am very thankful, and hope this will find you all so still. I hope your mother and Eli will have a pleasant and profitable trip. And may you and Miss Ann have a pleasant time at home. I wish I could be there with you. I shall ask General Bragg again about Christmas to let me go home. I learn that corn is worth three dollars a bushel and salt a hundred dollars a sack. I don't know what you will do. But the best we can of course. The Lord help us. I would write to Eli and Wes now but the boy is about to start. I will write to them in a day or two. My love to everybody. May God bless you all. Kiss Eli & Wes & the children for me. Your devoted

J. K. Callaway

P. S. I will send you a small piece of the telegraph wire which the yankees had on the battlefield. I send it as curiosity and a trophy.

N. B. When you write me hereafter address me in Hindman's Division. Withers has resigned and it is now Hindman's Division. *I am all right.*

Yours truly forever

J. K. C.

Mrs. D. B. C.

Camp of Wagon Train of 28th Ala.

Tuesday Evening Oct 6/63

My Dearest D.:

After returning my grateful thanks unto the Lord for his continued preservation of my life and health, I must tell you what a fine dinner I have just eaten. It consisted of beef tripes and corn bread. The beef was killed this morning and we eat the tripe for dinner. And, though it may seem strange to you, I think it was the best tripe I ever tasted. I will give you the process by which it is prepared so readily:

Take the tripe as soon as the beef is killed and wash it thoroughly in cold water; then *dip* it in boiling water so as to scald it, and then scrape it till it is perfectly clean, when it will look as white as a chicken; then wash it again in cold water in order to wrence it off clean. Then cook it, that is, boil it till it is perfectly tender, and then dip it in batter and fry it. Thus you may kill a beef for breakfast and eat the tripe for dinner. And it's too good for a soldier.

I have no particular news. Everything is, in the main, as it was when I wrote last. There was some cannonading yesterday, but I don't know what was done. They say we threw some shells into one of the enemy's forts and saw them out of it. I don't know *myself.* There was also a rumor in camp yesterday that a courier had been captured who had, on his person, a dispatch to Burnside stating that if *he,* (Rosecrans), did not get reinforcements in six days he "would be gone up". This though is rumor. There were two or three very heavy guns fired late last night, but I don't know for what purpose.

I got a letter today from Damaris dated September 23rd and 24th. They were not all well, three or four of the children were having chill and fever. Her letter is full of religion, full of prayer and faith. O how precious to me is such a sister! She sends her love to you and wish you to kiss "Dear little *Joseph* and *Temperance*" for her. She dwells on those names and prays that they may be "*Joseph* and *Temperance indeed*." She says that if she should be so unfortunate as to miss of heaven she will praise God even in torment for having had such pious parents. I feel a good deal like her. For I feel sure that if I am saved I shall owe my salvation to the pious precepts and example of my now sainted Father and Mother, whose faithful fervent prayers for me still rise like incens[e] to heaven, and God for Christ's sake is answering them. O, My dear, let us pray mightily & constantly and he will hear us. I am still afraid to say that "I know that my Redeemer liveth" yet "I can, I *do* believe" it. The Lord help my unbelief! Pray for me, my dear. Let us live nearer to God. Let us live more by prayer. "The Christian enters heaven by prayer." The Lord inspire us with deeper devotion, with continual hungering and thirsting after righteousness.

D. I sent you another book yesterday, entitled "Cosette" of Victor Hugo's series entitled "Les Miserables."[4] Be sure to let me know if you get it, and let me know how much postage you have to pay. The Post Master at Chickamauga says it will only be ten cents. I hope Father Garrett will not charge you so much this time.

You have not said yet how much you have read of those books I left with you? How do you like them? and what do you think of them? What do you think of Mr. Margrave and those over whom he had so much influence? Those characters are of course fictitious all of them, but they are portrayed to represent the author's opinions, and you find some very strong arguments to support those opinions which he does not declare as his own, because he can not bring scientific investigation to his support. Bulwer is a great writer and has a great reputation; and I am of opinion that he has chosen the novel or fictitious style in order to evade public censure, and preserve his great name, as an author, in public opinion while exciting the scientific world to the investigation of his very delicate question. And if this feels . . . of his The Strange Story—finds that public opinion would tolerate such a thing he will then come out in a scientific work on Metaphysics, setting forth an entirely new philosophy such as is hinted at in his novel. Which he is afraid to espouse until he feels of the popular mind.[5]

I will not close my letter till morning, so that I may give any news that may come in from the front tonight, which I will put in a post script. I am very well. May the Lord bless us with a ready peace & restoration to each other. Pardon our sins & save us in heaven for Christ's sake. Kiss the children. My highest regard to Misses Nellie, Ann & Julia. Good By.

Mrs. Dulcinea Callaway   J. K. Callaway

P. S. Wednesday Morning the 7th. There is no news. A rumor came in last night that some prisoners were captured yesterday who said the yankees are crossing the river. Have got all their large guns over. It is raining again this morning. Bad day to cook rations. I am quite well this morning & hope you are. Let me hear from you. The Lord bless you all. Good By.   J. K. C.

> Camp Wagon Train, 28 Ala.
> Chickamauga Creek
> Saturday Evening Oct. 10th 1863

My Dearest Love:

Your anxiously looked for letter of the 4th reached me today. I have been quarreling with our Post Master every day for a week and when he has brought me a letter which was not from the right one I have told him to go back. Today when he got here I took his old haversack (he carried the mail in it). I met him and took it away from him and looked over the whole mail, and just as I had despaired I recognized a certain brown envelope. I snatched it up and recognized the hand writing on the back, but I never read the superscription till I had read the contents of the letter several times. O you have no idea how it helps me to get a letter from you. Really it is all my solace. When I am writing to you it seems as if I were talking to you, and when I read your letters it seems like you were talking to me. O how I want to see you! I certainly never wanted to see you worse. I have had the blues for two weeks. My Bible and your letters are all the comforters I have. And when I get one letter it seems an age before I get another.

I have no news for you my Dear. The seige is still going on, though every-thing has been perfectly quiet today, and I am still with the wagon train at-tending to the cooking, and having a good time. I get plenty to eat, especially beef tripes, and have a tent to sleep in. My bed consists of a pile of hay on which I have a buffalo rug, a sheepskin, an oil cloth, a saddle blanket, five coverlets, two good blankets, a good quilt and a big feather pillow. Am I not comfortable? But my comrades are in line of battle among the rocks on the side of Missionary Ridge, with one blanket to the man without tents and eating cold and scant rations.

It is said that President Davis is here somewhere but I have not seen him. I suppose he is here, though. It is said that Rosecrans is being reinforced. And we are expecting Gen Bragg to open on him vigorously every day. I can't tell what he is waiting for. On Wheeler, perhaps.[6]

It is now about sun set and I will finish in the morning. Until then, with many kind wishes & kisses, Good Night.   J. K. C.

Sunday morning Oct. 11th 1863

My Dear, Through God's mercy I am very well this morning, for which I am very thankful, and I hope you are all so. It would grieve me indeed to know that you were unable to be up and appreciate this lovely Sabbath morn-ing. The weather has been beautiful for several days. This is what we want. Let us thank the Lord.

Everything is still very quiet. No firing now for about three days.

D. I sent you two papers the other day and your mother one. Let me know if you got them and if you have to pay any postage on them and how much. I suppose your mother and Eli have got home by this time? How did they enjoy the trip? How was T. pleased? I am glad that you and Miss Ann are having such a pleasant time. May it continue forever. Present my compli-ments to Miss Ann.

Well, I have written all that can be of any interest to you unless it be to tell you about my clothing. I have three pairs of Drawers, and three pairs of socks, one pair of the socks are worn nearly out and one pair is new. I have never worn them at all. I have four pairs of pants, two of cotton (those you sent me). My old uniform pants and a pair which I got from the Government the other day of good woolen goods. I have two domestic shirts and the one you made for me. I have lost that woolen shirt that I got from Mrs. Morrow. I need one or two heavy shirts and some yarn socks, and a vest or two. Though I have no way to carry them. My old Carpet Sack will not hold what I have already. That is why I lost my shirt and all my towels. But send them along. I'll do the best I can.

My Dear, As it is Sunday morning perhaps a few words on the subject of religion would not be improper. It's the all absorbing subject with me, and I hope it is so with you. But I can only say let us read the Word and pray much. The Lord has begun a good work. O may he continue it!

I should like very much to become a member of the Church again, and I know you would, but how shall we manage it? Our Chaplain—Mr. Graham—proposed to send my name to Prof. Moore but I told him to wait till I could hear from you. I see no chance but for us to go through probation again. But if you say so I will let the chaplain send my name up stating that our probation was out when we moved from Coffee, and write to Moore myself to call on you and get your name. By this means we may get into full connection at once, which I much prefer. Let me hear from you immediately on this subject. And may the Lord direct us in this thing!

My Dear have you made any arrangements for meat and bread for next year? If this difficulty here is settled in time I shall, if everything becomes quiet, try to get home again. I have not drawn any money since I left home. Nor do I know when I will.

My sincerest love to mother and Eli. Kiss T. & Joe for me. And may the grace of our Lord and Savior be with you all. Amen.

Your Devoted Husband
J. K. Callaway

Mrs. D. B. Callaway

Camp Wagon Train
Monday Evening, Oct. 13th 1863

My Dear Wife: I am sick! I am sick of our separation! Sick of the war! And I am sick anyhow. I had a little dumb chill yesterday morning, after I finished writing to you, and then had a slow fever till daylight this morning. I have had a severe headache felt very stupid all day today. I am afraid I am going to be sick sure enough.

A negro is going to start home tomorrow and I will send this by him. He will mail it at Selma.

I have been forgetting all along to tell you that I took supper with *Captain* Sam Prince the other night. I have seen him several times lately. He is Quarter Master of the 8th Miss. Regiment. He looks as dry and surly as ever. And you have been forgetting to tell me if you got those needles I sent you while we were at Chattanooga. How did you like them? And you do not say if you got the piece of Yankee telegraph. Did you?

I have no special news. Everything is quiet this evening, though there was some cannonading this morning. Our Pickets and those of the enemy are very close together but do not fire at each other, though they talk together, swear at each other, exchange papers &c. But Gen. Bragg has ordered all that kind of doing stopped. I hear that our cavalry was to take Shelbyville today.

My Dear, I wrote you the other day that I had sent you Damaris's letter, but didn't send it. I will send it in this that you may know how full of religion and prayer she is. Let us be like her. I thank God that I have such relatives. I know that the Lord has heard and is answering the prayers that have gone up to Heaven for me and my Soul thrills with joy at the thought of meeting all those dear relatives in heaven. I do bless God tonight and at all times for pious parents. And when I reflect that their sainted spirits are now perhaps my guardian angels and flutter with rapture around their returning prodigal son even while I write these lines, my soul is almost in ecstacy. My eyes are dim with tears of joy and gladness. I have a taste

> "Of all the ecstatic joys that spring
> Around the bright Elysian."

Blessed be God. I can begin now to "Rejoice in hope of the glory of God." My Dear, read the 23rd Psalm and you see the sentiments and comforts of the faithful Christian. Which I pray day and night to realize, and I trust I do, at least to some extent. Oh that I could adopt it as confidently as David did. Now read the 20th Psalm and you have my daily prayer for you and our afflicted country. "The Lord hear thee in the day of trouble."

Well, I believe I will quit till morning. I began a letter to you Saturday and finished it yesterday, and have commenced one today and will finish it tomorrow. So I have written to you every day for four days in succession. Do you write to me half so often? I am never satisfied only when I am writing to you or reading a letter from you. I suppose Eli will be coming back to the army soon and I want him to be sure to come to see me before he goes to his Regiment. He will find me—if I don't move—about a mile and a half from Chickamauga Station, where he will get off of the cars. Tell him to enquire for Hindman's Division Train and then for Manigault's Brigade train. It looks like raining this evening.

Well, I said I would quit till morning and so I will. Until then, with many kisses and good wishes and prayers for our mutual protection, I bid you Good Night.

J. K. Callaway

Tuesday Morning. Oct. 14th

I feel very well this morning. It is raining pretty smartly. It commenced about midnight and looks like it will rain all day.

There is no news this morning, except that I heard last night that all our artillery had been moved from the point of Lookout Mountain. I don't know what that means.

D. did Mrs. Hooks send any money by me when I was coming back from home? I have forgotten. I remember her speaking about it but I think I told her that the boys would be paid off some and would then have plenty of money. She wanted to send the money to Mark [Hooks] to buy some needles, I think. Mark came to me the other day and said she wrote to him that she sent him ten dollars by me; and I told him that she did not, and I don't think yet that she did.

Remember me kindly to all. Many kisses on this for you and the children. And may the Lord bless you. Your Devoted   J. K. Callaway

Mrs. Dulcinea B. Callaway

Wednesday Morning Oct. 14th [15th,] 1863

Logan did not get off yesterday and I will add another short Post Script. It rained all day yesterday and all night last night and is raining this morning. And it rains very hard too. Everything is flooded. Oh, how I do want to be at home in such awful bad weather. But I fear it [will] be a long time before I can get there to stay long at a time. No telling when we will ever have peace.

The devil must be "turned loose upon the earth for a season." But I ought not to complain at my present lot. I am out of all danger from the enemy and have a tent to stay in, plenty to eat, and a bed consisting of a pile of hay, four coverlets, two blankets, a buffalo rug, sheepskin, saddle blanket, oil cloth &c. While my comrades have to stay out yonder without tents and only one blanket to the man, eat cold and scant rations &c.

If Logan does not get off today I will mail this here and send it along. I am very well. No hopes of a furlough on this spell. My love to all. Tell Eli I think it time I was getting a letter from him.

May the Lord bless us all & restore peace to us.

Your very affectionate husband

J. K. Callaway

Camp Wagon Train

Wednesday Morning Oct. 21/63

My Dear Wife: Your long looked for favor of the 12th reached me day before yesterday, and I write again today. I am very well, thank the Lord, and hope this find[s] you all so. Everything quiet yet and I think now it will remain so for some time. I learn that President Davis told General Manigault that we would hold still and let our cavalry operate in rear of the enemy for some time. Although he said in his speech that our flag would be "planted on the banks of the Cumberland in thirty days." I hear also that General Bragg's Adjutant general told Col. Mitchell that Bragg will send home for clothing again as soon as things become a little more quiet. And General Bragg has published an order which says any noncommissioned officer or soldier who will get a recruit can have a forty day's furlough. And if it included officers I would make the contract, if he would agree to wait sixteen or eighteen years for the recruit. From all these facts I think all will be still for some time.

I have no other news, and only write, as you say, to let you hear from me. We have had a day or two of fine weather but this morning it is thundering and looks very much like rain. But so far as I am concerned let it rain, but oh, for the men out yonder. I am having a gay time. I am chief cook and bottle washer. No one has control over me. And I command all the cooks from the whole Brigade. And when the commissaries want a detail, or want my cooks to do anything out of their line, they have to ask *me*. Although some of them are as big as *majors.* And I sit in my tent out of the rain and read and write and eat as much as I please. Only walk round and see the cooks once or twice a day. I pay what all officers do for their rations: 85 cts. a pound for bacon, 20 for beef, 12½ for flour, 4 for meal, 35 for salt and 25 for rice. About $25 a month, and then my tobacco writing paper pens, ink, envelopes and other foolishness, takes about all my wages. But I think I'll send you a few hundred after a while.

It has now commenced raining, and I am gloomy. Oh, how I wish I was at home with you. I am sorry it was not me that was going home when you looked for me.

But give my love to all—especially to Mrs. Hooks—And Let us pray much and we will yet be permitted to live long together for God.

Your Loving
J. K. Callaway

Mrs. D. B. Callaway

CHAPTER TEN

Missionary Ridge

October 26–November 19, 1863

JOSHUA'S DAYS of comfort and plenty came to an end all too soon, and on October 25 he rejoined his regiment at the foot of Missionary Ridge. Here the soldiers had established a line of earthworks a short distance above the plain. General Manigault reported these works "of very inferior character, owing to the great deficiency of implements and the rough and rocky character of the ground." [1]

The lines of the opposing armies were close, and, although one soldier complained, "It is one of the most disagreeable places you ever saw," the view afforded by the Confederate position moved others to lyricism. "At night just after dark," Manigault wrote, "when all the camp fires were lighted, the effect was very grand and imposing. . . . Over and over again I have spent an hour or more in the quiet of the evening . . . admiring this grand illumination, thinking of home, family, and friends, or speculating as to the future." [2] Joshua, too, on October 26 and November 1 and 19, tells Dulcinea of the entrancing and enchanting views.

Toward the middle of November the Federals seemed to be moving about more than usual, although no outright immediate threat manifested itself, and Bragg continued to feel secure in his position atop Missionary Ridge. Manigault reported that by November 20 it became obvious the Federals would take some action shortly but that Bragg "trusted too much to the natural advantage of the ground he occupied, or was not fully informed as to the strength of the army he had opposed to him. Perhaps he underrated his adversaries." General St. John R. Liddell also asserted, "Danger was thickening fast around Bragg. But he seemed singularly indifferent." Liddell thought

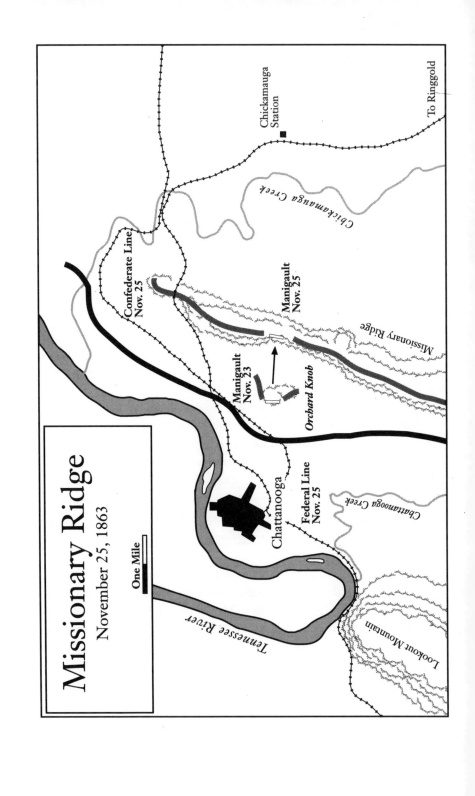

Missionary Ridge
November 25, 1863

One Mile

Tennessee River

Chattanooga

Lookout Mountain

Chattanooga Creek

Federal Line
Nov. 25

Orchard Knob

Manigault
Nov. 23

Manigault
Nov. 25

Confederate Line
Nov. 25

Missionary Ridge

Chickamauga Creek

Chickamauga
Station

To Ringgold

perhaps Bragg was so overwhelmed by the impossibility of wresting Chattanooga from the Federals that "this caused him to overlook the gathering storm."[3] Joshua noted that on November 18 the Federals had driven in the Confederate pickets on the far right, and he commented, "You need not be at all surprised to hear of some demonstration at any moment."

This group of letters reveals Joshua sick of soldiering. He longs to be home with his family; it delights him that Dulcinea joined the church at Summerfield, and he plans to do the same; his health remains good, but he complains of the paperwork that piled up while he was on detached duty; and he experiences a brief flare of ambition for immortality. Despite the hardships, Joshua looks for the best in his situation, as evidenced in his November 1 letter where he jumps from complaining about how miserable and lonesome he is to describing the beauty of the view from Missionary Ridge. He is reading Mary Elizabeth Braddon's sensational best-seller *Aurora Floyd,* and in the last letter in this group he refers to Dulcinea as "Lolly." This is probably a playful reference to the main character in the novel, Aurora, whose husband calls her Lolly. Aurora, or Lolly, is, like Dulcinea, or "Lolly," *adored* by her husband.

> Missionary Ridge
> Monday Oct 26th 1863

My Darling Wife:

Your highly interesting and *most* affectionate letter of last Sunday the 18th reached me late yesterday evening. I was actually delighted with it. It glows with love and the spirit of religion. It is a jewel. How can I bear longer separation from the idol of my heart! Life, under these circumstances, is becoming a burden; but with the love of God in my heart and you at my side life would be sweet under any circumstances.

To prove to you how heartily I endorse your action in regard to joining the church I will tell you that last night, after receiving your letter at dusk, I went to preaching, and after the sermon, an opportunity being offered, I joined myself. I shall write to Prof. Moore today and ask him to suffer me to cast my destiny with that of the church at Summerfield. And shall ask him to let my membership date from the day on which you joined, that we may be received into full connection together. And may the Lord hasten the happy time when the demon of war shall be driven from our bleeding land, and the angel of peace shall hover over us again with her silvery wings. And may you, my dearest love, and I go hand in hand through a long and peaceful life, stand together acquitted at the bar of God and then on the wings of angels fly away [to] heaven to cast our crowns at the feet of Jesus and spend eternity in singing his praises, followed by our dear little children. This is a delightful thought, an absorbing theme. Let us never lose sight of it. But let our lives, our precepts and example be such as to influence our children at the very dawn of reason to choose the way of the Lord. "Behold the eye of the Lord is upon them that fear him, upon them that hope in his Mercy."

Well, you see by the heading of this letter I am not at the wagon train. The cooking fraternity was all ordered in yesterday and the men are cooking their own rations now. And I am with the command at the foot of Missionary Ridge in full view of the yankee works. To stand on top of the Ridge and view the valley of Chattanooga, and reflect that its two hostile armies, whose tents so thickly dot the landscape as to present the appearance of one vast camp, while such a cloud of smoke overhangs as to lead a stranger to think there is a vast sea of fire concealed in the valley, to view the valley from the top of Ridge, I say, and reflect thus, and the scene is grand indeed. It is sublime.

I am glad to hear that you have engaged 50 bushels of corn, but you don't say who it's from nor what you have to pay. I am under many obligations to my friend Mr. Adams for his kind offers of assistance to you. Present him my highest regard and grateful thanks.

As to my clothing, my dear, I think I can do very well if you can furnish me a few pairs of woolen socks. I believe I told you that I had got a good pair of pants and lost my woolen shirt. I have now lost a pair of drawers, those you sent me.

I have a five dollar gold piece, D., for which I gave forty dollars in "Confed." If I had any chance I would send it to you. I have been offered six dollars in silver and fifty in "Confed" for it.

I am very well, thank God, and hope this will find you all so. Give my love to your mother and kiss T. and Joe for me. And all of you remember me in your prayers. May the Lord give us peace, upon *His own terms,* forgive our sins and restore us to each other soon is my constant prayer.

Your Devoted husband

J. K. Callaway

Mrs. Dulcinea B. Callaway

Same Date &c.

My Dear Eli,

Your very short letter is certainly excusable under the circumstances; I am very thankful to you even for a *line.* And I am sure you will excuse this when I tell you that this is all the paper I have. Nay more: you will even give me credit for being so punctual as to answer your letter promptly even though I have it to do on the back of D.'s. But I will write again soon.

I have no news except that there was some cannonading last night, they say; but I was asleep and did not hear it. If they had thrown their shells this way they might have awakened me. Some of them did wake and hear the shells passing, but I didn't.

I agree to your proposition to pray for peace, but I am disposed [to] let the Good Lord decide upon what terms we have it. We have been pray[ing] for peace upon our own terms for three years and the prospect becomes more gloomy. Now let us accept it on his terms and trust his goodness to do us well. We know he will give us justice, or our rights. Let us not ask more. "Blessed are they that trust in the Lord." Write again. Yours *truly*

E. W. B.   J. K. Callaway

P. S. My compliments to Charley Briggs. I hope he'll succeed in getting detached. J. K.

8 o'clock P. M.

My Dear, your favor of the[4] reached me this evening after I had written all the foregoing, and I must certainly let you know it.

I[t] brings the desired intelligence about needles papers &c. but have not said yet whether you [got] the book I sent you. "Cosette?"[5]

Of course I have no news more than I wrote today. However I can say the firing of artillery has been kept up all day from the point of Lookout Mountain; and tonight they are firing from the same place occasionally and the yankees are firing some from their forts.

They threw a few shells and solid shot over this way before dark, but none came near the 28th. But they could reach us here very easily. But I hope they will not do it.

I wrote you Monday about joining the church. You did perfectly. I prefer going in on probation myself.

Pray for me, my Darling. Pray that I may be saved from all my sin. And may our joy in the Lord be perpetual and may He hasten the happy time when we may be reunited to serve and rejoice in the Lord together, is [the] prayer of Your Devoted

J. K. Callaway

Well, My Dear Eli, I know you will pardon me for writing on the back of D.'s letter again. Paper is very scarce and very costly. Your esteemed favor of the 22 came in this evening and I must write a little.

You will learn all the news I have, from D.'s letter. I am down with the blues, Eli. I have not got more than half sense. I can't bear the thought of being [away] for 12 months yet.

I am tired to death of the war. I hope you will pray for me. I need more of the spirit that was in Jesus. O, Lord, sustain me! It really seems that longer separation from my Dear wife and children is unbearable.

I am at a loss to know what you mean by saying the Lord is preparing your soul for a different country, or "better land than this." I trust he [is] preparing us all for a better land, even a home in heaven. Blessed be his holy name forever. I rejoice in hope of his glory.

> "How long Dear Savior, Oh how long
> Shall this bright hour delay?
> Fly swift around, ye wheels of time,
> And bring the promised day!"

When we shall all sit down in his Kingdom. Let us pray without ceasing and trust in God. Write soon to your Bro.

E. W. Baker   J. K. Callaway

[Envelope: From: Lieut. J. K. Callaway, Co. "K" 28th Regt. Ala. Vols., to Mrs. J. K. Callaway, Summerfield, Dallas County, Alabama]

Missionary Ridge

Sunday morning Nov 1st 1863

My Dear Darling Wife:

I have not received any letter from you since I wrote you, and I write you this morning merely to kill *time,* which is the greatest burden I have. I am almost dead to see you and be with you. My patience is worn entirely out with the war. I am perfectly miserable; but God knows if I could see any prospect for peace, even a year hence, I could manage to bear it. But I see no prospect for it even ten years hence. The Lord help us!

I am well, thank God, and I hope this will find you all so. We have had any quantity of rain lately but this morning is clear and beautiful and clear. The sun is just above the top of Missionary Ridge, shedding golden light all over the valley, which is variegated with ten thousand autumn tints. And the yankee tents are so thick that their camp looks like a vast cotton field in the distance. The scene, the morning, is picturesque in the extreme. Just imagine a great valley, surrounded on all sides by a chain of mountains, of which you have a full view, decorated with myriads of the golden leaves of autumn, luxuriating in the morning sun, while the smoke, rising from the innumerable camp fires, gives a lazy haze and mellow tint to the light, and the only sound you hear is the hum of the army and the music from a dozen brass bands. Bless God for a lovely Sunday morning! But the more lovely the scene the more I love to compare it to the blessed quiet of home and *peace* and the company of my loved ones; and contemplate a little cottage home on some lonely island of the sea, with no human being near me but my beloved Dulcinea and little children. I long for such a home. I am as sick of the war as any man who ever deserted. But do not you think I have any notion of a similar course. No, never.

I got a letter from Sis and Nig the other day. They are all well. No news among them. I got a letter from Wes yesterday. He was well on the 26th. I suppose you have heard from him before this time.

I have not a word of news from any quarter, and I have not got sense enough this morning to make my letter interesting or long. I may, however, be in better order this evening. And as I have no way of sending this off till tomorrow, I will not seal it. Give my love to your mother and Eli. And kiss the children for me. Pray for me constantly. Your loving & devoted

J. K. Callaway

Mrs. D. B. Callaway

P. S. Tell Eli I will write to him some day if not today. I have been so busy, for 3 days, making out Must[er] and Pay rolls, Commutation accounts, recording furloughs for wounded men, registering a thousand other little things that had been left for me to do, making out Descriptive Lists, final Statements &c. &c. &c. (All of which I have to do,) that I have not had time to read but two or three chapters in my bible and as many in "Aurora Floyd,"[6] and only the Telegrams in a newspaper which I have had in my pocket for 3 days. But give him my unqualified love. I do have a severe time, I do all the writing for the whole concern, even the passes and a great many of the private letters to the wives of the men. At least half a dozen of them have asked me to write for them today. Good by.   J. K.

4½ o'clock P. M.

Well, my Dear, Sure enough I can write a little more this evening. Mr. George Cosby will start his boy home in the morning and I will send this by him.

I have just come from preaching. The Rev. Mr. Richards has just preached a fine sermon from the 18th verse of the 4 chapter of First Peter. "If the righteous scarcely be saved" &c. He contrasted the two great classes of mankind (the righteous and wicked) very strikingly. And showed how and why the former are scarcely saved and drew a very doleful picture of the places at which the ungodly and the sinner must appear. They will appear, first at the death scene, secondly at the judgement, and finally in hell. O, horror! He dwelled upon the great plan of the atonement. Showed how the plan was concealed in the secret counsels of God for four thousand years, and how even the angels looked down with pity on mankind, wondering how their salvation was to be effected, till all hope had well nigh expired and the darkness of despair was fast settling on the forlorn scene. Then drew a very vivid picture of the wonder, astonishment of the angels when at last the fact was revealed to them,—When they *saw* the second person of the "adorable Trinity" descend to earth and take our nature and assume our sins! Wonderful condescension! which when the angels discovered they made the golden arches and pillars of Heaven ring with a new song, even the song of redeeming grace and dying love. Now, my Dear, let us join the chorus and keep it up till old Earth shall resound with the soul thrilling song of redeeming grace and dying love, and our spirits shall at last be caught up on the strain and wafted to Heaven. Let us praise God always for this great salvation. I do now feel, thank the Lord, that I have an interest in it. May our lives correspond with our profession.

I believe I wrote you that I had lost my knife and fork, a shirt, my drawers and all my towels. If you get a chance send me some drawers, socks and a towel. I will probably get some woolen shirts from Mr. Abercrombie and pants from the Government and I need them.

I must tell you that we had a big chicken stew and slice potato pie for dinner. I am heavy on such dinners; and I feel a little heavy now from it.

Well, I believe I have made a good long letter after all my apology. Hope it will interest you.

Remember me kindly to all and Pray for me, and may God bless you all is my Devout prayer to the Lord of hosts

J. K. Callaway

[Envelope: From J. K. Callaway, Co. K 28 Ala, to Mrs. J. K. Callaway, Summerfield, Alabama]

Missionary Ridge
Sunday Nov. 4 1863

My Dear:

We have just come in off picket where we have been for 24 hours. Mr. John Suther starts home tomorrow and I send this by him. Enclosed I send you fifty (50) dollars. Be sure to let me know if you get it, and let me know how much you have on hand. I wrote to Eli two or three days ago in which I put a message for you, if he is gone when the letter gets there break it yourself, read it and then forward it to him.

Your letter of the 2nd reached me this morning. Eli's note, notice of his

6 day's furlough, was in it. I was in hopes he would get to stay at home till Christmas but alas! this cruel war.

I am glad you thought of Mrs. Hooks' money. I will pay it because *you* say I owe it. But I still think she didn't send it. I have not got the money now but expect to have in a day or two.

I have not a word of news unless it is that we have had fine weather for several days. True there is some moving about of the troops, but [I] know nothing of the object. Longstreet has gone in the direction of Knoxville, but I don't know what for.[7]

I am very well, thank God, and I do hope this will find you all so. T. does have a hard time. I have not seen Charlie Briggs and have not got the vests you sent.

Let us pray much for each other. Let me hear from you soon. My love to mother and the children, remember me kindly to Messrs Adams and [John] Beaty and any who may enquire after my welfare.

May the Lord have mercy upon us all and give us peace and the pardon of sins is the devout prayer of,

M[y] Darling Wife,
Your Devoted Husband
J. K. Callaway

Mrs. Dulcinea B. C.

P. S. I may fill the other side yet before I send it off. If I have any thing to write.

4½ P. M. Well, Dear, sure enough I will write a little. We have just now eat a very hearty dinner, Baked Beef, corn bread, stewed peaches, molasses and slice Potato Pie with butter in it. But bread and water would be far better if prepared by your own sweet hands and seasoned by your dear presence.

It is turning very cold with some appearance of snowy weather.

God Bless you my
Darling Wife
J. K. Callaway

On Picket
Thursday Nov 19/63

Dear "Lolly":

We are, as you see, on Picket today. But "My news column" will be short nevertheless.

I believe I forgot to say in last whom I was sending it by. Well I sent it by Lieut Mims, who started home on a twenty day's furlough Tuesday morning. I wrote the letter the day before and hence left out one very nice little circumstance which might be very interesting to you: The yankees have been camping on the other side of the River in a big flat for a long time, and it being a good place they have been collecting there for several weeks. Well, Monday night Bragg planted a battery of 17 guns on this side, and opened on their camp at daylight Tuesday morning, and scared the rascals nearly to death. Seventeen pieces made the place so hot that they got out double quick.

Yesterday morning I went down to the 20th Ala. and got some fellows to go up on the top of the Lookout Mountain. I can now say that I have been on a spot that [will] be one of the most renowned in all future history. I wish you could see it. The scene is *sublime beyond conception*. The height is so great that the country appears perfectly level. And the renowned Missionary Ridge looks precisely like a wave, about as high as your head, in an illimitable blue sea. I could not help thinking how travelers from all countries will come to stand on Lookout Mountain to see the valley of Chattanooga, and how that the poets and painters of future generations will stand there to have their geniuses inspired, and then immortalize the scene and the mountain in song and on canvas, and while I was musing thus I could not help feeling a spark of ambition, a desire to make my name as immortal in future history and as classic as that of Lookout Mountain. But, just at this point in my reverie, I saw a man step out of a house that stood at the foot of the mountain. I suppose he was a general, as they told me that some general had his Hd. Qrs there but he looked so small, a mere speck, that I could not tell he was there at all if he had not moved. And when I compared him to the mountain and then to the universe, and thought of his pride and ambition, I could not help smiling at his impetuosity and sighing at his insignificance. He reminded me of an ant trying to shake the earth, and my ambition cooled off and I would be perfectly content to be at home with my wife and never be thought of after I die.

Well, enough of that. Yesterday the yankees drove in our pickets away up on the right I learn and made some demonstrations, and last night, after we had gone to bed, we got orders to be ready to move at daylight this morning. But we did not move except to come out on picket; but there seems to be some moving about which I think is indicative of something. You need not be at all surprised to hear of some demonstration at any moment.

It is now 12 o'clock; and we will be relieved tomorrow. I will not write any more till then. But then I will finish my letter, and give you any additional news.

As ever your Devoted

J. K. Callaway

CHAPTER ELEVEN

Missionary Ridge

November 25, 1863

JOSHUA HAD MATURED since leaving home. His November 19 letter reveals a man who, despite a yearning for immortality, understands that for most people life offers more simple rewards. In his acceptance of those simpler rewards in the form of home and family, Joshua achieves a contentment that too often eludes those who seek it.

In the same letter, Joshua also foretold events of the next several days. On November 23 Federal general Ulysses S. Grant began his offensive against the Confederate-held heights around Chattanooga.

Grant's immediate objective was to capture Orchard Knob, a steep, timber-covered hill that lay between the opposing armies, picketed by the Twenty-eighth Alabama. The two sides made contact at about 5 P.M., and the vastly outnumbered advance Confederate soldiers were driven rapidly back into the main defenses of Orchard Knob. Here the Twenty-eighth "resisted obstinately, and with great gallantry." The commander of the regiment mistakenly believed he had orders to hold the position "at all hazards" and that the remainder of the brigade would join him. The Twenty-eighth clung to their defenses, fighting across the breastworks with bayonets, until the Confederates on both flanks had been driven off. Finding the odds against them irresistible, the regimental commander ordered a retreat. The Twenty-eighth Alabama lost about 175 soldiers, most of whom were captured along with the regimental colors. The Federals seemed satisfied with the possession of Orchard Knob, remaining there to turn and strengthen the position. The Confederates, although dismayed at their loss, did not deem the position important enough to mount the general engagement necessary to recover it.[1]

That night Joshua's weary and depleted regiment, relieved from picket duty, moved to the top of Missionary Ridge, where they began constructing timber breastworks on its brow, proceeding slowly because of the lack of tools. Brigade commander Manigault declared that "the protection obtained . . . was poor and insufficient, although every effort was made to make them as secure as possible." On the 24th, as positions were readied on Missionary Ridge, the left end of the Confederate line on Lookout Mountain collapsed. During the night Bragg repositioned the defeated Lookout Mountain troops on the far right of the Missionary Ridge line, where he expected the Federals to make their most determined effort. In this, Bragg read Grant correctly—that was the plan, although in the event, that is not what occurred.[2]

On the 25th, Grant ordered General William T. Sherman to attack the right end of the Missionary Ridge defenses, while General Joseph Hooker smashed the Confederate left. The two forces would roll up the Confederates along the ridge. Sherman, however, ran into insurmountable obstacles—the unexpected steep declivities in the land and General Patrick Cleburne. Ferocious fighting having failed to achieve Grant's expectations by midday, the Federal commander ordered General George Thomas's Army of the Cumberland to create a diversion at the center of the Confederate line. This diversion, Grant believed, would force Bragg to weaken his right, enabling Sherman to smash his way through.[3]

At 2 P.M. the Confederates on Missionary Ridge observed the Federals massing a large force in front of Hindman's division (commanded by General J. Patton Anderson), in which the Twenty-eighth Alabama resided. The troops belonging to this division held positions at both the foot and the crest of the ridge, an unsuitable arrangement that contributed to the coming disaster. When the enemy advanced at 4 P.M. the soldiers at the foot of the ridge fired and then, following orders, abandoned the breastworks and scampered up the steep slope to join their comrades. The Federals, seeing how easily (as they perceived it) they had driven off the first Confederate defense, became flushed with confidence and, without orders, forged on upward.[4]

The Confederates who had been positioned at the foot of Missionary Ridge arrived at the crest in no condition to fight. Those fortunate enough to reach the top were "broken down, exhausted & demoralized," Manigault testified. "For many minutes . . . both officers & men were so jaded & fatigued as to be utterly incapacitated for service. The moral effect," he lamented, "was to say the least, unfortunate." Colonel William F. Tucker, commanding the brigade posted to Manigault's left, corroborated Manigault's observation: "Many had to be carried off by the Infirmary Corps, while numbers of others . . . were so sick they could scarcely stand." Adding to the chaos, the soldiers had retreated as individuals and could not immediately find their proper place among the troops at the crest, causing "some confusion & mixture of commands." Tucker, too, reported the troops "somewhat demoralized."[5]

As these exhausted and frightened Confederates tried to catch their breath and composure, the Federals lunged up the slope. The configuration of the land in front of Hindman's division protected the enemy from Confederate fire; consequently, when they appeared suddenly within yards of the defenders' positions, little could be done to prevent the line being broken. General Zachariah C. Deas's brigade, on Manigault's right, appeared in need of reinforcement, so the division commander ordered the Thirty-fourth Alabama, anchoring Manigault's left, to their aid. As the regiment marched off to reinforce Deas, Tucker's troops to the left of Manigault's brigade gave way. The Federals quickly seized the artillery battery and turned it on Manigault's soldiers. The Twenty-eighth Alabama, now the extreme left of their brigade, changed front to face their attackers while the Tenth South Carolina on the right attempted to stave off Federals who had overpowered Deas's position. While these two regiments "stood their ground and were fighting manfully," Manigault noticed that "some disorder" existed in the center of his line and "men were leaving the ranks in alarm." They were not alone. "Soon a general disposition was evinced," General Anderson reported, "by all this portion of the line, to slough off by fragments from the line of breastworks towards the rear." This is rather an understatement of the panic and hopelessness that made these brave men turn tail and run.

Division commander Anderson finally received orders to retire from the field. Manigault rallied what was left of his brigade on a ridge about five hundred yards from the original line, and then positioned them to guard the

Shallow Ford Road while the wagons, artillery, stores, and wounded were evacuated. About 8 P.M. the weary brigade crossed the Chickamauga to join the rest of the army on its retreat to Dalton.[6]

Manigault's fellow brigade commanders held diverse views of their soldiers' performance at Missionary Ridge. Deas asserted "the Officers & men behaved well: and to other causes than want of courage & capacity on their part, must be attributed the disaster of that day." Tucker believed that if the enemy had been checked for just a couple of minutes, "they could have been swept from the hill or into eternity with scarcely an effort on [the soldiers'] part." Manigault was appalled by the conduct of his troops. There were disadvantages to be overcome, he acknowledged, "but even under these adverse circumstances they should have conducted themselves better. At the last moment even no necessity existed for the indecent haste, with which they abandoned the field to the enemy." These words are perhaps harsh when one considers what these soldiers had been through—Manigault's brigade alone had lost 558 men, killed, wounded, and missing between November 23 and 27.[7]

Joshua's performance during the battle earns him mention in his brigade commander's official report and praise for his bravery and gallantry from a fellow soldier.

Encampment 28th Ala. Regt. Inft.
Manigault's Brigade
Hindman's Division, Hardee's Corps
Army of Tennessee Near Dalton, Ga.
December 5th 1863

Mrs. J. K. Callaway,

It now falls to my unhappy lot to write you a short letter letting you know what has become of your much beloved and Devoted Husband Lieut. Joshua K. Callaway who fell in the late Battle on Missionary Ridge, mortally wounded while rallying his Company he was shot through the Bowels with a miney [sic] Ball. We picked him up, started off the field with him when he asked us to lay him down and let him Die. We laid him down. We were then compelled to leave him. I don't no [sic] that he is dead but feel satisfied that he is dead. In his Death the Country lost one of her Bravest sons, the Company to which he belonged a gallant and much beloved officer. Never can his place in the Co. be filled. I feel at a loss without him as we started out in a mess together and remained together till he was wounded. I have every Reason to belicvc that he is gone to a better land where there is no more war.[8] . . . left some clothing; also some bed clothing he left . . . 1 jacket 2 shirts 2 . . . also left a . . . there is nothing in the satchel though. It is locked and key gone. I want you to write to me as soon as you get this letter and let me know what disposition to make of his things his . . . clothes. I think I can send along also his . . . If it be your wish I will try and send all his things home his bedding will demand a good price here and if you are willing or rather I would I can sell them and send you the money. He has left one months [sic] pay account wich [sic] it will take to pay the debts he owes in the Regt wich [sic] I shall collect and pay his debts. The remainder I will forward on to you also will send you a final statement of the Ballance wages due him.

The company and officers deeply sympathize with you in his loss but what is your and our loss is his Eternal gain.

W. F. Aycock
Lieut. Co. K 28th Ala. Regt.

Epilogue

AND SO Joshua K. Callaway, aged twenty-nine, became one of the war's six hundred thousand statistics, his last moments or hours—unknown; his final resting place—unknown.

The war, and life, went on without Joshua. In 1868 Dulcinea and the children, along with her mother and brothers Eli and Dan, joined brother Wes in Hays County, Texas. Twelve years after Joshua's death, on January 19, 1875, Dulcinea married John A. Graves, a union that did not produce any offspring. In April 1883 Dulcinea died; she is buried in City Cemetery, San Marcos, Hays County, Texas. She was not quite fifty years of age.[1]

Joshua and Dulcinea's children, Amelia Temperance (called T throughout her life) and Joseph, grew to adulthood in Texas. Joseph married Ophelia Pierce in 1885, with whom he had seven children, and in 1887, four years after his mother's death, moved to the state of Washington. Here he served as a local preacher for the Methodist Church until poor health forced him to retire to a small farm in Eatonville, where he died on June 8, 1914. He is buried in the Eatonville, Washington, cemetery. "No words can be too strong," asserted his obituary writer, "to indicate his loyalty to the Church; his faithfulness to his charge and his sterling Christian character."[2]

T remained in Texas, and on December 21, 1881, she married John Smith Kellam in Oyster Creek, Hays County. A friend reporting the event declared, "Miss T. is an amiable intelligent lady. . . . Smith is an energetic, honorable young man, and gives evidence of making a successful voyage on life's tempestuous sea." In 1939 another newspaper article reported the celebration of their fifty-eighth wedding anniversary. Three years later, on September 16, 1942, T died, survived by her husband, children, and grandchildren. She is buried in Robstown Cemetery, Texas.[3]

T and John Smith Kellam produced five children—three sons, Otis Terrell, Joseph Ulmer, and Warren Smith, and two daughters, Eva Lucile (Lyon) and Opal Amelia (Douglass). The letters that Joshua wrote to Dulcinea during the Civil War were eventually distributed among T's grandchildren, the

168

offspring of Otis (Doris Jane Kellam), Eva (Betty Jo and Horace King Lyon), and Opal (Thomas C. Douglass Jr.).[4] The entire collection was cared for remarkably well, and eventually, through the efforts of Otis's daughter Doris Jane and her husband, Ralph Langley, the family decided the letters should be brought together again into one collection. After careful thought and research, they chose the Eugene C. Barker Texas History Center at the University of Texas, Austin, to be the caretakers of the letters.

In the 1980s, while searching for information on General Braxton Bragg and the Army of Tennessee, I found Joshua's letters and became fascinated with them. After returning several times to read them, and finding each time that they were even better than I remembered, I sought permission to publish the collection, which the family graciously granted.

And so it has come to pass that Joshua's "spark of ambition," a desire to make his name "immortal in future history," has been satisfied through his own lovingly preserved thoughts and words.[5]

APPENDIX: PERSONALITIES

Military units are of the Twenty-eighth Alabama Regiment, ages are as of 1862, and place of residence is Selma, Alabama, unless otherwise noted.

ANDERSON, JAMES PATTON, a native of Tennessee, had practiced medicine before serving in the Mexican War, after which he turned to politics. When the war came, he served first at Pensacola and then saw field service at Shiloh, Perryville, Murfreesboro, Chickamauga, and Chattanooga and in the Atlanta campaign, during which he was severely wounded, rejoining the army in time to surrender with it at Greensboro, North Carolina. Ezra J. Warner, *Generals in Gray: Lives of the Confederate Commanders* (Baton Rouge, 1959), 7–8.

AYCOCK, WILLIAM FRANCIS, enlisted at Perryville at the age of twenty-one. Although wounded in July 1864, he continued to serve in the Confederate army until the end of the war. *Compiled Service Records of Confederate Soldiers Who Served in Organizations from Alabama,* 508 reels (Washington, D.C.: National Archives), accessed at the Tutwiler Collection of Southern History and Literature, Birmingham Public Library, Alabama; *Confederate Service Records, 1861–1865,* Alabama Department of Archives and History, Montgomery.

BAKER, AMELIA (MILLIE) REGAN, was Dulcinea's mother. Joshua and Dulcinea, with their two children, were living with Amelia Baker when Joshua enlisted, and Dulcinea and the children continued to live there when he left for the war. Born in North Carolina, Amelia lived in Enterprise, Alabama, in 1850 and reported her age as forty-four. In 1860 she had aged only eight years, claiming to be fifty-two, and lived in Summerfield, Alabama. She was listed as a farmer, worth $400 in real estate and $3,184 in personal property, who owned three slaves (aged twenty-four, three, and two). Having married John Baker in 1828 in Robeson County, North Carolina, Amelia gave birth to nine children, eight in North Carolina and one in Alabama. She and John moved to Coffee County, Alabama, sometime before 1846. John died before 1850. Four of their sons fought in the Civil War. *1850 Federal Census; 1860 Federal Census;*

Mrs. H. K. Lyon, comp., "Joshua K. Callaway: His Ancestry and Descendants," type-script, Joshua K. Callaway Papers, Eugene C. Barker Texas History Center, University of Texas, Austin.

BAKER, DANIEL ASBURY, Dulcinea's brother, was born in North Carolina. In 1862 he was fourteen years old. It appears that he enlisted in Company C, Twenty-first Alabama Infantry, on September 22, 1862, in Talledega, for three years or the duration of the war. In May 1865 he was listed on the Roll of Prisoners of War that surrendered at Citronelle, Alabama, and was paroled at Meridian, Mississippi, on May 13, 1865. Other documents, however, report Baker as captured at Fort Gaines on August 8, 1864, and another asserts that he was exchanged on January 4, 1865. *1860 Federal Census; Compiled Service Records.*

BAKER, ELI W., was Dulcinea's brother. Born in North Carolina, he was twenty-two years old. The 1860 census listed him as attending school. Eli enlisted at Selma, Alabama, in April 1861 in Company C, Fourth Alabama Infantry. On June 27, 1862, he was wounded near Richmond, Virginia, resulting in a furlough through December. In May 1863 he received a wound at Chancellorsville but recovered only to be wounded again at Gettysburg on July 2, 1863, and "left in the hands of the enemy." After spending a few weeks at Fort Delaware, he was exchanged on July 31. He was on furlough through April 1864 and then placed on detached service in the commissary department in Selma in July 1864. He was paroled at the war's end. *1860 Federal Census; Compiled Service Records.*

BAKER, IRENE, Dulcinea's sister, was born in North Carolina. A teacher in 1862, she was twenty-four years old and married to Joshua's cousin, John Hanford Callaway. Lyon, "Joshua K. Callaway."

BAKER, JAMES D., was Dulcinea's brother, but he was not listed in the 1860 census with the Baker family. He may have joined the Fourth Alabama with Eli Baker and was described as being five feet five inches tall and having blue eyes and sandy hair and complexion. He took the Oath of Allegiance on May 5, 1865. In 1880 he was reported in Walker County, Texas, with a five-year-old son born in Alabama. *1880 Federal Census; Compiled Service Records;* Lyon, "Joshua K. Callaway."

BAKER, WESTON F., Dulcinea's brother, was born in North Carolina. The 1860 census listed him at seventeen years old as a student. His service record merely states that he enlisted as a private at Selma, Alabama, on February 6, 1863. By 1866 he moved to Hays County, Texas, followed by others of the family. *1860 Federal Census; Compiled Service Records;* Lyon, "Joshua K. Callaway."

BALEY [BAILEY], ANDREW D., enlisted at Selma, Alabama, in March 1862. *Compiled Service Records.*

BANKS, NATHANIEL P., was a Massachusetts political general with no military training. General Thomas J. Jackson easily defeated him during the 1862 Shenandoah Valley campaign. Banks later commanded at Port Hudson, but Callaway's report (July 5, 1863) of the capture of his army there in July 1863 was a false rumor about the fate of Port Hudson—perhaps wishful thinking on the part of the Southerners. Ezra J. Warner, *Generals in Blue: Lives of the Union Commanders* (Baton Rouge, 1964), 17–18; Patricia L. Faust, ed., *Historical Times Illustrated Encyclopedia of the Civil War* (New York, 1986), 38.

BARRON, ELIAS, enlisted at Perryville, Alabama, on March 29, 1862, at the age of eighteen. *Compiled Service Records.*

BEATY, JOHN, born in North Carolina, was a forty-four-year-old gin maker and owner of eight slaves. *1860 Federal Census.*

BEATY, THOMAS C., enlisted in Company I, Forty-seventh Alabama Infantry, on April 18, 1862, at the age of twenty-eight. According to his service record, he was paid thirty-four dollars on July 20, 1863, making it unlikely that he had been killed at Gettysburg, as Callaway had heard. However, his company's September–October muster roll, under the entry Present or Absent, merely reported, "not stated." *Compiled Service Records.*

BEAUREGARD, GUSTAVE TOUTANT, a Louisiana West Point graduate (1838), became a Confederate hero in April 1861 through his seizure of Fort Sumter. After the Battle of First Manassas in 1861 he angered President Davis, who quickly transferred the general to the West, a convenient place for inconvenient officers. As second in command to General Albert Sidney Johnston, Beauregard moved up to army command upon Johnston's death at the Battle of Shiloh in April 1862, but he did not enjoy the position for long. In late June 1862 he treated himself to an unauthorized sick leave, and Davis quickly took advantage of this to remove Beauregard from the command. It passed to General Braxton Bragg, Callaway's first corps commander. Although many authors refer to Beauregard as Pierre Gustave Toutant (P. G. T.), I use just G. T., as Beauregard himself did after dropping the Pierre as a young adult. Warner, *Generals in Gray*, 22–23; T. Harry Williams, *P. G. T. Beauregard: Napoleon in Gray* (Baton Rouge, 1955); Faust, *Historical Times Illustrated Encyclopedia*, 51–52.

BELL, THOMAS J., enlisted from Summerfield, Alabama, into Company I at the age of nineteen. *Compiled Service Records*.

BENNETT, RUBE, enlisted at Perryville, Alabama, at age nineteen. Apparently his bout with the measles debilitated him to the point of uselessness to the army—his discharge came through on July 1, 1862. *Compiled Service Records*.

BOGGS, ANDREW, enlisted at Selma, Alabama, at the age of eighteen. *Compiled Service Records*.

BOGGS, MISS, was Andrew Boggs's sister.

BOLLING, TULLY, enlisted at Perryville, Alabama, at the age of twenty-five. *Compiled Service Records*.

BRAGG, BRAXTON, a North Carolina West Point graduate (1837), resigned from the U.S. Army in 1856 to be a planter in Louisiana, after his marriage to Eliza (Elise) Brooks Ellis, a wealthy heiress. At the outbreak of war he became the Confederacy's first commander of the Gulf Coast from Pensacola to Mobile. In September 1862 he joined General Albert Sidney Johnston's army. After Johnston's death at Shiloh, General Beauregard assumed command of the army, and when Beauregard took an unauthorized leave of absence in June 1862, Bragg became commander of the Army of Tennessee. As its commander Bragg led the army during the Kentucky campaign, the Battle at Murfreesboro, the Tullahoma campaign, the campaign and Battle of Chickamauga, and at Lookout Mountain and Missionary Ridge. The debacle at Missionary Ridge prompted Bragg to resign the command, and shortly afterward President Davis summoned him to Richmond to act as military adviser. In late 1864 Bragg once again resumed field command at Wilmington, North Carolina, only to lose that important port in early 1865. Commanding the Army of Tennessee longer than any other general and leading it to its greatest achievements, Bragg proved to be an excellent disciplinarian and organizer but a poor field commander. Joshua Callaway served under Bragg throughout his military career, first in Bragg's corps and then in his army. Warner, *Generals in Gray*, 30–31; Grady McWhiney, *Braxton Bragg and Confederate Defeat*, vol. 1 (New York, 1969); Judith Lee Hallock, *Braxton Bragg and Confederate Defeat*, vol. 2 (Tuscaloosa, Ala., 1991).

BRECKINRIDGE, JOHN CABELL, a Kentucky lawyer born in 1821, served as vice president of the United States from 1856 to 1860 and ran for president in the 1860 election. When Kentucky declared its neutrality, Breckinridge became a leader of the Southern sympathizers in the state, and in November 1861 he received a commission as a Confederate brigadier general. Breckinridge served in a variety of positions and places, including secretary of war during the last few months of the war. Warner, *Generals in Gray*, 34–35; William C. Davis, *Breckinridge: Statesman, Soldier, Symbol* (Baton Rouge, 1974); Lucille Stillwell, *John Cabell Breckinridge* (Caldwell, Idaho, 1936); Frank H. Heck, *Proud Kentuckian, John C. Breckinridge, 1821–1875* (Lexington, Ky. 1976).

BRETT, JOHN, was married to Joshua Callaway's cousin Serena Callaway. Lyon, "Joshua K. Callaway."

BRIGGS, CHARLEY [CHARLES H.], enlisted as a private in Company C, Fourth Alabama Infantry, at Selma, Alabama, on April 26, 1861. He was an eighteen-year-old clerk who had been born in Virginia but now lived in Summerfield, Alabama. He suffered several episodes of various illnesses during his military career, including diarrhea, debilitas, and pericarditis. For a time in 1864 he served on detached duty as the medical purveyor of Longstreet's corps. *Compiled Service Records.*

BUELL, DON CARLOS, was born in Ohio in 1818 and graduated from West Point in 1841. Severely wounded during the Mexican War, Buell served as a staff officer at the headquarters of several military departments until the outbreak of the Civil War. He served primarily in the western theater, saving the day for General Grant at the Battle of Shiloh. Buell resisted Bragg's invasion of Kentucky in the autumn of 1862, but in the aftermath of the Battle at Perryville, Kentucky, Buell was relieved from command for being dilatory in following Bragg's army after the battle. On June 1, 1863, he resigned his commission and returned to civilian life. Warner, *Generals in Blue*, 51–52; Faust, *Historical Times Illustrated Encyclopedia*, 88.

BURNSIDE, AMBROSE EVERETT, an Indiana West Point graduate (1847), served in the regular army until 1853. When the Civil War began, he reentered the army, seeing varied service—brigade command at the Battle of First Manassas in 1861;

command of the successful expedition against the North Carolina coast; corps command at Sharpsburg; command of the Army of the Potomac during the Fredericksburg debacle and the infamous and abortive "Mud March"; command of the Department of the Ohio; the defense of East Tennessee and Knoxville against General Longstreet's laughable campaign; and corps command in General Grant's 1864 offensive against Richmond. After the embarrassment of the Crater incident at Petersburg, Virginia, Burnside resigned from the service. Warner, *Generals in Blue*, 57–58; William Marvel, *Burnside* (Chapel Hill, 1991).

BUTLER, WILLIAM LAVEL, enlisted at Marion, Alabama. Frequently cited for good conduct by his commanding officer, General Arthur M. Manigault, Butler was wounded and captured at Franklin, Tennessee, on December 17, 1864. Many years later an observer wrote of Butler's ordeal. "[He had been] shot clear through from side to side with a Minie ball. . . . The officer in charge of removing the wounded had him examined by the surgeon, whose opinion was that he had sufficiently recovered to be sent to prison. Butler knew his own condition and that to be removed that day while the snowstorm was raging would be certain death, so he said to the officer: 'This is murder to remove me now.' The officer replied: 'You are a prisoner and must go.' " The observer reported that Butler's retort "lacked a good deal of being Sunday school literature." Butler recovered enough to be the "Chief" of "Division 29" at Fort Delaware, where he was imprisoned, until his release on May 30, 1865. Arthur Middleton Manigault, *A Carolinian Goes to War: The Civil War Narrative of Arthur Middleton Manigault, Brigadier General, C. S. A.*, ed. R. Lockwood Tower (Columbia, S.C., 1983), 107; War Department, *War of the Rebellion: A Compilation of the Official Records of the Union and Confederate Armies* (Washington, D.C., 1880–1901), ser. 1, vol. 30 (pt. 2), 344 (hereafter cited as *OR;* unless otherwise noted, all citations are to ser. 1); *Compiled Service Records;* H. P. Figuers, "A Boy's Impressions of the Battle of Franklin," *Confederate Veteran* 23 (1915): 4–7, 44; *Southern Historical Society Papers* 19 (1891): 46.

CALLAWAY, AMELIA TEMPERANCE (ALSO TILL, TILLIE, T.), Joshua and Dulcinea's daughter, was born on April 3, 1858, in Summerfield, Alabama. In 1881 she married John Smith Kellam, a native of Van Buren, Arkansas, in Brazoria County, Texas. A contemporary news writer asserted, "Both parties are in their twenties and are well old enough to know what they are about. . . . Miss T. is an amiable intelligent lady, and we think will prove true to her vows. Smith is an energetic, honorable young man, and gives evidence of making a successful voyage on life's tempestuous sea." The couple shared more than sixty years of marriage and produced five children. Amelia died in 1942 in Nueces County, Texas, at the age of eighty-four. Her descendants became the custodians of the collection of letters written by her father, which they donated to the Eugene C. Barker Texas History Center, Austin, Texas. Lyon, "Joshua K. Callaway"; two unidentified news articles, courtesy of Ralph and Doris Langley, San Antonio, Texas.

CALLAWAY, CAMILLA (SIS), Joshua's sister, was born around 1838 and married E. D. (Ell) Godwin. Lyon, "Joshua K. Callaway."

CALLAWAY, (SARAH A.) DAMARIS, Joshua's sister, was born in Florida in 1832. She married Hope P. Powell and in 1860 lived in Newton, Dale County, Alabama, with her husband and four children. Lyon, "Joshua K. Callaway"; *1850 Federal Census.*

CALLAWAY, DULCINEA BAKER, Joshua's wife, was born in May 1833 in North Carolina. Dulcinea gave birth to three children: Amelia Temperance and Joseph J., both of whom reached adulthood, and a girl born in June 1860, who died sometime before 1862. In 1868 Dulcinea migrated to Texas with her mother, her children, and some of her brothers. On January 19, 1875, she married John A. Graves, in Hays County. They had no children. Dulcinea died in April 1883 at the age of forty-nine. She is buried in City Cemetery, San Marcos, Texas. Lyon, "Joshua K. Callaway"; *1860 Federal Census.*

CALLAWAY, ELISHA, Joshua's uncle, was born in Delaware. During the Civil War he lived in Macon, Mississippi. Lyon, "Joshua K. Callaway."

CALLAWAY, ELISHA W., Joshua's brother, was born in Alabama in 1828. Elisha was a surveyor and a teacher, who married Mary Pace Callaway, the widow of his cousin. It is believed that Elisha deserted Mary sometime before April 1863. Lyon, "Joshua K. Callaway"; *1850 Federal Census.*

CALLAWAY, J. (JONATHAN) HOSEA, a fifty-year-old cousin of Joshua's, was a farmer born in Georgia. He moved to Arkansas in 1860. Lyon, "Joshua K. Callaway."

CALLAWAY, JOHN HANFORD, a son of J. Hosea's, was married to Dulcinea's sister Irene. Both of them were teachers, and they moved to Arkansas probably shortly after

J. Hosea. John was born in Alabama in 1838. Lyon, "Joshua K. Callaway"; *1850 Federal Census.*

CALLAWAY, JOSEPH J., Joshua and Dulcinea's son, was born on January 18, 1862, in Alabama. In 1885 he married Ophelia Pierce in Hays County, Texas. They had seven children, five daughters and two sons. In 1887 they left Texas for the state of Washington, where Joseph worked as a local preacher for the Methodist church. When his health no longer permitted him to carry out his pastoral duties, Joseph retired on a small farm in Eatonville, Washington. It was here that he died on June 8, 1914. His obituary asserted: "No words can be too strong to indicate his loyalty to the Church; his faithfulness to his charge and his sterling Christian character." He is buried in the Eatonville cemetery. Lyon, "Joshua K. Callaway"; unidentified news article, courtesy of Ralph and Doris Langley, San Antonio, Texas.

CALLAWAY, JOSHUA K., was born on September 2, 1834, in North Carolina. In the 1850 census he worked as a mail carrier, and by 1860 he was a teacher. His father, Joseph Callaway, was a Methodist minister, born in 1800 in Hancock County, Georgia, and died in 1857 in Haw Ridge, Dale County, Alabama. Joseph married a woman named Temperance, born about 1805 in Georgia. Joseph and Temperance died within a few days of each other, cause and exact dates unknown, shortly after they had moved to Haw Ridge. Joshua married Dulcinea Baker probably sometime in 1857 in either Dale or Dallas County, Alabama. Joshua joined the army at Shelby Springs, Alabama, on March 29, 1862, at the age of twenty-eight. Beginning as first sergeant on October 28, 1862, he received a promotion to second junior lieutenant. His service record listed him "Absent sick" in November 1862; a report on efficiency of officers from August–September 1863 stated Callaway was "efficient, standing good. Absent from command 16 days with leave." Lyon, "Joshua K. Callaway"; *1850 Federal Census; 1860 Federal Census; Compiled Service Records.*

CALLAWAY, MARY J. S., was the daughter of Elisha Callaway and cousin to Joshua. Born in 1839, Mary began teaching at the age of fourteen in Noxubee County, Mississippi. After the death of her father she established a boarding school for girls, the Elisha Callaway Institute, which eventually became the Mississippi State University for Women. Lyon, "Joshua K. Callaway."

CALLAWAY, SAMANTHA M., Joshua's sister, was born in February 1841. She married Joseph J. Chancey, who was killed in the Civil War, and then married Andrew

Jackson Melton. She had children from both marriages, one of whom drowned in the Arkansas River. Samantha died in April 1907 in Oklahoma. Lyon, "Joshua K. Callaway."

CALLAWAY, TEMPERANCE, see Callaway, Amelia Temperance.

CALLAWAY, THOMAS, a cousin of Joshua, served in the Ninth Texas Regiment. Lyon, "Joshua K. Callaway."

CALLEN, OLD MR. JOHN, was a fifty-seven-year-old farmer born in North Carolina. Callen owned forty-seven slaves. He was probably a neighbor of the Bakers and Callaways. *1860 Federal Census.*

CAMILLA, see Callaway, Camilla.

CHANCEY, JOSEPH, was married to Joshua's sister Samantha. Lyon, "Joshua K. Callaway."

CHEATHAM, BENJAMIN FRANKLIN, was a farmer in his forties who had served in the Mexican War, joined the Confederate army in July 1861, and was promoted to major general in March 1862. As brigade, division, and corps commander, Cheatham served in every engagement of the Army of Tennessee from Shiloh to Atlanta. Warner, *Generals in Gray,* 47–48; Christopher Losson, *Tennessee's Forgotten Warriors: Frank Cheatham and His Confederate Division* (Knoxville, Tenn., 1989).

CLEBURNE, PATRICK RONAYNE, born near Cork, Ireland, was one of only two foreign-born officers to receive appointment as major general in the Confederate army. Immigrating to the United States in 1849, he eventually became a lawyer in Arkansas. At the outbreak of war he offered his services, serving as colonel of the Fifteenth Arkansas before receiving a promotion to brigadier general in March 1862 and then to major general in December of the same year. Known as a superb field officer, Cleburne ruined his chances for further promotion when he proposed the arming of slaves to fight for their further enslavement. Cleburne was killed at the bloodbath at Franklin, Tennessee, on November 30, 1864. Warner, *Generals in Gray,* 53–54; Howell Perdue and Elizabeth Perdue, *Pat Cleburne: Confederate General* (Hillsboro, Tex., 1973).

COCHRAN, WILLIAM T., was one of Joshua's messmates. Cochran enlisted at Perry-ville, Alabama, at the age of thirty-three. In August 1862 he was appointed commissary sergeant and dropped from the military roll in February 1864. Joshua described him as a great humorist, wit, and ventriloquist, a printer by trade, and full of yarns and anecdotes. "Muster Roll," Alabama Department of Archives and History, Montgomery, Alabama; *Compiled Service Records*.

COONS, LIEUTENANT, enlisted at Elyton, Alabama, at the age of thirty-two. He had a florid complexion, sandy hair, blue eyes, and was five feet five inches tall. He was captured on November 23 or 24, 1863, at Lookout Mountain and released from the Johnson's Island, Ohio, prison camp on June 13, 1865. *Compiled Service Records*.

COSBY, GEORGE, enlisted at Selma, Alabama, in August 1863. He was a private in Company K. *Compiled Service Records*.

COSTELLO, JUDGE P. D. (PIERRE), was captain of Company K, Twenty-fifth Alabama Infantry. Wounded severely at the Battle of Shiloh in April 1862, he recovered enough to fight and die at the Battle of Murfreesboro. The brigade report lists him as "Wounded Mortally December 31, 1862 during First Charge—Died of wound 4th January at Murfreesboro." At the time of his death he was a prisoner within Federal lines. *Compiled Service Records*.

DACUS, GEORGE B. S., enlisted as a private at Perryville, Alabama, at age thirty-three. *Compiled Service Records*.

DALLAS, BRYAN, enlisted as a sergeant at Selma, aged twenty. The 1860 census listed him as a student. *Compiled Service Record; 1860 Federal Census*.

DALLAS WARRIORS was a company of Alabamians raised in Dallas County, where Summerfield is located.

DAMARIS, see Callaway, (Sarah A.) Damaris.

DAN, see Baker, Daniel Asbury.

DAVIES, W. W., an officer of the Eighth Alabama Regiment, he and two others resigned from the Eighth in order to raise the Twenty-eighth Alabama, the regiment Callaway joined. *Daily State Sentinel*, Selma, Alabama, February 16, 1862.

DAVIS, JEFFERSON, was president of the Confederate States of America, 1861–65.

DEAS, ZACHARIAH CANTEY, was a native of South Carolina who moved to Alabama as a child. After serving in the Mexican War, Deas became a wealthy cotton broker prior to 1861. He raised the Twenty-second Alabama Regiment at his own expense and led his brigade of five Alabama regiments at Chattanooga. After the war Deas, like so many other southerners, moved to New York City, where he recouped his losses and became a prominent member of the stock exchange. Warner, *Generals in Gray*, 70–71; Richard N. Current, ed., *Encyclopedia of the Confederacy* (New York, 1993), 459.

DUNCAN, JOHNSON KELLY, was a Pennsylvania West Point graduate (1849) who cast his lot with the Confederacy. Duncan was in command of the coast defenses at New Orleans when the city fell to a Federal fleet and he was captured. Upon his release he served as chief of staff to General Bragg until his death from typhoid fever at Knoxville, Tennessee, in December 1862. Warner, *Generals in Gray*, 77–78; Current, *Encyclopedia*, 498.

E. D., see Godwin, E. D.

E. W., see Callaway, E. W.

EDWARDS, NATHAN, enlisted as a private in Company K at Perryville, Alabama, at the age of thirty-eight. *Compiled Service Records.*

EDWARDS, S. A., enlisted as second lieutenant of Company K at Perryville, Alabama, at age twenty-six. He resigned in June 1862. *Compiled Service Records.*

EL, see Godwin, E. D.

ELI, see Baker, Eli W.

ELL, see Godwin, E. D.

FARROR, HENRY, enlisted at Perryville, Alabama, as a private in Company K, at the age of thirty-four. He died in the General Hospital, Cholona, Mississippi, on August 30, 1862. His assets at the time amounted to $2.30. *Compiled Service Records.*

FORD, HOMER M., Joshua's messmate, enlisted at Perryville, Alabama, at the age of thirty-three. In October 1862 Ford became the regimental acting commissary. At the Battle of Chickamauga, General Manigault cited him for gallant conduct. At the close of the war he was a captain, surrendering under General Richard Taylor and paroled on June 9, 1865. *Compiled Service Records; OR*, vol. 30 (pt. 2), 344.

FORREST, NATHAN BEDFORD, a wealthy Tennessee planter, slave trader, and businessperson, raised his own battalion of cavalry in 1861. He fought throughout the western theater and has been assessed by some military critics as the foremost cavalry officer produced in America. However, Forrest often had problems with his superior officers and failed to serve them competently. Warner, *Generals in Gray*, 92–93; Robert Selph Henry, *"First with Most" Forrest* (New York, 1944); John Allan Wyeth, *That Devil Forrest: Life of General Nathan Bedford Forrest* (New York, 1959); Brian Steel Wills, *A Battle from the Start: The Life of Nathan Bedford Forrest* (New York, 1992); Hallock, *Braxton Bragg*, 100–102.

FOWLKS, A. M., enlisted at Marion, Alabama. Fowlks was born in Lewisburg, North Carolina, in November 1838, and the family moved to Marion in 1850. Beginning as a lieutenant in Company A, in 1863 Fowlks was promoted to major and assigned to General J. E. Johnston's staff, retained under General Hood, and returned to Johnston's staff again. After the war he became an entrepreneur of hardware and agricultural implements. *Compiled Service Records;* T. A. DeLand and A. Davis Smith, *Northern Alabama: Historical and Biographical* (Chicago, 1888; reprint, Spartanburg, S.C., 1976), 689.

FRAZER, JOHN WESLEY, was a West Point graduate from Tennessee. He resigned from the Eighth Alabama Infantry in order to raise and command the Twenty-eighth Alabama, Callaway's regiment. In May 1863 Frazer received appointment as brigadier general and was ordered to East Tennessee, where he was forced to surrender to General Ambrose B. Burnside. He remained a prisoner of the United States until the end of the war. Warner, *Generals in Gray*, 93; Current, *Encyclopedia*, 637.

GAY, THOMAS B., enlisted at Perryville, Alabama, at age forty-two. A farmer, he had a light complexion, blue eyes, auburn hair, and stood six feet one inch. On October 3, 1862, he was discharged as unfit for duty. The surgeon's report stated that Gay suffered a "general debility resulting from chronic diarrhoea followed by anasarca" and was currently suffering from pneumonia. *Compiled Service Records.*

GEORGE, ELI P., enlisted at Perryville, Alabama, at age twenty-seven, as first lieutenant of Company K. He was paroled on June 2, 1865, after surrendering with General Richard Taylor. *Compiled Service Records.*

GODWIN, E. D. (ELL, EL), was Joshua's brother-in-law, married to Camilla. He was born about 1838. Lyon, "Joshua K. Callaway."

GODWIN, LAM, enlisted as a private in the Thirty-third Alabama Infantry on March 13, 1862, at Greenville, Alabama, at the age of twenty. In May 1863 he was detailed as a teamster. *Compiled Service Records.*

GOYERS [GOYNES], JOSEPH, enlisted as a private in the Thirty-third Alabama Infantry on March 13, 1862, at Greenville, Alabama, at the age of twenty-five. He received a severe head wound at the Battle of Murfreesboro, on December 31, 1862. *Compiled Service Records.*

GRAHAM, W. W., was a chaplain. He resigned in October 1864. *Compiled Service Records.*

GRANT, ULYSSES SIMPSON, was an 1843 West Point graduate from Ohio. After service in Mexico, Grant's military career was checkered, as was his civilian life after leaving the U.S. Army in 1854. During the Civil War he came into his own, rising to the rank of lieutenant general and to the command of all the Union armies. His superb military judgment and skill gave the Northern armies the direction they needed to win a victory. Warner, *Generals in Blue,* 183–86; Faust, *Historical Times Illustrated Encyclopedia,* 320.

GREGORY, JAMES, was a thirty-two-year-old merchant, born in Connecticut, in partnership with A. W. Hawley. *1860 Federal Census.*

HALLECK, HENRY WAGER, was a New York West Point graduate (1839). He made the army his career until 1854, when he resigned to head a leading law firm in California. He reentered the army upon the outbreak of war. Serving in the West, Halleck commanded successful subordinates, especially Ulysses S. Grant, which brought him to the attention of President Lincoln. In July 1862 Halleck moved to Washington, D.C., after being appointed commander in chief, a post he held until March 1864, when Grant became commander in chief and Halleck was reassigned as chief of staff. The general is a distant cousin of the author. Warner, *Generals in Blue*, 195–97; Stephen E. Ambrose, *Halleck: Lincoln's Chief of Staff* (Baton Rouge, 1962).

HARDEE, WILLIAM JOSEPH, was a Georgia West Point graduate (1838). Hardee was a career soldier, serving in various positions in the U.S. Army, writing an army manual, (*Rifle and Light Infantry Tactics*), and serving as commandant at West Point. In 1860, while still an officer in the U.S. Army, Hardee became Georgia's purchasing agent of arms and munitions. In January 1861 he finally resigned from the U.S. Army and joined the Confederacy. Serving in the western theater, Hardee proved himself an outstanding corps commander. After the death of his wife, Hardee passed the responsibility for his four children on to his sister-in-law; when he remarried some years later, he chose a woman twenty-three years his junior, about the age of his daughters. Warner, *Generals in Gray*, 124–25; Nathaniel Cheairs Hughes Jr., *General William J. Hardee, Old Reliable* (Baton Rouge, 1965); Hallock, *Braxton Bragg*, 10–11.

HARGROVE, E., enlisted at Perryville, Alabama, at age forty-six. He was a private in Company K, discharged on July 1, 1862. *Compiled Service Records.*

HARPER, MICAJAH, was captain of Company A, Twenty-fifth Alabama Infantry. At the Battle of Shiloh he was killed during the second charge of his unit by a shot in the head. *Compiled Service Records.*

HARRIS, CHARLES R., enlisted at Perryville, Alabama, at age twenty-seven. He became captain of Company K but resigned on November 25, 1862, while home on sick leave. *Compiled Service Records.*

HAWLEY, A. W., was a thirty-four-year-old merchant from Connecticut, in partnership with James Gregory. *1860 Federal Census.*

HENDERSON, HOWARD A. M., enlisted in Walker County, Alabama, and became captain of Company E. He resigned on September 18, 1862, due to "chronic Bronchitis." His son wrote that Henderson was a commissioner for the exchange of prisoners at Cahaba, Alabama, during the last year of the war. *Compiled Service Records; Confederate Veteran* 30 (1922): 399.

HEWETT, G. W., enlisted in Company G as captain. He was wounded at the Battle of Chickamauga and furloughed for sixty days. His military record ends here. *Compiled Service Records.*

HILL, DANIEL HARVEY, was a West Point graduate from South Carolina. He served in the eastern Confederate armies until July 1863, when he was ordered to the Army of Tennessee. Hill's open and virulent criticism of General Braxton Bragg led to his being relieved from duty following the Battle of Chickamauga. Warner, *Generals in Gray*, 136–37; Hallock, *Braxton Bragg*, 94–97.

HINDMAN, THOMAS CARMICHAEL, a thirty-five-year-old general from Tennessee, was not an ideal commander. He fought in the western theater until receiving a severe wound at Atlanta that put him out of the war. Hindman proved an unpopular officer. Upon his replacement of General Withers, one soldier declared, "All I have to fear now is our new general." General Manigault believed Hindman to be "a scheming, maneuvering, political general, with whom it was dangerous to come in contact": "Morally, he stood deservedly low in the opinions of most of the officers of the Army . . . the cunningest, most slippery intriguer that I ever met with." Manigault also charged that the division slipped from first-rate in point of numbers, drill, efficiency, and discipline to third-rate under Hindman's administration. Warner, *Generals in Gray*, 137–38; Charles T. Jones Jr., "Five Confederates: The Sons of Bolling Hall in the Civil War," *Alabama Historical Quarterly* 24 (1962): 179; Manigault, *Carolinian Goes to War*, 78; Hallock, *Braxton Bragg*, 40, 48, 54–62, 103, 136, 145.

HOOKER, JOSEPH, was a West Point graduate from Massachusetts. He served in various command positions with the eastern Union armies until he was sent with two army corps as reinforcement to Chattanooga in November 1863, after the Union defeat at Chickamauga. Warner, *Generals in Blue*, 233–35; Faust, *Historical Times Illustrated Encyclopedia*, 369–70.

HOOKS, MONROE MARK, enlisted as a private in Company I at Selma, Alabama, in March 1862. *Compiled Service Records*.

HOPE, see Powell, Hope.

HOPKINS, FRANCIS M., enlisted as captain of Company I in Selma, Alabama, in March 1862. He was an assistant professor in the male department of the Centenary Institute and was instrumental in forming Company I in the Selma/Summerfield area. General Manigault cited him for gallant conduct at the Battle of Chickamauga. On November 23, 1863, he was captured near Chattanooga and imprisoned at Johnson's Island, Ohio, on December 1, 1863. *Compiled Service Records; OR*, vol. 30 (pt. 2), 344; Thomas McAdory Owen, *History of Alabama and Dictionary of Alabama*

Biography, 4 vols. (1921; Spartanburg, S.C., 1978), 1:216; *Daily State Sentinel,* Selma, Alabama, February 23, 1862.

HOSEA, see Callaway, J. (Jonathan) Hosea.

J. HOSEA, see Callaway, J. (Jonathan) Hosea.

JACKSON, THOMAS JONATHAN (STONEWALL), was a Virginia West Point graduate (1846). Jackson resigned from the U.S. Army in 1852 to teach at the Virginia Military Institute. When the war began, this eccentric soldier quickly became a household name, North and South. He was christened "Stonewall" at the Battle of First Manassas. Many of Jackson's military exploits were brilliant: the Shenandoah Valley campaign, the Battle of Second Manassas, and his flank march at Chancellorsville, which resulted in his death, were all mentioned by Joshua Callaway in his letters. Warner, *Generals in Gray,* 151–52; Current, *Encyclopedia,* 830–35.

JOE, see Callaway, Joseph.

JOHN AND IRENE, see Callaway, John Hanford, and Baker, Irene.

JOHNSTON, JOSEPH EGGLESTON, was a Virginia West Point graduate (1829). He served in the U.S. Army until April 1861, when he resigned to serve with the Confederacy. He commanded the Confederate forces in Virginia until his wounding at Seven Pines in May 1862, when the command passed to General Robert E. Lee. (Callaway's reference is to the series of battles leading up to Seven Pines.) President Davis then sent Johnston to the western theater, where his performance as department commander highlighted his feuding with Davis. In late 1863 Johnston took command of the Army of Tennessee upon General Bragg's resignation, and in July 1864 he, in turn, was replaced by General John Bell Hood. Near the end of the war he returned to field command to oppose General William T. Sherman's march through the Carolinas, surrendering to Sherman two weeks after Lee's capitulation to General Grant at Appomattox Court House, Virginia. Warner, *Generals in Gray,* 161–62; Craig L. Symonds, *Joseph E. Johnston: A Civil War Biography* (New York, 1992).

KIMMEY, MACE [MASON C.], enlisted as captain of Company A, Thirty-third Alabama Infantry on February 20, 1862, at Elba, Alabama, at the age of thirty-eight. He was wounded at the Battle of Perryville, Kentucky, on October 8, 1862, captured, and later exchanged near Vicksburg, Mississippi, on November 15, 1862. From July to December 1863 he was detached on recruiting service, rejoining the command in April 1864. On April 20, 1865, he was reported captured at Macon, Georgia. *Compiled Service Records.*

LEACH, BILL, enlisted at Perryville, Alabama, on March 7, 1863, as a private in Company K. *Compiled Service Records.*

LEE, ROBERT EDWARD, was a Virginia West Point graduate (1829) and a career soldier. At the start of the war he resigned to join the Confederacy. Lee spent the first months of the war in a series of positions, including military adviser to President Davis. After General Johnston's wounding at Seven Pines in May 1862, Lee took command of the Army of Northern Virginia, leading it to fame, glory, and, ultimately, defeat. Warner, *Generals in Gray,* 179–83; Current, *Encyclopedia,* 916–20.

LIDDELL, ST. JOHN RICHARDSON, of Mississippi, attended West Point for one year before dropping out, possibly because of his low class standing. He began the war as a volunteer aide-de-camp for General Hardee and served as confidential courier to General Albert Sidney Johnston before receiving an appointment as brigadier general in July 1862. After fighting at Perryville, Murfreesboro, and Chickamauga, he was transferred to the Trans-Mississippi. He later wrote his version of the war, an often caustic and witty memoir. Warner, *Generals in Gray,* 187–88; St. John Richardson Liddell, *Liddell's Record,* ed. Nathaniel C. Hughes (Dayton, Ohio, 1985).

LINCOLN, ABRAHAM, was president of the United States of America, 1861–1865.

LOCKET, THEOPHALUS W., enlisted at Perryville, Alabama, at the age of seventeen as a private in Company K. *Compiled Service Records.*

LONGSTREET, JAMES, was a South Carolina West Point graduate (1842). Longstreet occasionally performed magnificently on the battlefield. However, he made a poor subordinate, sulking during General Lee's offense at Gettysburg and sabotaging General Bragg's command at Chattanooga in late 1863. In November 1863 he was sent off to Knoxville, where he proved to be completely incompetent in independent command. His memoir of the war, *From Manassas to Appomattox,* is largely fiction and wishful thinking. Warner, *Generals in Gray,* 192–93; Hallock, *Braxton Bragg,* 79–81, 107–8, 122–26, 175–76.

McCown, John Porter, was a Tennessee West Point graduate (1840). McCown was a career soldier who resigned in May 1861 to join the Confederacy. He spent the war in the western theater. In May 1863 most of his division was ordered from Bragg's Army of Tennessee to Mississippi. Earlier, Bragg had preferred charges against McCown for disobedience of orders, and he believed McCown to be unfit for command. Warner, *Generals in Gray*, 199–200; Faust, *Historical Times Illustrated Encyclopedia*, 457–58.

McMillen, William, enlisted at Selma, Alabama, at age nineteen as a private in Company I. McMillen died at Corinth, Mississippi, in June 1862. *Compiled Service Records.*

Manderson's Shop was owned by John Manderson, forty-five, a master cordwainer born in Ireland. *1860 Federal Census.*

Manigault, Arthur Middleton, had no formal military training, although he had served in the Mexican War. He began his Civil War career as an aide to General Beauregard at Fort Sumter; he then became colonel of the Tenth South Carolina Infantry, commanding the first military district in South Carolina. After the Battle of Shiloh he was ordered to the West with his regiment, one of few eastern units sent to the western theater, and served in the Army of Tennessee until his wounding at the Battle of Franklin in November 1864. Joshua Callaway spent nearly all of his military career under Manigault. Warner, *Generals in Gray*, 210–11; Manigault, *Carolinian Goes to War.*

Martin Family was probably Henry, sixty-three, and Ann, fifty-four, farmers, born in North Carolina. *1860 Federal Census.*

May, Benjamin W. and William H. Both of these men enlisted at Elyton, Alabama, as privates in Company D. Benjamin was nineteen, William twenty-nine.

Mims, George A., enlisted at Selma at the age of nineteen as a sergeant in Company I. He was captured near Chattanooga on November 23 or 24, 1863, and imprisoned at Rock Island, Illinois, on December 5. On September 19, 1864, he escaped from the prison hospital. The manner of his escape is unknown. *Compiled Service Records.*

MIMS, JOSEPH A., enlisted at Selma as second lieutenant of Company I, a unit he was instrumental in raising. He was wounded at Lovejoy Station, Georgia, on July 22, 1864. *Compiled Service Records; Daily State Sentinel,* Selma, Alabama, February 12, 1862.

MITCHELL, JULIUS C. B., raised nine of the companies that made up the Thirteenth Alabama Infantry, resigned his position with that unit, and organized the Thirty-fourth Alabama Infantry. After the Battle at Missionary Ridge he received a surgeon's certificate of disability and was transferred to conscription duties. *Compiled Service Records.*

MONTGOMERY, JOHN A., was a son of John and Hannah Montgomery (see below). He enlisted at Selma, Alabama, at the age of twenty-one as a private in Company I or J. John was born in North Carolina and in the 1860 census was listed as a clerk, probably in his parents' saddle/harness shop. He was wounded during the evacuation of Corinth, Mississippi, and received a discharge. He subsequently served in the quartermaster department at Selma until mustered out in the spring of 1865. After the war he settled in Texas, married Cecilia Cocker, and engaged in farming and real estate until his death in May 1932. *Compiled Service Records; Confederate Veteran* 40 (1932): 354.

MONTGOMERY, JOHN AND HANNAH MOORE, were natives of North Carolina who moved to Summerfield in 1847. They owned a saddle/harness business, and he served as the local Methodist Episcopal minister. John died in 1863. DeLand and Smith, *Northern Alabama,* 695.

MORGAN, JOHN HUNT, born in Alabama, served in the army during the Mexican War. Upon his discharge he became a manufacturer and merchandiser in Lexington, Kentucky, until the Civil War began. As a colorful and legendary brigadier general of cavalry Morgan led several raids into Tennessee, Kentucky, Indiana, and Ohio, where he was captured and imprisoned in 1863. After escaping and making his way south, Morgan again received command of cavalry. On September 4, 1864, he was killed during a surprise attack by Union cavalry. Warner, *Generals in Gray,* 220–21; James A. Ramage, *Rebel Raider: The Life of General John Hunt Morgan* (Lexington, 1986).

NABORS, WILLIAM M., enlisted at Elyton, Alabama, at the age of thirty-six as a captain in Company D. He served throughout the war, surrendering under General Richard Taylor, and receiving his parole on June 22, 1865. *Compiled Service Records.*

NAT, see Pace, Nathaniel.

OLD ROSEY, see Rosecrans, William Starke.

ONEAL [O'NEAL], JESSE, was in Company A of General Nathan Bedford Forrest's Regiment of Alabama Cavalry. *Compiled Service Records.*

OSBORN, WILLIAM C., was one of Joshua's messmates. A twenty-seven-year-old farmer, enlisted at Perryville, Alabama, as a private in Company K, Osborn remained with the army only a few months. On July 24, 1862, he was discharged as unfit, suffering heart palpitations and being "subject to prostrating paroxysms" brought on by the hot weather and a "highly wrought nervous temperament." Osborn was five feet eleven inches tall and had a light complexion, blue eyes, and light hair. *Compiled Service Records.*

OVERTON, GEORGE W., a fifty-year-old brickmason, enlisted at Selma as a private in Company I. The Overtons were close neighbors of the Baker-Callaway household. George had been born in Georgia, his wife Elizabeth in South Carolina. They had six children living at home, aged twenty-two, seventeen, fifteen, thirteen, five, and three, at the time George enlisted in the army. George Overton was captured on January 5, 1863, at Murfreesboro, Tennessee, and sent to City Point, Virginia. On April 2, 1863, he was paroled from the prison into General Hospital, Petersburg, Virginia, suffering from febrile typhoid. He died on April 6 of erysipelas, a highly contagious acute infectious disease characterized by fever and chills and a rapidly spreading bright red inflammation of the skin caused by streptococcus. This ailment finished off many hospitalized sick and wounded Civil War soldiers. *1860 Federal Census; Compiled Service Records.*

OVERTON, JOHN F., was a son of George Overton (see above). He enlisted at Summerfield in March 1863, at the age of eighteen, as a private in Company I and was paroled at Montgomery, Alabama, on May 22, 1865. John Overton was six feet two inches tall and had dark hair, blue eyes, and a dark complexion. *Compiled Service Records.*

OVERTON, THOMAS W., another son of George and Elizabeth, was a twenty-two-year-old brickmason when he enlisted in the army. *1860 Federal Census.*

PACE, NATHANIEL, was married to Callaway's cousin Clarissa Callaway. Lyon, "Joshua K. Callaway."

PHILLIPS, JOSEPH, enlisted at Selma, Alabama, in March 1862, at the age of twenty-three, as a private in Company I. *Compiled Service Records.*

POLK, LEONIDAS, was a North Carolina West Point graduate (1827) who had never served his country—he resigned from the army immediately after graduation to study for the ministry. Polk combined the ministry with planting, and when he became Episcopal bishop of the Southwest in 1838, a position that entailed much traveling, he left his wife, Frances Ann Devereux Polk, and their children to manage on their own for extended periods of time. At the outbreak of war, Polk's old friend President Davis appointed him major general. Serving in the West, Polk was at Shiloh, the Kentucky campaign, Murfreesboro, and Chickamauga. Polk never forgot his civilian position and conducted himself always as though he were in charge, often disobeying or ignoring orders from his military superiors. He was never an outstanding combat leader, and his behavior during the Chickamauga campaign and battle led General Bragg to remove him from the Army of Tennessee. Following Bragg's resignation, Polk returned to the army, only to be killed by a cannon shot at Pine Mountain on June 14, 1864, during the Atlanta campaign. Joseph Howard Parks, *General Leonidas Polk, C. S. A.: The Fighting Bishop* (Baton Rouge, 1962); *OR*, vol. 30 (pt. 2), 54–55, 731; ibid., vol. 52 (pt. 2), 533–35; Warner, *Generals in Gray*, 242–43; Hallock, *Braxton Bragg*, 9, 17–18, 61–62, 71–74, 78, 90–91.

POPE, JOHN, was a Kentucky West Point graduate (1842) and a career soldier. In early 1862 he opened the upper Mississippi River by capturing Madrid and Island No. 10. In May, he commanded the left wing of the army under General Halleck in the advance on Corinth, and in June he was transferred to the East to take over the Army of the Potomac, which he led to an unmitigated defeat at Second Manassas. He was subsequently assigned to command the Department of the Northwest, effectively removing him from further participation in the war effort. Warner, *Generals in Blue*, 376–77; Faust, *Historical Times Illustrated Encyclopedia*, 593.

POWELL, HOPE, was Joshua's brother-in-law, married to Sarah A. Damaris Callaway. Lyon, "Joshua K. Callaway."

PRICE, STERLING, spent most of his adult life as a career politician, with time out to serve in the Mexican War. He became a soldier again in May 1861, seeing action at Wilson's Creek and Pea Ridge before joining Beauregard's forces. His military career proved unillustrious. Warner, *Generals in Gray*, 246–47; Manigault, *Carolinian Goes to War*, 29; Current, *Encyclopedia*, 1251–52.

PRINCE, SAM[UEL], enlisted at Enterprise, Mississippi, on October 18, 1861, at the age of thirty-five, as captain of Company K, Eighth Mississippi Infantry. In May 1862 he was assigned the duties of assistant quartermaster, but by July he was reported "sick at hospital." In April 1864 he applied to resign while absent on sick leave, and he retired on May 3, 1864.

RATLIFF, WILLIAM M., was Joshua's messmate. He enlisted at Perryville, Alabama, in March 1862, at the age of thirty-six, as a private in Company I. Ratliff died in June 1862. *Compiled Service Records.*

REESE, CARLOS, JR., was a captain in Company C. He served as assistant quartermaster in Manigault's brigade. *Compiled Service Records.*

REID, JOHN COLEMAN, was born in 1824 in Tuscaloosa County, Alabama, and in 1861 was practicing law. In October 1861 the secretary of war commissioned him a colonel and authorized him to raise a regiment of infantry, the regiment Joshua Callaway joined. General A. M. Manigault frequently cited Reid for coolness and courage, "splendid bearing on the field," and conduct aiding success in battle. General T. C. Hindman praised Reid as "a gallant and efficient officer." A biographer described him as a "man of marked characteristics . . . as brave a man as ever followed his country's flag, and, at the same time . . . the tenderest and most sympathetic. . . . Through every battle and skirmish to the close, the same kindness and affectionate tenderness for his men in camp and on the march, and the same invincible coolness in battle, characterized Colonel Reid in an eminent degree." Manigault, *Carolinian Goes to War*, 60, 107; *OR*, vol. 30 (pt. 2), 344; *Compiled Service Records;* DeLand and Smith, *Northern Alabama*, 669–70.

ROSECRANS, WILLIAM STARKE, an Ohio West Point graduate (1842), had resigned from the army in 1854. He began his Civil War career as an aide on General McClellan's staff and then moved on to field command. His defeat of General Lee in 1861 led to the creation of the state of West Virginia. The year 1862 found Rosecrans in the western theater, where he saw service at Corinth and Iuka before taking command of the Army of the Cumberland in October 1862. In December 1862–January 1863 he defeated General Bragg at Murfreesboro, and in June–July 1863 he forced Bragg out of the Tullahoma area into Chattanooga. Advancing again, Rosecrans and Bragg met at Chickamauga in September, where Bragg's Army of Tennessee routed the Union army. General Grant replaced Rosecrans in October 1863, and Rosecrans spent the remainder of the war commanding the Department of Missouri. Warner, *Generals in Blue*, 410–11; Faust, *Historical Times Illustrated Encyclopedia*, 642–43.

SAMANTHA, see Callaway, Samantha M.

SAVAGE, DAN [DANIEL R.], enlisted in Company K, Thirty-third Alabama Infantry, on March 13, 1862, at Greenville, Alabama, at the age of twenty-five. He died in the hospital at Winchester, Tennessee, on January 1, 1863.

SAVAGE, JAMES, was a sixty-year-old Alabama farmer, born in North Carolina. *1850 Federal Census*.

SELLICK, JAMES B., enlisted at Marion, Alabama, at thirty-nine years of age, as a Lieutenant in Company A. *Compiled Service Records*.

SHERMAN, WILLIAM TECUMSEH, was a West Point graduate from Ohio. He left the U.S. Army in 1853 but answered the call when the Civil War began. He became a close friend and confidant to General Grant, and when Grant was called to Washington to take overall command of the armies in the field, Sherman assumed command of the forces in the western theater. He is probably most famous, and infamous, for his March to the Sea in late 1864. Warner, *Generals in Blue*, 441–44; John F. Marszalek, *Sherman: A Soldier's Passion for Order* (New York, 1993).

SIS, see Callaway, Camilla.

SKINNER, A. MARSH, enlisted in Company K at Perryville, Alabama, in March 1862 at the age of twenty-eight. He died in June 1862, leaving Susanah E. Skinner widowed. *Compiled Service Records*.

SMITH, EDMUND KIRBY, was a Florida West Point graduate (1845). A career soldier, Smith resigned his U.S. Army position to join the Confederacy in April 1861. He was seriously wounded at First Manassas and upon recovery received assignment to the District of East Tennessee. Following the Kentucky campaign, Smith took command of the Trans-Mississippi Department, where he repelled the Red River invasion. Nearly the last Southern general to surrender, Smith was the last survivor of the Confederacy's full generals, dying in 1893. Warner, *Generals in Gray*, 279–80; Current, *Encyclopedia*, 1472–74.

SMITH, JAMES R., enlisted at Perryville, Alabama, in March 1862, at the age of eighteen. He served as corporal and sergeant of Company K. Joshua Callaway described Smith's bravery at the Battle of Chickamauga, and Smith's name also appears on the Roll of Honor in the official reports of the battle. *Compiled Service Records; OR*, vol. 30 (pt. 2), 534.

STARK [STARKE], B. W., enlisted in Company A, Eighteenth Alabama Infantry, at Elba, Alabama, on July 22, 1861. In March 1862 he became captain of his company, but a few weeks later, at 11 A.M. on April 6, he was wounded—"Throat dangerously"—at the Battle of Shiloh. He resigned from the army in July 1862 to take up the post of judge of probate of Coffee County, Alabama. *Compiled Service Records.*

T., see Callaway, Amelia Temperance.

TEMPERANCE, see Callaway, Amelia Temperance.

THOMAS, see Callaway, Thomas.

THOMAS, GEORGE HENRY, was a West Point graduate from Virginia. Although a southerner, Thomas took his oath of allegiance to the United States seriously and refused to join the Confederacy when the war came. He served throughout the war in the western theater. At Chickamauga he earned the nickname "Rock of Chickamauga" for his courageous stand while the rest of the army, including its commander, scampered back to Chattanooga. At the Battle of Missionary Ridge, it was Thomas's troops that broke Bragg's line, sending the Confederates, in their turn, scampering for safety. At Franklin and Nashville in late 1864 Thomas virtually destroyed the Confederacy's Army of Tennessee. Warner, *Generals in Blue*, 500–502; Faust, *Historical Times Illustrated Encyclopedia*, 754.

TILLIE, see Callaway, Amelia Temperance.

TRAPIER, JAMES HEYWARD, was a South Carolina West Point graduate (1838). He resigned from the army in 1848 and joined the Confederate army at the outbreak of the war. His lack of military acumen prompted General Bragg to have him removed from command in the western army in late 1862. Trapier held a series of minor posts in South Carolina for the remainder of the war. Manigault, *Carolinian Goes to War*, 30; Warner, *Generals in Gray*, 309–10; Current, *Encyclopedia*, 1613–14.

TUCKER, WILLIAM FEIMSTER, commanded a company of Mississippi infantry at First Manassas, but shortly thereafter he and his command were transferred to the western theater, where he eventually rose in rank to brigadier general. A wound received during the Atlanta campaign ended his active field duty. Warner, *Generals in Gray*, 311.

TUCKER, WILLIAM R., enlisted in Walker County, Alabama, in February 1862, at the age of forty-one, as a private in Company E. He was promoted to second junior lieutenant on October 3, 1862, but in August 1863 he was "Court martialed for advising and persuading a soldier to desert. Cashiered. Absent from command 5 days without leave." Joshua Callaway describes this event and its aftermath. *Compiled Service Records*.

UNCLE ELISHA, see Callaway, Elisha.

UNCLE ELISHA'S DAUGHTER, see Callaway, Mary J. S.

VAN DORN, EARL, was a Mississippi West Point graduate (1842) and a career soldier. After joining the Confederate forces in 1861, he led the Army of the West to two defeats before being transferred to command General Pemberton's cavalry. At Spring Hill, Tennessee, on May 7, 1863, Van Dorn was murdered by a Dr. Peters for having "violated the sanctity of his home." Warner, *Generals in Gray*, 314–15; Robert G. Hartje, *Van Dorn: The Life and Times of a Confederate General* (Nashville, 1967).

VAUGHN, FREDERICK B., enlisted at Selma, Alabama, at the age of twenty-four as first sergeant of Company I. *Compiled Service Records*.

VAUGHN, HENRY, enlisted at Selma, Alabama, at the age of nineteen as a private in Company I. He was discharged in June 1862. *Compiled Service Records*.

W. F., see Baker, Weston F.

WARREN, SIDNEY, enlisted as second lieutenant colonel in Company F, Thirty-third Alabama Infantry, on March 11, 1862, at Brandon's Store, Alabama. He died on July 6, 1862. *Compiled Service Records.*

WATERS, RUBEN R., enlisted at Perryville, Alabama, at the age of eighteen as a private in Company K. Waters was captured at Murfreesboro, Tennessee, on January 9, 1863, and sent to Camp Morton, Indiana, in February. *Compiled Service Records.*

WES, see Baker, Weston F.

WESTON, see Baker, Weston F.

WHEELER, JOSEPH, a Georgia West Point graduate (1859), joined the Confederacy at the start of the war. In July 1862 General Bragg appointed him chief of cavalry, a post he retained throughout Bragg's tenure as commander of the Army of Tennessee. Although Wheeler was active throughout the war, he proved somewhat careless in many areas, including the cavalry's foremost responsibility, intelligence. Warner, *Generals in Gray,* 332–33; John P. Dyer, *"Fightin' Joe" Wheeler* (Baton Rouge, 1941); Hallock, *Braxton Bragg,* 51, 60–61, 110–12.

WILSON, JOHN T., enlisted at Marion, Alabama, in January 1862 as lieutenant (second, subsequently promoted to first) of Company A. An 1863 report stated his performance was "tolerably efficient—Standing good." *Compiled Service Records.*

WINN, DR. P. C., enlisted at Shelby Springs, Alabama, on March 1, 1862, as acting surgeon. In February 1863 he sent his resignation papers from Vaccination and Pest-House, Rome, Georgia, and they were accepted by the president on March 31, 1863. *Compiled Service Records; Southern Historical Society Papers* 22 (1894): 270.

WITHERS, JONES MITCHELL, was an Alabama West Point graduate (1835) who resigned within a year of graduation to study law. He saw service during the Mexican War but resigned immediately after hostilities ceased. When the Civil War began, he again entered military service. Withers received high commendation from Generals Bragg and Polk for his actions at Murfreesboro. In August 1863 General Hindman took over Withers's Division, and Withers took charge of the Alabama reserve forces until the end of the war. Warner, *Generals in Gray,* 342–43; Current, *Encyclopedia,* 1736–37.

WOOD, PLEASANT G., enlisted at Selma, Alabama, as first lieutenant of Company I. Born near Centerville, Alabama, in 1832, he was practicing law when the war began. An 1863 evaluation reported him "very efficient. Standing good." He was promoted to captain at Missionary Ridge, and at the close of the war he held the rank of lieutenant colonel of the Twenty-eighth Alabama, having received three field promotions for bravery. *Compiled Service Records;* DeLand and Smith, *Northern Alabama,* 673; Walter M. Jackson, *The Story of Selma* (Birmingham, Ala., 1954), 196.

NOTES

INTRODUCTION

1. Joshua K. Callaway to Dulcinea Baker Callaway, On Picket, November 19, 1863, Joshua K. Callaway Papers, Eugene C. Barker Texas History Center, University of Texas, Austin.

2. Mrs. H. K. Lyon, comp., "Joshua K. Callaway: His Ancestry and Descendants," typescript, Barker Center.

3. Ibid.

4. W. Brewer, *Alabama: Her History, Resources, War Record, and Public Men, from 1540–1872* (1872; Tuscaloosa, Ala., 1964), 185–86, 207. Statistics on the percentages of slaves in the population were calculated by Robert Pace.

5. Lyon, "Joshua K. Callaway"; Thomas McAdory Owen, *History of Alabama and Dictionary of Alabama Biography*, 4 vols. (1921; Spartanburg, S.C., 1978), 1: 215–16; Jesse M. Richardson, ed., *Alabama Encyclopedia and Book of Facts* (Northport, Ala., 1965), 152.

6. U.S. Bureau of the Census, *Eighth Census, 1860*, Population and Slave Schedules (ms, microfilm).

7. Lyon, "Joshua K. Callaway."

8. *Daily State Sentinel*, Selma, Alabama, February 16 and 23, 1862.

9. U.S. National Archives, "Regimental Return for October 1862, Twenty-eighth Infantry," *Compiled Service Records of Confederate Soldiers Who Served in Organizations from Alabama*, 508 reels, National Archives and Records Administration, Washington, D.C.; *Confederate Service Records, 1861–1865*, Alabama Department of Archives and History, Montgomery.

10. Brewer, *Alabama*, 634; I. W. McAdory, "Memorandum: Company 'H'[,] 28th Alabama Regiment[,] Manigaults [*sic*] Brigade[,] Army of the [*sic*] Tennessee," Alabama Department of Archives and History, Montgomery, 1; Arthur Middleton Manigault, *A Carolinian Goes to War: The Civil War Narrative of Arthur Middleton Manigault, Brigadier General, C. S. A.,* ed. R. Lockwood Tower (Columbia, S.C., 1983), xi–xii, 14–15, 42; *Confederate Veteran* 7 (1899): 407; War Department, *War*

of the Rebellion: A Compilation of the Official Records of the Union and Confederate Armies (Washington, D.C., 1880–1901), ser. 1, vol. 10 (pt. 1), 789; vol. 10 (pt. 2), 461, 549; vol. 16 (pt. 2), 764; vol. 20 (pt. 1), 659; vol. 20 (pt. 2), 419, 432; vol. 23 (pt. 2), 735, 942, 959; vol. 30 (pt. 2), 15; vol. 31 (pt. 2), 659; vol. 31 (pt. 3), 617 (hereafter cited as *OR*; unless otherwise noted, all citations are to ser. 1); John Crittenden to Bettie Crittenden, May 31, 1864, John Crittenden Letters, Barker Center.

    11. John Crittenden to Bettie Crittenden, July 5, November 26, 1862, Crittenden Letters. For additional information on the health of Civil War Americans, especially Southerners, see Judith Lee Hallock, "'Lethal and Debilitating': The Southern Disease Environment as a Factor in Confederate Defeat," *Journal of Confederate History* 7 (1991): 51–61.

    12. This communication between the home community and the army was not unique to the Alabamians. As an example, Robert Maberry has found the same pattern among Texas troops serving in the Confederate northwest. Robert Maberry Jr., *Texans and the Defense of the Confederate Northwest, April 1861–April 1862: A Social and Military History* (Ph.D. diss., Texas Christian University, 1992), 269.

    13. Mary E. Braddon, *Aurora Floyd*, 3 vols. (London, 1863; reprint, New York, 1979); Victor Hugo, *Les Misérables*, trans. Charles E. Wilbour, introduction by Paul Benichou (New York, 1964), ix; Edward Bulwer, *A Strange Story* (n. p., 1861); Timothy Shay Arthur, *The Withered Heart* (Philadelphia, 1857).

CHAPTER 1: Corinth, April 13–May 24, 1862

    1. C. R. Harris, "Record of Events, March 29–April 30, 1862," Capt. Comdg. Co. K, Twenty-eighth Regimental Data, Alabama Department of Archives and History, Montgomery.

    2. Steven E. Woodworth, *Jefferson Davis and His Generals: The Failure of Confederate Command in the West* (Lawrence, Kans., 1990), 103; Wiley Sword, *Shiloh: Bloody April* (New York, 1974), 92; Shelby Foote, *The Civil War: A Narrative*, vol. 1, *Fort Sumter to Perryville* (New York, 1958), 382; T. Harry Williams, *P. G. T. Beauregard: Napoleon in Gray* (Baton Rouge, 1955), 150.

    3. E. B. Long and Barbara Long, *The Civil War Day by Day: An Almanac, 1861–1865* (Garden City, N.Y., 1971), 209, 213; Grady McWhiney, *Braxton Bragg and Confederate Defeat*, vol. 1, *Field Command* (New York, 1969), 256; Thomas Lawrence Connelly, *Army of the Heartland: The Army of Tennessee, 1861–1862* (Baton Rouge, 1967), 176.

4. Manigault, *Carolinian Goes to War,* 16.

5. Ibid., 16, 19, 20; Connelly, *Army of the Heartland,* 176–77; Foote, *Civil War,* 1:381; Williams, *Beauregard,* 152.

6. Joshua's inexperience led him to exaggerate. There were in reality about forty thousand soldiers at Corinth.

7. Throughout the letters, religion becomes increasingly important to Joshua. The persuasion by Bible and tract organizations, and the great religious revival that swept the Southern armies following the Confederate defeats of the summer of 1863, caught Joshua's interest and enthusiasm. James I. Robertson Jr., *Soldiers Blue and Gray* (Columbia, S.C., 1988), 170–89; Bell Irvin Wiley, *The Life of Johnny Reb* (Baton Rouge, 1978), 174–91.

8. These notes were not found among the letters.

9. This incident took place during one of General Earl Van Dorn's abortive and tardy flank movements during the Federal advance on Corinth in the spring of 1862. Stanley F. Horn, *The Army of Tennessee* (Norman, Okla., 1941), 451 n. 6.

10. Confederate military hospitals had been established in these towns.

CHAPTER 2: Corinth to Tupelo, June 2–July 6, 1862

1. McWhiney, *Bragg,* 258; Thomas L. Snead, "With Price East of the Mississippi," in *Battles and Leaders of the Civil War,* ed. Robert Underwood Johnson and Clarence Clough Buel, 4 vols. (New York, 1956), 2:717–34, 720; Foote, *Civil War,* 1:384; Long and Long, *Day by Day,* 218–35.

2. Connelly, *Army of the Heartland,* 177; Williams, *Beauregard,* 153; Mark Mayo Boatner III, *The Civil War Dictionary* (New York, 1959), 176.

3. Williams, *Beauregard,* 158; McWhiney, *Bragg,* 264–65; Manigault, *Carolinian Goes to War,* 21.

4. Callaway's Twenty-eighth Alabama was brigaded with the Tenth and Nineteenth South Carolina Regiments in Manigault's Fourth Brigade.

5. Blythe's Mississippi Regiment was brigaded with the Twenty-eighth Alabama until the army reached Tupelo, where it was exchanged for the Thirty-fourth Alabama. The change pleased Manigault, as he received nearly 800 soldiers in exchange for 250. Manigault, *Carolinian Goes to War,* 21.

6. The rest of this letter is missing.

7. Frequent rumors of recognition by the European powers circulated throughout the Confederacy, reflecting the high hopes held by many. For a full account of Con-

federate diplomacy and hopes for recognition, see Frank Lawrence Owsley, *King Cotton Diplomacy: Foreign Relations of the Confederate States of America*, rev. by Harriet Chappell Owsley (Chicago, 1959).

8. Callaway is referring to the series of battles that raged around Richmond, Virginia, between armies led by General Joseph E. Johnston and General George B. McClellan (May 4–June 1), and to the Shenandoah Valley campaign, Virginia, brilliantly executed by General Thomas Jonathon (Stonewall) Jackson (May 3–June 8). Callaway's reference to Johnston whipping "the yankees out of Virginia" is wishful thinking. Long and Long, *Day by Day*, 213–19.

9. He names only three.

10. Richmond, Virginia, capital of the Confederate States. This may be an allusion to the fact that Beauregard had left.

11. By "camp news" Callaway meant rumors.

12. "Acquaint now thyself with him, and be at peace: thereby good shall come unto thee."

13. The Battle of Chickahominy, also known as Gaines's Mill, was fought on June 27, 1862, the third of the Seven Days' battles around Richmond, Virginia. The writer obviously misdated this letter.

14. Some of this letter is indecipherable.

15. On the retreat from Corinth there were skirmishes with Federal cavalry at Boonesville on June 6 and 11. Long and Long, *Day by Day*, 223, 225.

16. The victory Callaway celebrated was McClellan's "changing his base of operations" to Harrison's Landing as a prelude to a complete withdrawal of Federal troops from the area of Richmond and the failure of the first attempt to reach the capital city by way of the Virginia peninsula. Ibid., 236.

17. Callaway appended a note to Dulcinea's brother.

18. Many soldiers from the western theater were sent to the army in Virginia, with no corresponding transfer of troops from the East to the West. Richard M. McMurry, *Two Great Rebel Armies: An Essay in Confederate Military History* (Chapel Hill, 1989), 88–89.

CHAPTER 3: Tupelo to Smith's Cross Roads, July 13–September 1, 1862

1. McWhiney, *Bragg*, 266–67; Connelly, *Army of the Heartland*, 197–200; Woodworth, *Davis and His Generals*, 128–29. See also James Lee McDonough, *War in Kentucky: From Shiloh to Perryville* (Knoxville, Tenn., 1994).

2. McWhiney, *Bragg*, 267–68.

3. Ibid., 261–62, 268.

4. Connelly, *Army of the Heartland,* 194–95, 197–98; Woodworth, *Davis and His Generals,* 131, 134.

5. McWhiney, *Bragg,* 268–71; Long and Long, *Day by Day,* 243; Connelly, *Army of the Heartland,* 203–4.

6. Callaway is referring to a July 13 raid by General Nathan Bedford Forrest and 1,000 cavalry troops on an important depot and garrison on a Federal line of supply along the Nashville and Chattanooga Railroad. Forrest reported he captured 1,200, killed 29, and wounded 120; his own losses were 25 killed and 40–60 wounded. Connelly, *Army of the Heartland,* 201–2; Brian Steel Wills, *A Battle from the Start: The Life of Nathan Bedford Forrest* (New York, 1992), 76.

7. Callaway appended a letter to Dulcinea's brother.

8. During the summer of 1862, the Confederates sent raiders into Missouri to harass Federal outposts. They disrupted Union forces and supplies throughout the state but did not come close to clearing them out of Missouri.

9. A reference to the Battle of Cedar (or Slaughter) Mountain, Virginia, on August 9, 1862.

10. In addition to the successful raid on Murfreesboro by Forrest, General John Hunt Morgan captured a Federal garrison at Gallatin, Tennessee, on August 12, and shortly afterward he made fools (and prisoners) of the Union cavalry sent to capture him in the "Hartsville Races" episode. Connelly, *Army of the Heartland,* 202–3; Long and Long, *Day by Day,* 250; McDonough, *War in Kentucky,* 57–60.

11. A southerner who sympathized with and supported the Northern cause. East Tennessee proved to be a highly Unionist area. Unlike west and middle Tennessee, east Tennessee held a very small population of slaves. Its inhabitants primarily owned small, self-sufficient farms. When the state seceded in June 1862, east Tennesseans tried unsuccessfully to form a separate state. Confederate authorities, both civil and military, cracked down hard on the area. Military occupation, martial law, mass arrests, forced loyalty oaths, and confiscation of property became common. Thousands of the region's people fled to Kentucky, where many enlisted in the Union army; many of those who remained in Tennessee turned to guerrilla warfare.

12. The clothing had been issued by the Confederate War Department.

CHAPTER 4: Kentucky Campaign, September 27–November 9, 1862

1. Manigault, *Carolinian Goes to War,* 51. For a discussion on Bragg's supply problems and lack of support from Richmond, see Judith Lee Hallock, *Braxton Bragg and Confederate Defeat,* vol. 2 (Tuscaloosa, Ala., 1991), 159–60; Richard D. Goff, *Confederate Supply* (Durham, N.C., 1969), 188–93.

2. St. John Richardson Liddell, *Liddell's Record,* ed. Nathaniel C. Hughes (Dayton, Ohio, 1985), 83.

3. McWhiney, *Bragg,* 285–86.

4. McAdory, "Memorandum," 9; *OR,* vol. 16 (pt. 1), 983.

5. McWhiney, *Bragg,* 288–310, 322; Manigault, *Carolinian Goes to War,* 41–42.

6. McWhiney, *Bragg,* 319.

7. Manigault, *Carolinian Goes to War,* 42.

8. Ibid., 52. For a full account of the Kentucky campaign, see McDonough, *War in Kentucky,* 117–314.

9. U.S. National Archives, "Regimental Return for October 1862, Twenty-eighth Infantry," *Compiled Service Records;* "Company K Muster Roll," October 31, 1862, Alabama Department of Archives and History, Montgomery.

10. The Confederates actually took four thousand prisoners.

11. The letter breaks off here.

12. From the scanty clues provided by Joshua, one physician believes Callaway may have had an intestinal infection such as typhoid fever. Harris D. Riley Jr., M.D., personal communication to author, December 6, 1991.

13. Dropsy is an archaic term for the accumulation of fluid outside the circulatory system or outside the blood vessels. It can be caused by many ailments, including typhoid fever, malnutrition, liver disease, and heart failure. Ibid.

CHAPTER 5: Shelbyville, February 1–May 1, 1863

1. See letter dated July 7, 1863, Chapter 7; Receipt for eighty dollars collected by Callaway at Selma, Alabama, on January 18, 1862, proving he was not with the army at this time but was at his home in Summerfield, just above Selma.

2. Manigault, *Carolinian Goes to War,* 72, 73.

3. John Crittenden to Bettie, Fall Creek, Tennessee, February 26, 1863, Crittenden Letters.

4. During the war the Alabama legislature set aside $11.8 million in public funds for the relief of the state's poor families, and many counties took a similar action. Callaway's reference to "committee money" may refer to one of these legislative acts. H. E. Sterkx, *Partners in Rebellion: Alabama Women in the Civil War* (Cranbury, N.J., 1970), 146–47. See also *Daily State Sentinel,* Selma, Alabama, February 16, 1862.

5. At this time there was a strong Copperhead movement in the northern states, especially in the western area. In Ohio, Clement L. Vallandigham attacked the Federal government so vociferously that he was expelled from the Union and sent into

the Confederate lines held by the Army of Tennessee. For further reading, see Frank L. Klement, *The Limits of Dissent: Clement L. Vallandigham and the Civil War* (Lexington, Ky., 1970).

6. During the six months of relative inactivity in the Tullahoma area, the Army of Tennessee received many recruits, raising its numbers higher than ever before. Thomas Lawrence Connelly, *Autumn of Glory: The Army of Tennessee, 1862–1865* (Baton Rouge, 1971), 69; Hallock, *Braxton Bragg*, 15.

7. This letter ends here.

8. In mid-March 1863, rumors reached the Army of Tennessee that General William S. Rosecrans was retreating from Murfreesboro to Nashville. To confirm the rumors, Bragg ordered cavalry reconnaissance. As usual, the cavalry reports merely exacerbated the confusion. General Earl Van Dorn reported that Rosecrans had withdrawn some troops to Nashville, but he was preparing an offensive; General Joseph Wheeler declared Rosecrans was withdrawing entirely from the area; General William Martin found the Federals firmly in place at Murfreesboro, and General John Morgan agreed; and General Wharton insisted a withdrawal was under way. Rosecrans was not retreating from Murfreesboro. Connelly, *Autumn of Glory*, 119–20.

9. In the next section of the letter, a considerable portion of the page is missing. It proved impossible to piece together what Joshua had written.

10. Dulcinea is probably pregnant.

11. The letter breaks off here.

12. It appears that Dulcinea may have suffered a miscarriage.

13. General John C. Breckinridge and his division were headed for Mississippi to aid in the defense of Vicksburg.

14. For an account of the Kentucky campaign, see Chapter 4.

15. See note 13.

16. See note 14.

17. Arkansas Post, also known as Fort Hindman, was located on the Arkansas River, about fifty miles upstream from Vicksburg. It fell to Federal general John A. McClernand on January 11, 1863. Nearly all of the Confederate defenders were captured. Boatner, *Dictionary*, 24–25; Patricia L. Faust, ed., *Historical Times Illustrated Encyclopedia of the Civil War* (New York, 1986), 23.

18. See note 14.

CHAPTER 6: Shelbyville, May 9–June 26, 1863

1. Connelly, *Autumn of Glory*, 116; Manigault, *Carolinian Goes to War*, 74.

2. Manigault, *Carolinian Goes to War*, 73.

3. The Battle of Chancellorsville, Virginia, May 1–4, 1863.

4. Callaway was mistaken about a "great victory" in Mississippi.

5. Date is indecipherable.

6. From October 1862 until its fall on July 4, 1863, General Ulysses S. Grant kept steady pressure on Vicksburg, Mississippi. The Confederate government made feeble and disjointed efforts to defend this important post on the Mississippi River. Its eventual loss on July 4, 1863, severed the Trans-Mississippi from the rest of the Confederacy.

7. General Nathaniel P. Banks held Port Hudson, Louisiana, under siege from mid-March 1863 until its surrender on July 8, 1863.

8. Carving rings from shells seems to have been a favorite pastime among the troops. "The boys are all engaged in making things out of clam shells," another soldier in Manigault's brigade told his wife. "They are of a beautiful white and when finished off neatly look well." John Crittenden to Bettie, Fall Creek, Tennessee, May 30, 1863, Crittenden Letters.

9. Many Alabama soldiers served in the eastern armies, as did Dulcinea's brother Eli. The Battle of Chancellorsville, Virginia, took place on May 1–4, 1863, as General Joseph Hooker attempted to reach Richmond by pushing his Federal army past General Robert E. Lee's Confederates. Hooker withdrew after a close encounter with an enemy shell caused him to lose his senses and his nerve. Stonewall Jackson suffered his mortal wound here. Hallock, *Braxton Bragg,* 160–61; McMurry, *Two Great Rebel Armies,* 88–89; Long and Long, *Day by Day,* 348. For a full account, see Ernest B. Furgurson, *Chancellorsville 1863: The Souls of the Brave* (New York, 1992).

10. Timothy Shay Arthur wrote *The Withered Heart* in 1857. This American editor, writer, and publisher wrote more than seventy moral and didactic novels promoting thrift, family life, religion, and temperance. Arthur's only great success proved to be his 1854 *Ten Nights in a Barroom,* which rivaled *Uncle Tom's Cabin* in popularity, and, like Harriet Beecher Stowe's work, it was dramatized and played throughout much of the country. Stanley J. Kunitz and Howard Haycraft, eds., *American Authors, 1600–1900* (New York, 1938), 38–39; Allen Johnson, ed., *Dictionary of American Biography,* 10 vols. (New York, 1957), 1:377–78.

11. The quote is from Robert Southey's (1774–1843) "The Curse of Kehama," published in 1810. John Hayward, ed., *The Oxford Book of Nineteenth-Century English Verse* (London, 1965), 181.

CHAPTER 7: Tullahoma to Chattanooga, June 29–August 2, 1863

1. Hallock, *Braxton Bragg,* 13–22.

2. Manigault, *Carolinian Goes to War,* 74–76.

3. Ibid., 77.

4. McAdory, "Memorandum," 3.

5. July 4, 1863, was a sad day indeed for the Confederacy. Vicksburg fell to General Grant, opening the Mississippi River to the Union forces; Bragg's army retreated across the Tennessee River; and General Robert E. Lee's army began its retreat from Gettysburg, Pennsylvania.

6. Lee's ill-advised and unsuccessful raid into the North ended in defeat at Gettysburg, Pennsylvania, on July 1–3.

7. Fort Donelson was on the Cumberland River, not the Mississippi.

8. Port Hudson, on the lower Mississippi River, fell on July 9 after a two-month siege. With the loss of Vicksburg on July 4, it became impossible to hold Port Hudson any longer.

9. Following the fall of Vicksburg, General William T. Sherman turned his attention to General Joseph E. Johnston's Confederate army at Jackson, Mississippi. Under continual pressure Johnston abandoned Jackson to the Federals on July 16. Long and Long, *Day by Day,* 380–86.

10. This was Eli's third wounding in battle. See Appendix, Baker, Eli W.

11. Plagued by desertions from the army, Bragg was reluctant to issue furloughs during this period. Hallock, *Braxton Bragg,* 29–32.

12. This may well have been the same hanging described by another Army of Tennessee soldier at Chattanooga. Sam Watkins wrote that he had seen a fellow Confederate shot by a firing squad. "This shooting business wasn't a pleasant thing to think about," he testified. "But Yankees—that was different," he believed; "I wanted to see a Yankee spy hung. I wouldn't mind that. I would like to see him agonize." So he went to the hanging place. A scaffold had been erected, two coffins were on the platform, and the ropes dangled from the crossbeam above. When the guard approached, Watkins saw two little boys:

But [I] did not see the Yankees that I had been looking for. The two little boys were rushed upon the platform. . . . "Are they the spies?" I was appalled; I was horrified; nay, more, I was sick at heart. One was about fourteen and the other about sixteen years old. . . . The ropes were promptly adjusted around their necks. . . . The youngest one began to beg and cry and plead most piteously. It was horrid. The older one kicked him, and told him to stand up and show the Rebels how a Union man could die for his country. Be a man! The charges and specifications were then read. The props were knocked out and the two boys were dangling in the air. I turned off sick at heart.

Sam R. Watkins, *"Co. Aytch": A Confederate Soldier's Memoirs* (New York, 1962), 95–96.

13. This is the first stanza of Thomas Gray's (1716–71) "Elegy Written in a Country Churchyard," published in 1751. The poem, considered one of Gray's finest, has remained a popular favorite. William Harmon, ed., *The Top 500 Poems* (New York, 1992), 327–32; Ian Ousby, *The Cambridge Guide to Literature in England* (Cambridge, England, 1993), 388–89.

CHAPTER 8: Chickamauga, August 27–September 24, 1863

1. Manigault, *Carolinian Goes to War,* 78–79; Hallock, *Braxton Bragg,* 56; Charles T. Jones Jr., "Five Confederates: The Sons of Bolling Hall in the Civil War," *Alabama Historical Quarterly* 24 (1962): 179.

2. Hallock, *Braxton Bragg,* 53–78.

3. Manigault, *Carolinian Goes to War,* 91–93.

4. Ibid., 93–94.

5. Ibid., 94–95; *OR,* vol. 30 (pt. 2), 348.

6. Manigault, *Carolinian Goes to War,* 95; *OR,* vol. 30 (pt. 2), 348.

7. Manigault, *Carolinian Goes to War,* 95–96; *OR,* vol. 30 (pt. 2), 348.

8. Manigault, *Carolinian Goes to War,* 97; *OR,* vol. 30 (pt. 2), 348; Hallock, *Braxton Bragg,* 72.

9. Manigault, *Carolinian Goes to War,* 98–99; *OR,* vol. 30 (pt. 2), 349.

10. Manigault, *Carolinian Goes to War,* 101; *OR,* vol. 30 (pt. 2), 349; Hallock, *Braxton Bragg,* 75.

11. Manigault, *Carolinian Goes to War,* 99–100.

12. Ibid., 102–3.

13. *OR,* vol. 30 (pt. 2), 350, 534; *Southern Historical Society Papers* 13 (1885), 367–68.

14. McAdory, "Memorandum," 4.

15. Quinine is used to relieve symptoms of malaria, colds, and fevers. Dulcinea may have been unable to obtain it, since by 1863 medical supplies of all sorts were scarce and expensive in the South.

16. Half of this sheet is missing.

17. Half of this sheet is missing.

CHAPTER 9: Behind the Lines, Chattanooga,
September 30–October 21, 1863

1. McAdory, "Memorandum," 4; Manigault, *Carolinian Goes to War,* 124, 125; see letter dated September 24, 1863, Chapter 8.

2. Davis to Bragg, June 29, 1872, Braxton Bragg Papers, Lincoln National Life Foundation Archives, Fort Wayne, Indiana. For a full discussion of the rampant dissension in the ranks of the higher echelons of the Army of Tennessee, see Hallock, *Braxton Bragg,* 88–126.

3. Eli was home on furlough following the Battle of Gettysburg, where he was captured and briefly held prisoner before being exchanged at the end of July 1863.

4. Victor Hugo completed *Les Misérables* on May 19, 1862. The first three parts, including "Cosette," had already appeared in April and May, and the last two parts were published in June. Translations quickly appeared worldwide, and it met with particular success in the United States. Victor Hugo, *Les Misérables,* trans. Charles E. Wilbour, introduction by Paul Benichou (New York, 1964), ix.

5. Edward Bulwer published *A Strange Story,* introducing the concept of occult powers, in 1861. Five years later Bulwer, who was born in London, became Baron Lytton and henceforth signed himself Bulwer-Lytton. Bulwer-Lytton's best-known novel is *The Last Days of Pompeii,* published in 1834. Frank N. Magill, *Survey of Modern Fantasy Literature,* 5 vols. (Englewood, N.J., 1983), 4: 1843–47; *World Book Encyclopedia* (Chicago, 1988), 2: 708.

6. Bragg relied on a three-pronged cavalry raid, under the general direction of General Joseph Wheeler, to further reduce the Federal supplies and rations. The trio of horse generals, however, failed to coordinate their efforts and accomplished nothing more than filling their own pockets with plunder and harassing civilians. For a fuller discussion, see Hallock, *Braxton Bragg,* 110–12; Connelly, *Autumn of Glory,* 268–70.

CHAPTER 10: Missionary Ridge, October 26–November 19, 1863

1. Manigault, *Carolinian Goes to War,* 125.

2. John Crittenden to Bettie Crittenden, Camp near Chattanooga, September 27, 1863, Crittenden Letters; Manigault, *Carolinian Goes to War,* 128–29.

3. Manigault, *Carolinian Goes to War,* 129; Liddell, *Liddell's Record,* 158.

4. He has left out the date.

5. See Chapter 9, n. 2.

6. Callaway had a copy of *Aurora Floyd* within a few months of its 1863 publication. This novel, along with *Lady Audley's Secret*, published in 1862, made Mary Elizabeth Braddon rich and famous. Although her feminist heroes created a "huge moral storm," the author was greatly admired by fellow writers such as Tennyson, Dickens, Thackery, and Henry James. In 1913, at the age of eighty, Braddon saw *Aurora Floyd* as a silent film. Mary E. Braddon, *Lady Audley's Secret* (1862; London, 1985); introduction by Jennifer Uglow, frontispiece, x.

7. In early November General Bragg and President Davis decided General Longstreet should leave the Chattanooga area and proceed with his troops to Knoxville. Although this move greatly depleted the Army of Tennessee, Longstreet's performance under Bragg, and his overt and covert attempts to replace Bragg as army commander, promised little in the way of cooperation had he remained at Chattanooga. Manigault succinctly summed up Longstreet's career: "In Virginia, General Longstreet's reputation stood very high," he reported. "I do not think that the impression he made in the West was a very favorable one." Many would agree with this fine understatement. Hallock, *Braxton Bragg,* 120–26; Manigault, *Carolinian Goes to War,* 127; Judith Lee Hallock, *General James Longstreet in the West: A Monumental Failure* (Forth Worth, Tex., 1995); Jeffry D. Wert, *General James Longstreet: The Confederacy's Most Controversial Soldier* (New York, 1993), 340–58.

CHAPTER 11: Missionary Ridge, November 25, 1863

1. Manigault, *Carolinian Goes to War,* 131–32, 143; George E. Brewer, "History of the Twenty-eighth Alabama Regiment," ms, c. 1915, Alabama Department of Archives and History, Montgomery, 33–34; *OR,* vol. 31 (pt. 2), 251, 281, 298.

2. John Hoffman, *The Confederate Collapse at the Battle of Missionary Ridge: The Reports of James Patton Anderson and His Brigade Commanders* (Dayton, Ohio, 1985), 37, 58–59; Hallock, *Braxton Bragg,* 132–34.

3. Hallock, *Braxton Bragg,* 138.

4. Hoffman, *Collapse,* 41, 61; Hallock, *Braxton Bragg,* 139–40.

5. Hoffman, *Collapse,* 60–61, 71–72.

6. Ibid., 41–43, 63–65, 71.

7. Ibid., 55, 65, 68, 72. For full accounts of the battles, see Peter Cozzens, *The Shipwreck of Their Hopes* (Chicago, 1994), and Wiley Sword, *Mountains Touched with Fire* (New York, 1995).

8. From here on this letter is difficult to decipher.

EPILOGUE

1. Lyon, "Joshua K. Callaway."

2. Ibid.; unidentified newspaper article, n.d., private collection of Doris and Ralph Langley.

3. Lyon, "Joshua K. Callaway"; three unidentified newspaper articles, December 23, 1881, December 21, 1939, and n.d., private collection of Doris and Ralph Langley.

4. Lyon, "Joshua K. Callaway."

5. See Chapter 10, letter dated November 19, 1863.

BIBLIOGRAPHY

MANUSCRIPTS AND COLLECTIONS

Bragg, Braxton. Papers. Lincoln National Life Foundation Archives, Fort Wayne, Indiana.

Callaway, Joshua K. Papers. Eugene C. Barker Texas History Center, University of Texas, Austin.

Compiled Service Records of Confederate Soldiers Who Served in Organizations from Alabama. 508 reels. National Archives and Records Administration, Washington, D.C.

Confederate Service Records, 1861–1865. Alabama Department of Archives and History, Montgomery.

Crittenden, John. Letters. Eugene C. Barker Texas History Center, University of Texas, Austin.

Harris, C. R. "Record of Events, March 29–April 30, 1862." Alabama Department of Archives and History, Montgomery.

McAdory, I. W. "Memorandum: Company 'H'[,] 28th Alabama Regiment[,] Manigaults [*sic*] Brigade[,] Army of the [*sic*] Tennessee." Alabama Department of Archives and History, Montgomery.

Riley, Harris D., Jr. Letter to author, December 6, 1991.

U.S. Bureau of the Census. *Federal Census, 1850.*

———. *Federal Census, 1860.*

NEWSPAPERS

Daily State Sentinel, Selma, Alabama

PUBLISHED PRIMARY SOURCES

Brewer, George E. "History of the Twenty-eighth Alabama Regiment," ms. Alabama Department of Archives and History, Montgomery, c. 1915.

Confederate Veteran.

Hoffman, John. *The Confederate Collapse at the Battle of Missionary Ridge: The Reports of James Patton Anderson and His Brigade Commanders.* Dayton, Ohio, 1985.

Johnson, Robert Underwood, and Clarence Clough Buel, eds. *Battles and Leaders of the Civil War.* 4 vols. New York, 1956.

Liddell, St. John Richardson. *Liddell's Record.* Edited by Nathaniel C. Hughes. Dayton, Ohio, 1985.

Longstreet, James. *From Manassas to Appomattox: Memoirs of the Civil War.* 1896. Bloomington, Ind., 1960.

Manigault, Arthur Middleton. *A Carolinian Goes to War: The Civil War Narrative of Arthur Middleton Manigault, Brigadier General, C. S. A.* Edited by R. Lockwood Tower. Columbia, S.C., 1983.

Southern Historical Society Papers.

War Department. *War of the Rebellion: A Compilation of the Official Records of the Union and Confederate Armies.* 128 vols. Washington, D.C., 1880–1901.

SECONDARY SOURCES

Ambrose, Stephen E. *Halleck: Lincoln's Chief of Staff.* Baton Rouge, 1962.

Arthur, Timothy Shay. *The Withered Heart.* Philadelphia, 1857.

Boatner, Mark Mayo, III. *The Civil War Dictionary.* New York, 1959.

Braddon, Mary E. *Aurora Floyd.* 3 vols. London, 1863. Reprint, New York, 1979.

Brewer, W. *Alabama: Her History, Resources, War Record, and Public Men, from 1540–1872.* 1872. Tuscaloosa, Ala., 1964.

Bulwer, Edward. *A Strange Story.* N.p., 1861.

Connelly, Thomas Lawrence. *Army of the Heartland: The Army of Tennessee, 1861–1862.* Baton Rouge, 1967.

———. *Autumn of Glory: The Army of Tennessee, 1862–1865.* Baton Rouge, 1971.

Cozzens, Peter. *The Shipwreck of Their Hopes.* Chicago, 1994.

———. *This Terrible Sound.* Chicago, 1992.

Current, Richard N., ed. *Encyclopedia of the Confederacy.* New York, 1993.

Davis, William C. *Breckinridge: Statesman, Soldier, Symbol.* Baton Rouge, 1974.

DeLand, T. A., and A. Davis Smith. *Northern Alabama: Historical and Biographical.* Chicago, 1888. Reprint, Spartanburg, S.C., 1976.

Dyer, John P. *"Fightin' Joe" Wheeler.* Baton Rouge, 1941.

Faust, Patricia L., ed. *Historical Times Illustrated Encyclopedia of the Civil War.* New York, 1986.

Foote, Shelby. *The Civil War: A Narrative.* 3 vols. New York, 1958–1974.

Furgurson, Ernest B. *Chancellorsville 1863: The Souls of the Brave.* New York, 1992.

Goff, Richard D. *Confederate Supply.* Durham, N.C., 1969.

Hallock, Judith Lee. *Braxton Bragg and Confederate Defeat.* Vol. 2. Tuscaloosa, Ala., 1991.

———. *General James Longstreet in the West: A Monumental Failure.* Fort Worth, Tex., 1995.

———. "'Lethal and Debilitating': The Southern Disease Environment as a Factor in Confederate Defeat." *Journal of Confederate History* 7 (1991): 51–61.

Harmon, William, ed. *The Top 500 Poems.* New York, 1992.

Hartje, Robert G. *Van Dorn: The Life and Times of a Confederate General.* Nashville, 1967.

Hayward, John, ed. *The Oxford Book of Nineteenth-Century English Verse.* London, 1965.

Heck, Frank H. *Proud Kentuckian, John C. Breckinridge, 1821–1875.* Lexington, Ky., 1976.

Henry, Robert Selph. *"First with the Most" Forrest.* New York, 1944.

Horn, Stanley F. *The Army of Tennessee.* Norman, Okla., 1941.

Hughes, Nathaniel Cheairs, Jr. *General William J. Hardee, Old Reliable.* Baton Rouge, 1965.

Hugo, Victor. *Les Misérables.* Translated by Charles E. Wilbour. Introduction by Paul Benichou. New York, 1964.

Jackson, Walter M. *The Story of Selma.* Birmingham, Ala., 1954.

Johnson, Allen, ed. *Dictionary of American Biography.* 10 vols. New York, 1957.

Jones, Charles T., Jr. "Five Confederates: The Sons of Bolling Hall in the Civil War." *Alabama Historical Quarterly* 24 (1962): 133–221.

Klement, Frank L. *The Limits of Dissent: Clement L. Vallandigham and the Civil War.* Lexington, Ky., 1970.

Kunitz, Stanley J., and Howard Haycraft, eds. *American Authors, 1600–1900.* New York, 1938.

Long, E. B., and Barbara Long. *The Civil War Day by Day: An Almanac, 1861–1865.* Garden City, N.Y., 1971.

Losson, Christopher. *Tennessee's Forgotten Warriors: Frank Cheatham and His Confederate Division.* Knoxville, Tenn., 1989.

Maberry, Robert, Jr. *Texans and the Defense of the Confederate Northwest, April 1861–April 1862: A Social and Military History.* Ph.D. diss., Texas Christian University, 1992.

McDonough, James Lee. *War in Kentucky: From Shiloh to Perryville.* Knoxville, Tenn., 1994.

McMurry, Richard M. *Two Great Rebel Armies: An Essay in Confederate Military History.* Chapel Hill, 1989.

McWhiney, Grady. *Braxton Bragg and Confederate Defeat.* Vol. 1, *Field Command.* New York, 1969.

Magill, Frank N. *Survey of Modern Fantasy Literature.* 5 vols. Englewood, N.J., 1983.

Marszalek, John F. *Sherman: A Soldier's Passion for Order.* New York, 1993.

Marvel, William. *Burnside.* Chapel Hill, 1991.

Ousby, Ian. *The Cambridge Guide to Literature in England.* Cambridge, England, 1993.

Owen, Thomas McAdory. *History of Alabama and Dictionary of Alabama Biography.* 4 vols. 1921. Spartanburg, S.C., 1978.

Owsley, Frank Lawrence. *King Cotton Diplomacy: Foreign Relations of the Confederate States of America.* Revised by Harriet Chappell Owsley. Chicago, 1959.

Parks, Joseph Howard. *General Leonidas Polk, C.S.A.: The Fighting Bishop.* Baton Rouge, 1962.

Perdue, Howell, and Elizabeth Perdue. *Pat Cleburne: Confederate General.* Hillsboro, Tex., 1973.

Ramage, James A. *Rebel Raider: The Life of General John Hunt Morgan.* Lexington, Ky., 1986.

Richardson, Jesse M., ed. *Alabama Encyclopedia and Book of Facts.* Northport, Ala., 1965.

Robertson, James I., Jr. *Soldiers Blue and Gray.* Columbia, S.C., 1988.

Sterkx, H. E. *Partners in Rebellion: Alabama Women in the Civil War.* Cranbury, N.J., 1970.

Stillwell, Lucille. *John Cabell Breckinridge.* Caldwell, Idaho, 1936.

Sword, Wiley. *Shiloh: Bloody April.* New York, 1974.

———. *Mountains Touched with Fire.* New York, 1995.

Symonds, Craig L. *Joseph E. Johnston: A Civil War Biography.* New York, 1992.

Warner, Ezra J. *Generals in Blue: Lives of the Union Commanders.* Baton Rouge, 1964.

———. *Generals in Gray: Lives of the Confederate Commanders.* Baton Rouge, 1959.

Watkins, Sam R. *"Co. Aytch": A Confederate Soldier's Memoirs.* New York, 1962.

Wert, Jeffry D. *General James Longstreet: The Confederacy's Most Controversial Soldier.* New York, 1993.

Wiley, Bell Irvin. *The Life of Johnny Reb.* Baton Rouge, 1978.

Williams, T. Harry. *P. G. T. Beauregard: Napoleon in Gray.* Baton Rouge, 1955.

Wills, Brian Steel. *A Battle from the Start: The Life of Nathan Bedford Forrest.* New York, 1992.

Woodworth, Steven E. *Jefferson Davis and His Generals: The Failure of Confederate Command in the West.* Lawrence, Kans., 1990.

Wyeth, John Allan. *That Devil Forrest: Life of General Nathan Bedford Forrest.* New York, 1959.

INDEX